Medicine in Maryland

Medicine in Maryland

The Practice and Profession, 1799–1999

Jane Eliot Sewell

THE JOHNS HOPKINS UNIVERSITY PRESS

Baltimore & London

© 1999 The Johns Hopkins University Press
All rights reserved. Published 1999
Printed in the United States of America on acid-free paper

1 3 5 7 9 8 6 4 2

The Johns Hopkins University Press
2715 North Charles Street
Baltimore, Maryland 21218-4363
www.press.jhu.edu

Library of Congress Cataloging-in-Publication Data
will be found at the end of this book.
A catalog record for this book is available from the British Library.

ISBN 0-8018-6127-6

To Lou,
with love

Contents

Contents

Illustrations appear after page 120.

Preface

When I first began to discuss a bicentennial project with the Medical and Chirurgical Faculty of Maryland, three significant questions came to mind. First, why not focus solely on contemporary medical issues? Why bother with history? The answer seems simple. We can understand where we are only by understanding how we got here, building upon the past to create the institutions with which we are so familiar, and how we solved or failed to solve the problems we encountered along the way.

If we do not get that vision of the past from books and articles by professional historians, we will construct it from less reliable sources. We each have a version of who we are and of our society. Sometimes our version comes from popular magazines, the evening news, local legends, or even historical novels or TV miniseries. I suggest that it behooves us to get it right, to have as solid a foundation for our view of the past as we have for our view of the present.

If a history were to be written, why should it focus almost exclusively on medicine? My answer to this second question is that revolutionary changes have taken place in human lives over the last two hundred years, and medicine is closely linked with some of the most important of these developments. We live longer and healthier lives. Our society has experienced a tremendous expansion in medical knowledge and treatments. Because these changes have been ubiquitous, medicine touches everyone in complex and frequently crucial ways that are often linked to key points of our existence. Two hundred years ago, these points were normally just birth and death. Now our lives are regularly punctuated by medical encounters across a wide range of professions.

We all have personal medical narratives, the stories of our illnesses and encounters with those who have treated us. These are important narratives, our autobiographical versions of history, and most of us are ready to relate them on a train, at a dinner party, or in a doctor's waiting room. These stories are meaningful to us and powerful in shaping our medical decisions—so powerful that they have come to play a major role in modern American media and culture. It is hard to surf TV without finding one or more medical dramas, either fictional or documentary, at any time of the day.

The third question, to which there are at least two answers, is, Why concentrate on one state? The short answer is that the Medical and Chirurgical Faculty of Maryland is celebrating its two hundredth anniversary in 1999, and such occasions always prompt us to reflect on the past. In this case, the Faculty decided that its past was worthy of a professional historical study that would go beyond an internal history of the organization and its most distinguished members. As the historian of medicine chosen to write this study, I was pleased that the Faculty opted for a critical work that would range beyond the practices of qualified physicians and their institutions. Thus, the state boundary became even more important because I was able to explore both the geography and what I consider to be the "archaeology" of medical practices throughout Maryland over two centuries. A state study enabled me to get beneath the surface of the grand national histories of medicine and to uncover some of the crucial processes of change in this sector of our society.

Some of those changes were national and international in scope. Two hundred years ago, for instance, medicine in Maryland was relatively simple and home based; there were few therapeutic choices. Today, medicine in Maryland is highly complex and largely based outside the home; there are many therapeutic options. About those trends there is very little that is particular to Maryland; this is a pattern that can be seen in each of the fifty states, although the time span varies from region to region. When, however, one scratches the surface of those megatrends, one finds innumerable aspects of a Maryland medical system that are particular to this state.

One element that repeatedly emerged was the manner in which diversity and complexity shaped Maryland medicine. Frequently, this diversity emerged in exclusive situations; certain groups found it difficult to receive medical treatment, and their needs linked up with those of marginalized practitioners to establish alternative institutions. While these institutions often operated quite separately from mainstream medical facilities, frequently there was discourse between them. Sometimes they exchanged ideas, sometimes students received part of their training in alternative institutions, and sometimes institutional mergers took place. These interactions were also an important part of the history.

Diversity and complexity were important for another reason. Diversity contributed in a fundamental way to the creativity of Maryland medicine, just as a broad gene pool contributes to hybrid strength. Thus, it was important that there were many different types of medical institutions, practitioners, and patients. It was important, too, that the United States has a federated government, with many powers and functions reserved to the states. That made it possible for Maryland to have a medical system in some ways distinctive from that of other states, even those that were neighboring and similar in many regards. The diversity of policies and programs that this has encouraged has frequently been lamented, but it has a saving grace: it contributes to creativity. Some of these innovations are in medical services, a much neglected subject.

Studied at the state level, we can see the ongoing fluctuation in our medical institutions between a centralization that favored efficiency and a decentralization that always looked inefficient but that favored creativity. This ebb and flow of centralizing tendencies continues today, reshaping our medical institutions and therapies. It is one of the major themes of this book.

An alternative approach to this subject would involve biographical sketches of practitioners, which has been a fruitful strategy in such well-conceived books as Henry Sigerist's *The Great Doctors*. But the history of medicine is more than the biographies of individual doctors and scientists, however prominent. We need to understand the patients, as well as the practitioners; the institutions, as well as the creative individuals; the nurses, dentists, and public health professionals, as well as the lauded leaders of Maryland medicine.

Another potential approach would be to focus entirely on the state's major city, Baltimore, and its capital, Annapolis. To do so, however, would be to exclude from the history all of those Marylanders who populated the rural areas and small towns of the state. They were numerous and important; they reveal additional elements of diversity and complexity that would have been overlooked in a city study.

A third approach has been to concentrate on individual—normally leading—institutions. In Maryland, this would have produced a dual study of the Johns Hopkins Medical Institutions and the University of Maryland Medical Centers. Both have been the subjects of detailed institutional histories, and I draw upon them heavily in the chapters that follow. To appreciate more fully the entire range of medicine and its history, I am convinced that we should look beyond the most prominent institutions, just as we look beyond the giants of medical innovation and look outside the large urban centers.

When we do look at the wider picture, we find a medical setting interlaced with class, race, gender, religious, and regional differences. Over the past century, Maryland medicine has maintained a high profile in the world, a profile chiefly associated with the University of Maryland Medical Centers and the Johns Hopkins Medical Institutions. These dominate the state's largest city. Renowned as they are, however, they have never been able to service all of the state's population. Throughout this relatively small state, important differences have always been starkly defined: east and west, north and south, rural and urban; Baltimore itself is like a number of separate towns or villages, concentrated but never fully integrated. Historians have tended, when discussing a state or region, to label it as western, midwestern, southern, or eastern. By doing so, they have obscured or overlooked important internal differences, variations that have been absolutely integral to making the place what it was. Maryland's particular conglomeration of differences gives it a distinctive position in the region and in the history of medicine.

Although this is not a book about medical firsts, Maryland has a large share of these accomplishments, and I touch upon some of the most noteworthy events of the past two centuries. Several of them have already earned well-deserved places in national and international medical histories, even though Maryland has never been on the cutting edge as a modern, urbanized state. It has always straddled North and South. Although it is located on the eastern seaboard and was thus settled early, Maryland never developed a cosmopolitan center of the size and significance of New York City or Philadelphia. Like those cities, however, Baltimore was a trade center linking internal transportation systems with sea carriage and national and international markets. For most of the first century covered in this book, the bulk of the trade involved an exchange of agricultural products for the manufactured goods that Marylanders and other Americans wanted. Some of Maryland's crops were produced using slave labor, and that "peculiar institution" split the state and many of its families, just as it did the nation. As the abolitionist movement gathered force in the early to mid–nineteenth century, these divisions became ever more acute.

Because of the scope of this book, which ranges over two hundred years, I was unable to go into great depth on any aspect of the history and certainly could not cover all dimensions of the state's medical heritage. I give an important role in my narrative to the development of medicine in the state's leading city, Baltimore; that story includes events at Johns Hopkins and the University of Maryland. But even within the city—in keeping with one of the main themes of the book—I have tried to illuminate facets of other medical systems and other institutions. Also, I have attempted to enrich that narrative with accounts revealing something about medicine as practiced beyond Baltimore, ranging from the Eastern Shore to the low mountains of Western Maryland.

The book begins when medicine was practiced entirely outside of the hospital and was almost entirely domestically based. That was a time of great tension within medicine, as a multitude of sects emerged and competed for the allegiance of the public. The early years of the Medical and Chirurgical Faculty were spent amid heated struggles over professional authority, licensure, and treatment. Chapters 2 and 3 present a view of medicine as it entered the hospital in the nineteenth century, and chapters 4 and 5 examine changes that occurred as medical education moved out of the office of the individual physician and into the professional setting of the hospital. The book then turns to public health, a facet of medicine that has received far less attention from historians than its far-ranging contributions to human health deserve. Chapter 8 is a brief survey of some of the leading medical developments since World War II, an era in which medical knowledge, training, and treatment have all expanded dramatically. In the modern era, too, national and state institutions have established new relationships and frequently struggled over jurisdiction and resources.

The sources essential to a history of medicine in this state are terribly uneven. There are rich and well-organized deposits in the Alan Mason

Chesney Medical Archives at the Johns Hopkins University, and I have found other materials of interest in the school's Welch Library and the library of the Johns Hopkins School of Public Health and Hygiene. The University of Maryland Health Sciences and Human Services Library contains some useful catalogues and bulletins, as well as collections of pamphlets and papers on the medical school, the hospital, the school of pharmacy, and the dental school (the first in the world). There are also valuable materials at the Shepherd and Enoch Pratt Hospital and at the Sinai Hospital. The U.S. National Archives provided some relevant records, but far more useful were the State Archives at Annapolis, Maryland. Some of the county medical societies have preserved materials of historical interest; others, unfortunately, have none. Similarly, some of the hospitals outside Baltimore have collected historical records and compiled their own histories. But here, too, the sources are uneven.

I was able to find scattered materials in some of the county historical societies, including the Frederick Historical Society and the Saint Mary's County Historical Society. The Stonestreet Museum in Rockville and the Civil War Medical Museum in Frederick had some written records and useful artifacts. Most important in terms of documents was the Maryland Historical Society, where the collections are unusually well organized and preserved. A few Maryland physicians who take an energetic interest in their heritage have also compiled biographical records of the profession in their part of the state.

Other sources included the extensive newspaper collections at the Enoch Pratt Free Library, as well as the materials preserved in the library's Maryland Room. The Maryland Room collections include pamphlets, clippings, and reports on medical schools, hospitals, and events in public health.

I began my research at the richest collection in the state, the Medical and Chirurgical Faculty of Maryland. In the extensive library of the Faculty, there are informative primary and secondary sources. Without a well-funded attempt to preserve and reorganize them, the state's and the nation's medical historians are likely some day to find these materials relatively inaccessible. For this current study, however, unlimited access to the Faculty's library provided absolutely invaluable resources.

Using these sources, I have written a study of medicine in Maryland that I hope will provide its readers with a better understanding of how medical practice has changed over the previous two centuries and how the complexities of geography, class, race, gender, religion, and professional development have shaped that process. During those two hundred years, some groups gained power, wealth, and status only to see their positions decline as the environment changed in ways that challenged their expertise. Some have regained their standing, while others never recovered. As this suggests, the history of medicine in this state has not been one of linear progress for any group of practitioners or their patients. To explore those developments in greater detail, we must now look back to the end of the eighteenth century, a time when Maryland's population was small and mostly scattered about the state on farms and in small towns. Annapolis, the state capital, had been surpassed in population by the thriving port of Baltimore, where there were merchants hoping soon to exceed the commerce of their northern rivals in Philadelphia and New York City.

Acknowledgments

M y first thanks go to my husband, Lou Galambos, who has unfailingly supported and sustained this project from beginning to
end. He is a great editor and a great friend. Margaret Burri has overseen
the book and given me unusually liberal access to library facilities at the
Medical and Chirurgical Faculty of Maryland. I am deeply grateful to her
and the Faculty for providing moral and financial support while leaving
matters of interpretation and evaluation in the hands of the author. My
advisory board consisted of Gert Brieger, Ronald Fishbein, A. McGee
Harvey, Ronald Walters, and Theodore Woodward. I had received considerable help from Professors Brieger and Walters in graduate school,
and their careful reading of this manuscript is much appreciated. Drs.
Fishbein, Harvey, and Woodward each understood different aspects of
medicine in Maryland and were patient enough to share their insights
with me. The board helped me avoid numerous errors; any that remain
are my responsibility.

Rich Behles at the University of Maryland Health Sciences and Human Services Library was immensely helpful and generous, as was Nancy
McCall at the Alan Mason Chesney Medical Archives at Johns Hopkins.
They provided me with just the kind of assistance and direction that
every author needs.

Jessica Nehrling was an extremely talented and vigorous research associate who will be another wonderful Maryland doctor in a few years. Julie Kimmel and Nora Kay Zelizer, too, devoted great skill and energy to the research on this study. I also received kind assistance from many of Maryland's county medical societies and the physicians who are members, as well as their spouses and receptionists. Similarly, several of the county historical societies provided useful material; the staffs at the Frederick, Saint Mary's, and Montgomery societies were especially helpful. The Maryland Historical Society is one of the main repositories of well-organized and well-preserved materials, especially for the late eighteenth and early nineteenth centuries. The staff was unfailingly knowledgeable and helpful. Kari Appler, Russel Kujan, and Susan Harman at the Medical and Chirurgical Faculty assisted with photocopying and my library work.

At the Johns Hopkins University Press, I received valuable and prompt help from Robert Brugger, Jacqueline Wehmueller, Linda Forlifer, Barbara Lamb, and Mary Eleanor Macsherry. They worked on a tight schedule without complaints and with impressive professionalism.

I am blessed with many good friends and family members who have demonstrated substantial interest in this book. They include Ornumah, Shahda, Jonathan, Christopher, and Timothy Walker, Denise and Jennifer Galambos, Mark Connor, Peg Crist, Mary Fissell, Kathy Craig, Brian Balogh, and Cindy Truelove. I thank them all for the various kinds of support they provided.

Finally, I thank my daughter Katherine for waiting until this manuscript was finished before making her entrance at the Greater Baltimore Medical Center.

Medicine in Maryland

Conflicts and Compromises

Domestic Medicine, Orthodoxy,

Sectarianism, and Quackery,

1799–1899

O n the morning of April 9, 1793, William Faris woke up with pains
in his hip. Faris, an Annapolis, Maryland, silversmith, was in such
pain that he could not get up and had to use a pair of crutches borrowed
from a neighbor. Over the next three weeks, he received several home
visits from Drs. Shoas and Murray, who prescribed "drops of loam, volatole tincture, and gum guaracum." He apparently made a good recovery,
but on July 8 he recorded in his diary that his wife "had a very queer fit
of the Ague and Fever." The next day, which was a "fine day," his wife
"took Bark."

Apparently her illness was subsequently not a cause of serious concern
because William made no further mention of her health until February 20, 1794, when he noted: "Mrs. Faris is very unwell. She went to bed
after Diner in the evening. I think she is a littel better. She swetted a littel in the evening." For a fortnight, she did poorly, suffering from fever
and a hacking cough. Again, the family doctors were consulted, and
Dr. Murray made house calls and sent medicine to the home. Mrs. Faris
took wine drops at night and bark during the day. She was also blistered
repeatedly. By early March, her husband observed, she was better.[1]

As the Faris family's diary indicates, medicine in Maryland during the
late eighteenth century was informal, almost entirely domestic, and, by
our standards, very unspecialized. A sense of the lack of specialization

in medicine and in the society generally is evinced by an advertisement
that appeared on the front page of the *Maryland Journal and Baltimore Advertiser* on November 30, 1779. The notice announced: "An Apothecary's
Shop For Sale, in Piscataway, in Prince George's County, in Maryland,
the Shop Furniture and Medicines, with complete Set of instruments,
and a few Books in Physick and Surgery, of the late Doctor Joseph Ader-
son, deceased. The Shop Furniture is large and elegant, and the Quantity
of Drugs fully sufficient for an extensive Practice, all well laid in, and in
good Order and Preservation." This advertisement appeared in a mainstream newspaper rather than a professional journal, a useful measure
of the lack of specialization. Moreover, the practice on the market was
clearly intended to be owned and run by a practitioner who would serve
as apothecary, physician, and surgeon. In Great Britain, the guild system
and the Royal Colleges of Physicians and Surgeons attempted to maintain boundaries between the different branches of medicine, but that set
of institutions seems to have had little influence in America.[2]

Just as medical practice remained relatively unspecialized, so, too, did
medical education. Samuel Stringer Coale, who had been appointed a
surgeon at the time of the American Revolution, was in many ways characteristic of the early practitioners in the formal sector of the medical
profession. Coale had studied, probably very briefly, at the College of
Philadelphia, which, at its establishment in 1765, was the first medical
school in the United States.[3] Returning to his home state of Maryland
in 1775, Coale set up a medical practice in Baltimore and the following
year a small manufacturing enterprise specializing in saltpeter, a widely
used preservative. For a time, he served as physician at Baltimore's Almshouse, which was one of the few institutions offering medical attention
in the state at that time.[4] Service to a charitable organization offered little
direct remuneration, but it was a means of making social and economic
contacts within the local community and building a private practice.

At that time, Coale and others who were interested in medicine could
study to become a doctor in Maryland only through apprenticeship, but
those conditions would soon change. As the century drew to a close,
ferment over education was bubbling through the state's medical profession. A small coterie of local physicians attempted to launch a medical
school similar to the one in Philadelphia. New York, too, was emulat-
ing the Philadelphia institution. But in Maryland, this and several other
efforts to develop more formal professional organizations foundered.

Many of the "regular" practitioners in Maryland and in other states to
the north had come to believe that apprenticeship was no longer serving

the best educational interests of their profession. The training was too variable, too dependent on the individual practitioner and apprentice. Apprentices had long learned medicine much as they learned how to garden, cook, or shoe a horse. But now the leaders of the medical profession wanted to distinguish their endeavors from those of artisans and housewives. They wanted a more formal, standardized system of training based on the deeply rooted body of knowledge, dating back to classical antiquity, which provided them with guiding therapeutic principles.

In the late 1790s, humoral theory, passed down from ancient Greece and repeatedly refined over many centuries, formed the core of medical thought and action. Central to the theory was the idea that all nature consisted of the four elements—fire, water, earth, and air—and that these elements possessed the qualities of hot, cold, wet, and dry. Health existed when these elements were in balance, and disease resulted from imbalance; hence, treatments were aimed at restoring balance. In the case of certain fevers, for example, the practitioner bled his patients to deplete their vital force and reduce the fire element.

Also central to the medical theory of eighteenth-century therapeutics was the ancient concept that the human body could sustain only one state of illness at any one time. Thus, the chief aim of many therapies was to produce dramatic symptoms that would eliminate the primary malady. To achieve such dramatic symptoms, drastic measures were commonly applied. Those efforts were directed toward achieving *depletion.* Therefore, physicians performed venesection, often letting blood in large quantities to the point of inducing collapse in the patient. This was thought to reduce inflammation and the physiological tension in the main blood vessels.[5] When people were bled enough, their physical status quickly and visibly changed. This, too, was an indication of successful treatment. A second key element of the so-called heroic regimen was aimed at *elimination;* powerful purgatives, laxatives, and emetics were used to produce diarrhea or vomiting and hence to flush out the system. Another therapeutic mainstay was *blistering,* which was an important part of the treatment Mrs. Faris received. The physician heated a glass cup over a flame and applied the cup directly to the patient's skin. The large, painful blister that resulted normally seeped fluid, a sign that the physician was producing the desired results.

Various harsh chemicals were used to cleanse the body's system and to produce other presumably therapeutic effects. One set of chemicals that was widely used consisted of mercurial compounds such as calomel. They frequently caused dramatic initial reactions that convinced the physicians as well as their patients that something was being achieved. Over the long term, these toxic medicines commonly caused serious side effects, often signaled by the patients' gums turning black and their teeth falling out. Today these treatments make us shudder, but many of us have inherited some of the notions of that time. The belief persists, for instance, that medicine must taste bad and treatments must cause pain to be effective. Like humoral theory, some elements of the inherited ideas of stoicism also remain with us in our presumably scientific era.

This widely accepted body of knowledge was an important part of the intellectual and cultural setting of Maryland when the state's physicians began to search for new means of formalizing their profession. That is not to imply that the mystery of medicine had been reduced to a simple dogma that was transplanted to the colonies, including Maryland, from England. To the contrary, the eighteenth-century body of medical knowledge was anything but simple; it was diverse and constantly changing according to local circumstances. The fundamental ideas were so broad and flexible that they lent themselves to highly varied applications based in part on regional, state, and local conditions. Some of the traditional remedies were available locally, and people of higher income in Maryland could also afford imported chemicals or plants. To a considerable extent, however, physicians, like their patients, had to adapt to their local environments, using materials that were at hand. That included several of the harsh chemicals that were employed in the Old World and could be produced in the United States, but American doctors also relied very heavily on indigenous plants. Sassafras was used extensively, as were ipecac and cinchona.[6]

Cinchona was an ancient Native American therapy that was adopted by both "regular" and "irregular" practitioners, as was tobacco. Housewives and physicians often had elaborate herb gardens that provided valuable medicinal ingredients, as well as flavor for foods. Several examples of these gardens have been preserved and cultivated in Maryland. The Stonestreet Museum in Rockville maintains an herbal garden representing the one that once served the medical needs of the family doctor who resided in its medical office, as well as his family's culinary needs; another can be seen at the Shiplap House in Annapolis.[7]

Home remedies were extremely important because doctors were scarce and relatively expensive. While no statistics are available, it is evident that housewives, friends, and neighbors provided the bulk of medical attention to Marylanders, as they did to the residents of other states. Court records indicate that women as well as men practiced medicine in colonial Maryland during the seventeenth century. Many of the drugs they used had been long employed in the colonies and Europe and continued to be used well into the eighteenth and nineteenth centuries. They included antimony as a purgative, juniper berries as a diuretic, lime juice to treat scurvy, and spirits of vitriol (sulfuric acid) for a variety of ailments, including epilepsy.[8] Some of the herbal materia medica used in America could be found in such herbals and self-help guides as Nicholas Culpeper's *Pharmacopoeia Londinenis* (originally published in England in 1649), which was widely used in the United States. But whether their sources were the printed word or folklore, Americans employed their herbal guidelines like recipes — subject always to the inclinations and experience of the cook, as well as the materials available. Herbal remedies were a common part of the domestic pharmacopoeia long before herbalism emerged as a distinct medical sect.

Once a sect began to take shape, however, regular medical men recognized a potential threat on the horizon. Home remedies in the hands of women had been relatively little cause for concern. But herbalism or botanic medicine practiced increasingly by men, who were often being remunerated for their services, represented an obvious challenge to the authority, status, and income of Maryland physicians. The desire on the doctors' part to protect their profession prompted them to organize, just as did their interest in promoting medical education. Proud of their intellectual inheritance, they expressed no doubts about their ability to further the public interest. Through a formal institution, they hoped in 1799 to realize their objectives.

A Medical and Chirurgical Faculty or Society

Maryland physicians had tried before to establish a formal professional organization and failed. Dr. John Archer, who was also a minister of the Presbyterian Church, had opened a "Medical Hall," known as the Harford Medical Society, where as many as fifty medical students were trained in the closing years of the eighteenth century.[9] But this type of local institution — and the other incipient medical societies — could not serve the interests of the entire state. Nor could it compete with such a successful and respected venture as the College of Medicine in Philadelphia.

In the state's leading city of Baltimore, where there was a greater concentration of physicians, there were intense and mounting discussions of education, irregular practice, medical fees, and medical licensing. Physicians increasingly looked toward an organizational response. Here, too, their initial efforts to develop a sustainable and effective medical society were disappointing. Such leaders as Dr. Charles Frederick Wiesenthal, who emigrated from Germany in 1755, were familiar with the manner in which European doctors had organized and the ways their societies had protected their professional interests. He and others were determined to emulate those models in Maryland.[10]

In 1779, Wiesenthal, Dr. Coale, and six other practitioners mounted a public protest. Because of the privations of war, doctors were experiencing unusual problems in collecting their fees. Lacking a fixed currency and suffering wartime inflation, they were no longer willing to settle their accounts in depreciated bills. Often, they found that their efforts would never be remunerated. "It must be confessed," they announced, "that the Gentlemen of the Faculty in this town [of Baltimore], have suffered more in respect to their bills since the commencement of the present war, than any other class of men in the community." Now they thought "it proper to inform the Public, that from the fluctuation of prices, and unfixt value of money, they find it necessary to charge for their services, in country produce, or by way of barter." Barring that, they would accept bills at less than their face value, "at such advance as will bear a proportion to the prices of the necessaries of life at the time of payment." Eager not to destroy the good will of the community, they assured the public that "the indigent sick may, nevertheless, apply and they shall be attended to, as usual, with tenderness and charity."[11]

This collective effort was followed a few years later by the creation of a proto-organization, "a medical establishment." Wiesenthal and Dr. Elisha John Hall of Frederick County launched this plan through the pages of the *Maryland Journal and Baltimore Advertiser.* Between November 1785 and December 1788, they discussed in the paper their desire for medical reform and repeatedly aired their concern about the prevalence of quackery.[12] One doctor, writing from the town of Frederick in November 1785, said that he had intended to write on the "Subject of a medical Establishment" but had become so incensed by the prevalence of irregular practitioners that he felt compelled to discuss that instead. "I am really provoked," he wrote, "at the Credulity of the People of this Vicinity, in trusting to, consequently in supporting a Number of villainous Quacks, who are imposing on them daily."[13]

The following month, a lengthy letter of response appeared in the same paper, denouncing quackery and calling for legislative action.

"There is no difference," the author insisted, "between a man who offers a dose, uncertain what its effects may be, solely for a premium, and one who presents his pistol to your breast, and demands your money, except the first is the most to be dreaded of the two: The highwayman may be satisfied with your purse, while the obdurate heart of the quack, insensible to every finer sensation, continues to thirst after lucre, even at the expense of your life." The time had come, the writer believed, to launch a formal, organized attack on quackery: "Let a petition from a number of very respectable inhabitants be presented to the General Assembly, remonstrating against the present proceedings, and pray for amendment; —let a number of Physicians be incorporated, whose abilities and characters may be unquestionable, with power to frame their own by-laws, for their own better government; the corporation being the most proper judges of what may be necessary." [14]

A further communication from Baltimore—probably from Charles Wiesenthal but signed "A Citizen"—impressed upon readers the value of professional medical societies, journals, and schools, as had been amply demonstrated in Europe.

> Medical societies have ever been viewed of such consequence, that the supreme authority of almost every nation in Europe have been very assiduous in promoting their importance. Shall America be less attentive to so weighty a matter? . . . Philadelphia at this time furnishes the best school of physic in America—Massachusetts and Connecticut have of late made some progress towards medicinal institutions—Shall Maryland be insensible to the advantages of such establishments? Her consequence, as a commercial State, is already established far and wide . . . . To create *a reputation for literature,* as she has done for commerce, is within her abilities, and ought to be her next ambition; and one would imagine, that this necessary pride will not permit her to be the last for encouraging Arts and Sciences, particularly the necessary ones of Physic and Surgery.

Such Maryland institutions would protect medicine's boundaries, provide a local base for medical education, and create a path for professional advancement. "At present we are indebted to the European or neighbouring States for our education . . . . Large sums of money are expended in foreign countries for the improvement of youth, when, by little attention, the students may have as great, if not superior, advantages at home, with much less trouble and expense." [15]

These published missives continued, and by 1788 Wiesenthal apparently decided that they had prepared the way for a meeting of Maryland's physicians. Their agenda: the best way to present their petition to the General Assembly asking for better regulation. The physicians of Baltimore had already organized themselves into a medical society with that avowed purpose, but Wiesenthal, the Baltimore society's president, wanted physicians from throughout the state to gather on December 15, 1788, at Stark's Tavern in Baltimore. If they could not attend, he said, they should send him their ideas about this plan. Despite Wiesenthal's careful and extended preparation, this attempt at organization failed. Neither their educational efforts nor their lobbying at the state legislature was successful, and the society collapsed in 1790.[16]

Although their early societies were short-lived, the needs and common interests of Maryland doctors continued to press them toward the creation of a permanent organization. In 1798, they launched yet another organizational effort, and at last they succeeded. This time, the state legislature passed "An Act to establish and incorporate a medical and chirurgical faculty or society in the state of Maryland" (January 20, 1799). As the preamble to the act of 1798, chapter 105 read:

> Whereas it appears to the general assembly of Maryland, that the establishment and incorporation of a medical and chirurgical faculty or society of physicians and surgeons in the said state will be attended with the most beneficial and salutary consequences, by promoting and disseminating medical and chirurgical knowledge throughout the state, and may in future prevent the citizens thereof from risking their lives in the hands of ignorant practitioners or pretenders to the healing art.[17]

Perhaps concerned that Baltimore might dominate the new society, the legislature wrote an element of geographical diversity into the law. Section IV of the act of incorporation stated

> that it shall and may be lawful for the said medical faculty, or any number of them attending, (not less than fifteen,) to elect by ballot twelve persons of the greatest medical and chirurgical abilities in the state, who shall be styled the Medical Board of Examiners for the State of Maryland, seven of whom shall be residents of the western and five of the eastern shore of Maryland, whose duty it shall be to grant to such medical and chirurgical gentlemen as they, either upon full examination, or upon the production of diplomas from some respectable college, may judge adequate to commence the practice of the medical and

chirurgical arts, each person so obtaining a certificate to pay a sum not exceeding ten dollars, to be fixed on or ascertained by the faculty.[18]

With this provision, the state had given to the regulars in medical practice jurisdiction over entry to their profession.[19] Expertise—that is, "the greatest medical and chirurgical abilities"—justified removing that power from the hands of lay persons or their elected representatives. It remained to be seen, however, whether the Faculty's jurisdiction would be exclusive and how the profession would deal with "ignorant practitioners or pretenders to the healing art."

The Faculty's initially incorporated members were recruited fairly evenly from across the state in the following numbers:[20]

Saint Mary's County	5	City of Annapolis	4
Kent County	5	Queen Anne's County	5
Anne Arundel County	5	Worcester County	5
Calvert County	5	Frederick County	5
Charles County	5	Harford County	4
Baltimore County	5	Caroline County	5
Talbot County	4	City of Baltimore	9
Somerset County	5	Washington County	5
Dorchester County	5	Montgomery County	6
Cecil County	5	Allegany County	3
Prince George's County	5		

By ensuring that all the counties of Maryland were adequately and as far as possible evenly represented, the society could perhaps engender a sense of unity or comity among the state's physicians. Unity and good geographical coverage would also help the organization protect the profession's political standing in Annapolis.

There were other practical considerations. At the end of the eighteenth century, the journey to Baltimore or Annapolis from several of the counties was a time-consuming and arduous undertaking. But the core of the organization, located in Baltimore and conducting its political efforts in Annapolis, needed to keep in touch with activities throughout the state. The answer was to decentralize; examiners for the Medical and Chirurgical Faculty (Med Chi) were chosen to oversee their own areas and to ensure that applicants for licensure from the Faculty were suitably qualified. They were also charged with the task of reporting unlicensed medical practice to the Faculty so that the organization could conduct proceedings of censure. At first, the Faculty's leaders thought the society should collect this sort of information and discuss these issues at regular gatherings in the state capital. The first was held on June 3, 1799, and the second, two years later, also in Annapolis. But after the attendance was disappointingly low at the third meeting, the Faculty decided to relocate and hold annual gatherings in Baltimore.[21]

The Faculty had to remain active if it was going to achieve one of its primary goals, establishing licensing as a requirement for practicing medicine in Maryland. The act of incorporation stated that "no person, not already a practitioner of medicine or surgery, shall be allowed to practice in either of the said branches and receive payment for his services, without having first obtained a license, certified as this law directed, under penalty of fifty dollars for each offence . . . one half for the use of the faculty, and the other for that of the informer."[22] But this seemingly explicit provision was actually like a patent for an invention; it would have to be enforced in practice to prevent "ignorant practitioners or pretenders" from continuing to sell their medical services. From 1820 until after the Civil War, in state by state, such laws broke down, enabling a wide variety of healers to conduct a wide variety of medical practices.[23] In Maryland, as it turned out, medical "pretenders" were still relatively rarely reported or fined. The respected physicians who acted as censors for the Faculty—men such as John Archer Sr.— were found to fall short when it came to supplying the names of offenders.[24] Since the censors ordinarily lived and worked in the same small communities as the "imposters" and their patients, it is easy to understand why the censors were inclined to turn a blind eye to what was happening.

Another way in which an official organization tried to bring unity to the medical profession was in the delicate area of fees. Bill collection in Maryland was an almost ubiquitous problem, but it was especially difficult (then and now) in the caring professions. As we saw above, physicians had found it difficult to collect the money they were owed when war depreciated the currency; even in peacetime, however, creditors experienced problems because of inflation and the lack of a uniform currency. In the early decades of the nineteenth century, physicians made some progress in setting standard fees for their services. But many patients still could not pay in cash, and they perforce used the barter system.

We can see an example of this in the account books of Dr. William E. Seth, who lived and practiced on the Eastern Shore of Maryland in the late eighteenth and early nineteenth centuries. Seth, who joined the Medical and Chirurgical Faculty in 1801, listed his official fees as follows:

September 29, 1807: Night visit $3.50, plus medications, total $5.24.
September 4, 1810: House call, plus medications, total $2.25.
September, 1810: Letter of Advice in Pleurisy $1.00
September, 1811: Vaccinating three children $3.00
September, 1812: Night visit $2.67, plus medications, total $3.25.

In fact, these records are misleading; much of Seth's remuneration came in the form of cider, rum, brandy, meat, and livestock.[25]

This problem persisted through the entire century. Dr. Lewis Woodward (1848–82), who practiced in Westminster, Maryland, recorded some of his economic difficulties in an 1880 letter to his brother: "I believe I have . . . generally plenty to do," he wrote. "Of course, a good deal of it is not very remunerative having to take my share of charity patients with the rest. The very low rate of charges here is a drawback to anyone desiring to become rich, but as my inclination is not in that direction that does not worry me." Without becoming "rich," Woodward managed to build a substantial practice before he contracted diphtheria from one of his patients and died of complications from the infection.[26]

Even with the Medical and Chirurgical Faculty behind them, physicians were not in a strong position to standardize their fees. The association included only a portion of the regular and clearly none of the irregular practitioners. Moreover, the regulars often could not command the unquestioning respect of the population; only rarely could trained physicians provide a measure of care and treatment that manifestly surpassed that provided by domestic and other healers.

The Thomsonian Challenge

The Faculty had good reason to conclude that it had failed to convince even the state legislature that its services clearly surpassed those of its irregular rivals. By the 1830s, Med Chi seemed to be making important strides toward medical regulation, but in 1838 the legislature passed a new law that undercut the Faculty's program. The offending measure was "an act to authorise the Thomsonians or Botanic Physicians, to charge and receive compensation for their services and medicine." This was a crushing blow that seemed to undo most of what the regulars thought they had accomplished in 1799.[27] They had for some time been openly hostile to Thomson's followers, the first sect to pose a substantial threat to their primary position in the state.[28]

Although many of the medical sects—including homeopathy and hydropathy—originated in Europe, they blossomed in greater profusion in America. As medical historian James Cassedy has remarked, American attitudes toward medical practitioners and their therapies reflected the diversity of the country's population as well as the need for everyone to attempt to be his or her own doctor.[29] People had that opportunity if they followed the teachings of Samuel Thomson (1769–1843), who in 1805 began to devote his career solely to the propagation of his concepts of proper medical practice. Although Thomson did not establish a sect, one developed around his ideas and then spread rapidly from his home in Alstead, New Hampshire, throughout the Northeast, the South, and the Midwest. In many ways his system was not greatly different from that of the regular medical profession, except that he used herbal remedies instead of mineral-based drugs and was more assertive about the natural power of the body to heal itself. As a young man, Thomson had developed an interest in the plants that grew in his vicinity and had been mentored by a woman who was an herbal healer. Of all the plants he studied, lobelia (*Lobelia inflata*) was his favorite and came to hold the most prominent place among his prescribed remedies. Lobelia, a powerful emetic, had long been part of the materia medica of Native Americans. It could readily be harvested in most parts of the United States and was thus an inexpensive treatment available to most Americans.

Thomson was an accessible, self-made man. He began as an apprentice to local root, herbal, and regular doctors, trying to glean what knowledge he could while eking out a meager living on his family farm. In 1790, he married and soon turned his attention to treating his own family in times of illness. After experimenting with elements of both regular and herbal medicine, he decided that the remedies he was able to concoct himself from herbs were more efficacious than anything else that was available. He developed treatments based on lobelia and steam baths for such maladies as scarlet fever and measles. His reputation as a healer soon spread, and by 1805 he had left farming and was devoting himself solely to his art. In 1806, he opened an infirmary in Boston, and by 1810 he was manufacturing the remedies for which he would seek and obtain patent protection in 1813.[30]

While Thomson largely accepted humoral theory as modified by Galen, he rejected the harsh therapies employed by the regular medical profession, believing that they diminished the body's ability to heal "in its cold state of disease." Instead, he sought to increase the body's vital heat by restoring the digestive powers. In addition to his signature plant lobelia (also appropriately known as pukeweed), Thomson used a variety of hot botanicals such as red pepper, as well as restoratives and steam treatment to stimulate patients' body heat.

His patented regimen began with steaming. This was normally done by sitting the naked patient wrapped in blankets on a chair over a tub of water in which red-hot stones were placed. This was followed by a six-stage program employing emetics, purgatives, enemas, and additional sweating. Lobelia combined with red pepper and brandy produced vomiting and perspiration, indicating that the stomach was cleansed and the body heat rising. After more steaming, the patient was again given red peppers along with ginger or black pepper; more perspiration resulted. Then the healer could administer one or more of a variety of botanicals that included bayberry, the root of white pond lily, the inner bark of hemlock, the root of marsh rosemary, the leaves of witch hazel, the leaves of red raspberry, and "squaw weed." Their purpose was to "scour the stomach and bowels." Next came a choice of bitters aimed at correcting the bile and restoring the patient's digestion; these comprised balmony, bitterroot, poplar bark, barberry, and goldenseal root. This was followed by tonic plants prepared in sugar and brandy and finally by Thomson's renowned and widely used Rheumatic Drops, which consisted of wine or brandy, gum myrrh, and cayenne pepper.[31] All this was part of Thomson's effort to provide an alternative to the harsh mineral remedies and the bleeding and blistering of the regular medical men!

While this alternative may not seem particularly mild to the present-day reader, it appealed to many nineteenth-century Americans. The accessibility and affordability of Thomsonian treatments made them very attractive. So, too, was the possibility that every man could be his own doctor, which was at that time often a practical necessity. Anyone who could pay twenty dollars was provided with the rights to Thomson's 1813 patent. Although that was a considerable amount of money to raise in one sum, it was vastly less expensive than paying for the repeated visits of a physician over many years. According to Thomson, by 1839 he had sold 100,000 "family rights."[32] Moreover, Thomsonianism freed people from being subjected to the social pretensions of some members of the educated medical profession, a prospect that resonated with the culture of Jacksonian America. Thomsonian rhetoric customarily reserved its own reverential tones for references to General Jackson.[33]

Although Thomsonians prided themselves in being able to practice medicine alone, they, like members of the other sects that emerged, welcomed the support of the like-minded and organized themselves into "friendly societies." These associations presented an organized rival standing in opposition to the regular profession. In addition to sharing information, these societies lobbied state legislatures to change licensing laws that placed control of medical practice in the hands of the regulars.[34] Maryland had a substantial Thomsonian following, whose members formed the Third Branch of the Thomsonian Friendly Botanical Society in March 1835. As the assembled botanics explained, they were forming the society "believing the Botanic System of Medicine as discovered and practiced by Doc. Samuel Thomson to be the most efficatious as well as the most simple and cheap of any known to us."[35] By January 1836, James Stabler of Elkton, Maryland, was writing with enthusiasm: "The Thomsonian system is about as far a head of the old practice, as the Himalaya's [*sic*] are above the Sugar Loaf, or small hill, and the Botanic fraternity number some hundreds of converts from the old school of quite as much gumption as most that remain behind them."[36]

The same month that the Maryland Thomsonians organized their Friendly Society, the regulars launched their direct attack on the sect on the floor of the House of Delegates. Led by Dr. Williams of Worcester County, they thwarted the Botanic effort to pass a "Bill to Incorporate the Thomsonian National Infirmary" in Baltimore. There were harsh words from both camps. Addressing the delegates, Williams denounced the Thomsonians as "men destitute of intelligence, good sense, or moral worth, who can raise twenty dollars for a Thomsonian book." They employed, he said, "common domestic, old woman remedies . . . . This system originated with a man by the name of Thomson, who according to his own narrative, was born in obscurity and bred in ignorance. It appears that his early life was characterized by two very remarkable dispositions, one was a curiosity to learn the qualities and names of plants, the other an unconquerable repugnance to work."[37]

Not to be outdone, the friendly Thomsonians countered: "The present law-protected system of Calomelising and blood-letting, maugre its boasted antiquity, is still in its swaddling-clothes, and notwithstanding the sanction which it has by law, it is in a rapid decline, and will die, rot and be forgotten in less than half a century." By contrast, "the Thomsonians solicited no 'legislative sanction' for their practice; its own intrinsic merits constitute the only claim it puts forth for public patronage."[38] While the state legislature may or may not have understood the "intrinsic merit" of Thomsonianism, it was willing to give the people of Maryland what apparently many of them wanted. It passed the 1838 act granting the sect rights similar to those of the regulars to treat patients and be paid for services. Much to the chagrin of regular practitioners, several states in addition to Maryland protected the irregulars and their societies, hospitals, and schools.

Despite the protection it received, Thomsonianism—like other enthusiasms that swept through nineteenth-century Maryland—began to fade from popularity after the founder and the first generation of practitioners started to pass from the scene.[39] When Isaac Briggs Jr. of Baltimore became ill in 1873, he reported on the situation in that city. He was suffering from "an obstinate spell of the Jaundice," due, he thought, to "my night exposure to cold and malaria from that most horrible disgusting and abominable of all basins—the basin of Baltimore." Unable to work, he treated himself with a "powerful Livor Invigorator," but, he grumbled, "How quick 2 or 3 good Thomsonian courses would set me all right again—but alas! There are no Thomsonian practitioners left in Baltimore that I can hear of—all dead that I formerly knew."[40]

Phrenology

Phrenology, which had more to do with diagnostics than therapeutics, became a highly popular sect during the middle decades of the nineteenth century. It long outlasted some of its competitors and even attracted many believers during the twentieth century. Phrenology was a pseudoscience that could be found in practice in a wide range of institutions, from highly respected university laboratories to the local pharmacist's shop.[41]

Viennese physician Franz Joseph Gall laid down the main conceptual constructs of phrenology in the 1790s. Although T. M. I. Forster, an English physician, coined the term *phrenology* in 1815, Gall formulated the set of concepts that put together a theory of the brain and a study of character. He deemed certain specific areas of the brain responsible for certain personality traits and concluded that these areas could be measured accurately by examining the human head. During the nineteenth century, phrenology went through numerous modifications in Europe and the United States. By the 1860s, the work of Pierre-Paul Broca, among others, had begun to provide clinical evidence in support of cerebral localization. But during this era, phrenology's influence went far beyond clinical and scientific ventures. It found deep resonance in Victorian society and was applied in an effort to access intelligence, tendencies toward criminality, romantic compatibility, and a host of other aspects of human behavior. In America, it influenced psychiatry and neurology, penology, and education.[42]

Proponents of this new science postulated that rather than the brain being a unitary organ, it was in fact composed of thirty-seven distinguishable faculties that were responsible for various aptitudes or propensities. This idea caught on quickly in Maryland. The first meeting of the Baltimore Phrenological Society on February 17, 1827, drew nine men, six of them medical doctors. From the start, they established the fundamentals of their doctrine:

> 1. That the brain is an aggregate of organs, and, as an organic system, constitutes exclusively the organ of the mind.
> 2. That the mind possesses a number of distinct and innate faculties each of them dependent on a particular material organ for its manifestation—the power of each faculties [*sic*] manifestation being in proportion to the *size* of its cerebral organ.
> 3. That it is possible, *in most instances,* to determine the existence of these internal organs, by corresponding developments on the skull; and hence be led to establish, a priori, the Education most suitable to be given to, and the Profession best adapted for, different individuals.[43]

The society kept detailed case studies of individuals. The reports contain measurements of the different areas of the skull, ranging from "very small" to "very large." These results provided indications, phrenologists assumed, of the degree of development of each of the thirty-seven faculties, including "combativeness, secretiveness, self-esteem, benevolence, marvellousness, weight, and language."[44] The report on Sergeant Bosworth of Fort McHenry explains the man's rapid remarriage after the death of his wife by reference to "the thickness of this man's neck and protuberance of the part where amativeness is located."[45] Although phrenology did not influence medicine in Maryland to the extent that Thomsonianism and other sects did, it remained an active element in the state's medical culture long after scientific medicine had taken over the lead role in shaping the medical profession.

The Expansion of Homeopathy

With the decline of Thomsonianism, the regular physicians in Maryland were not left in peace; another popular sect arose to challenge their therapeutic authority. Eclecticism enjoyed a brief period of expansion, but it was soon overshadowed by homeopathy, which, like phrenology, was an imported therapy.[46] This prominent sect was the brainchild of a regular German medical practitioner, Samuel Christian Friedrich Hahnemann (1755–1843). Hahnemann was a well-educated man who was fluent in several languages and had traveled extensively around Europe. He believed in the importance of balancing a sound diet, fresh air, and exercise to maintain good health and to promote healing. These were not particularly novel concepts in the eighteenth century, but then Hahnemann began to extend and elaborate on his concepts of proper therapy. Early in his career, he became disenchanted with the practices of the regular medical profession, especially with excessive bloodletting and the drugs that were being employed. His enquiring mind set him to work on the first of many series of pharmacological experiments, starting with himself as the clinical subject. In 1810, he published the results of his trials and his alternative theories in the *Organon of Medicine,* a book that went through five editions before his death in 1843.[47]

Hahnemann was critical of the fundamental way in which drugs were used. He recognized that numerous pharmaceutical preparations were valuable, but he questioned the common practice of the regular profession of combining several drugs in one dose (polypharmacy). He also believed that such medications served only as a means of "hushing up of the symptoms." He concluded that "all the usual palliatives have a secondary action that increases the patient's suffering, and the old school physicians have to keep repeating them in stronger doses to obtain the same relief. The relief is never lasting, and the symptoms always return worse than before."[48]

After several years of experimentation, Hahnemann arrived at the two main conclusions that came to be the signature of his system. *Similar similibus curantur,* or "likes cure like"—meaning that homeopaths should prescribe a specific medicine that, when given to a healthy person, most closely mimics the symptoms of the disease in its natural state. In his *Organon,* Hahnemann gave lengthy descriptions of how the homeopath should accomplish this end and paid special attention to the minute details of all symptoms. The father of homeopathy also arrived at a "law of infinitesimals" that has distressed the regular medical and scientific communities for nearly two centuries. Hahnemann believed that in illness the body was especially sensitive to drugs and that unbelievably tiny amounts were most effective.[49]

Unlike Thomsonianism, homeopathy was not intended to be practiced by the common man. In fact, its adherents claimed specialized knowledge and a sound theoretical base, much as did the members of the orthodox profession. Homeopaths studied the effects of their remedies and dosages in tests that they referred to as "provings." Their theory and practice combined to give them and much of the public the impression that they were every bit as scientific as the regular medical profession, and this argument was widely used in their favor.[50]

Homeopathy established a sound reputation in New York during the 1832 cholera epidemic, and its standing was strengthened further in the epidemics of 1848 and 1852. During each of these crises, its treatments were widely preferred over orthodox efforts.[51] Given the nature of cholera's symptoms, this preference seems quite understandable; depletion could hardly have appeared a desirable therapeutic choice.

The scientific claims of homeopathy probably had far less to do with its success, however, than did the particular nature of its therapeutics. The little white "sugar pills" that contained Hahnemannian preparations such as belladonna, aconite, and arsenicum were tasteless and produced no visible side effects. Homeopaths eschewed the bleeding, blistering, and harsh drugs of the regular professionals, whom they termed the "allopaths." Instead, homeopaths supplemented their remedies with advice about diet and exercise. This gentle regimen was especially appealing to women and children. Dr. John Ellis, who published *Family Homoeopathy* in 1879, was quite aware of why this therapeutic system was so popular. He had been professor of the theory and practice of medicine at the New York Medical College for Women.[52]

Throughout the northeastern states, homeopathy appealed in a special way not only to women and children, but also to members of the middle and upper classes. It included in its fold many more well-educated, articulate, and respected men and women than had Thomsonianism. In Maryland, as elsewhere, homeopathy attracted an important supportive elite. During the 1870s and 1880s, Henry Janes, the business partner of well-known philanthropist Enoch Pratt, was deeply committed to Maryland's homeopathic dispensary. Janes was certain that the statistics for homeopathic treatments and cures could easily demonstrate the superiority of that system over that of the allopathic physicians.[53]

While homeopathy enjoyed its greatest popularity in the states to the north of Maryland (especially in New York and Pennsylvania), Maryland continued to have a substantial homeopathic following in the late nineteenth century. Quite a number of regular physicians turned to homeopathy for at least part of their therapeutic armamentarium.[54] One was

Dr. Samuel Harper (1805–71). Harper, who was born in Queen Anne's County, received his medical degree from the University of Maryland in 1827. He promptly joined the Medical and Chirurgical Faculty, and by 1829 he was serving as one of the organization's Eastern Shore Censors, monitoring and reporting on unlicensed practitioners. Harper developed a busy practice embracing patients from Caroline, Queen Anne's, and Talbot Counties. He became a prominent citizen, acted as a justice of the peace in Caroline County, and dabbled in local politics.

In 1858, Harper moved to Kent County. His practice took on a different hue when he started to advertise himself as a homeopathic physician. News of this soon reached the Medical and Chirurgical Faculty, which withdrew his membership on the grounds of his "alleged union with homeopathists." While this professional slight might have severely damaged a medical man's reputation and thus his practice, that was not the case with Harper. He continued to thrive and was extremely popular among his patients on the Eastern Shore.[55]

Homeopathy, too, continued to have a strong following on the Eastern Shore. Dr. Thomas Cooper, who spent his whole life on the Delmarva Peninsula, was by the 1880s heavily committed to Hahnemann's style of therapeutics. Cooper had moved to Chestertown in Kent County, and in January 1884 he attended a meeting in Wilmington, Delaware, at which the Homeopathic Medical Society of Delaware and the Peninsula was established. Cooper was elected vice-president and was joined in his enthusiasm for the sect by his three physician brothers, who had all become officers of the society by 1887.[56]

Unlike Thomsonianism, homeopathy held its own in Maryland until the end of the nineteenth century. Its continued popularity, like that of the other sects, can to a large degree be explained by the dreadful nature of the regular therapeutic triad of bleeding, blistering, and purging.[57] Neither the regulars nor the homeopaths had reliable data on the efficacy of any particular therapy; under those circumstances, who can fault the Marylanders of that era who opted for the mildest therapy which anecdotal evidence suggested might give them a chance of recovery. The same could be said for their interest in hydropathy, osteopathy, naturopathy, and chiropractic, all of which were dissenting schools of healing that developed in reaction to the mainline profession and its therapies.[58]

Under pressure from the sects and determined to vindicate their profession, some regular physicians had, by the middle of the nineteenth century, begun to rethink their own approach to therapy. This movement began in Germany and France and then spread to the United States. Increasingly, physicians became convinced of what many of their patients already knew: experience was often more valuable than traditional theory when it came to treatment. As John Harley Warner explained, there was a change in the "therapeutic perspective" as the physicians turned away from rationalistic systems and toward empiricism.[59] This new perspective helped arm them against the sects and, even more importantly, began to militate against heroic measures and thus improve the public image of the profession.

Midwifery and Domestic Medicine

Like the homeopathic physicians, midwives were outside the confines of regular practice, but their relationships with the regulars were often co-operative. In Maryland, as in Europe at that time, midwifery and domestic medicine were intimately related. Both lay in the province of women, and this had been the case since time immemorial. Commonly, the same experienced women in the local community who were called upon to assist in childbirth were the ones who possessed the broadest knowledge of herbal remedies, poultice applications, and the steps to take when coping with dying family members.

Midwives learned on the job. Sometimes they had worked as young women with an already experienced midwife; sometimes they simply learned because they were the only women available in small communities; often they had had substantial personal experience of birthing. In remote areas, midwives often had to work alone, but wherever possible, parturient women gathered around them female relatives, friends, and neighbors to assist them in their ordeal. Female friends provided comfort and support; the midwives brought their skill and reassurance.[60]

Usually midwives were called in to assist at a birth when labor pains began, and they stayed in the household until the baby was delivered. In situations where the midwife determined that the birthing process was not going well and that there were complications, she frequently called in a doctor, but in many remote areas no assistance was available, regardless of what happened. Often the midwife returned to check up on the mother or remained in the house for a few hours or days after birth to assist with domestic chores and to care for the baby and the mother during her recovery. Midwives were paid a fee for their services, or, where cash was not forthcoming, they accepted payment in kind, an especially common practice in rural areas. Payment operated on a sliding scale; wealthier families paid more, poorer ones less. Sometimes midwives' payments were supplemented by grateful members of the extended family when they lived nearby.[61]

Midwives' skills, like those of most practitioners, were far from uniform, a fact that increasingly concerned their critics in Europe and the United States. The opponents of midwifery could certainly find instances in which dirty, drunken, or incompetent women seemed to be responsible for the untimely demise of a mother or an infant. But these widely publicized anecdotes were doubtless exaggerated. For the most part, midwives used their specialized knowledge and experience to save lives as well as to care for individuals involved in what was mostly a normal, healthy process. In the early nineteenth century, many were able to perform *version*—the manipulation of the fetus in utero—to turn a breech or otherwise badly positioned baby into the head-down position most conducive to childbirth. This valuable skill, rarely possessed at that time by physicians, undoubtedly reduced maternal and infant mortality and morbidity. Midwives were also able to induce labor by administering ergot, a substance that was derived from a fungal growth on rye grain and was readily available in the United States. By the late eighteenth and early nineteenth centuries, physicians had begun to recognize that ergot could be used to bring on preterm delivery in cases where the mother had a tiny or a malformed pelvis. Ergot was also useful in stemming postpartum hemorrhages because it brought about contraction of the uterus, thus saving lives as well as accelerating postpartum recoveries by preventing excessive blood loss.[62]

Maryland's midwives also used their special techniques and herbs to expel unwanted fetuses, and this posed a clear threat to the medical profession. In this case, the midwives were directly competing with the doctors, and their widely acknowledged ability to eliminate unwanted pregnancies also aroused concerns about patients' safety. By 1867, the medical practitioners of Maryland had been able to persuade the state to eliminate those concerns. The legislature responded with "an act for the protection of the public against medical imposters and for the suppression of the crime of unlawful abortion." With strong support from the American Medical Association, the effort to impose legal controls on abortion became a national movement.[63]

Midwifery in Maryland and the rest of the United States did not have the kind of quasi-professional standing that it had in Europe, so its practitioners were unable to react very effectively when doctors started to make claims of authority over birthing. This was true even though the midwives occasionally drew support from the sects. Their opposition to the harsh medications and methods of the regular medical profession sometimes elicited faint calls for unity. Thomas Hersey, for example, believed that women were best suited to assisting other women during childbirth. Hersey, who said he was a "practicing physician of the botanic order, formerly Surgeon in the U.S. Army," published a Thomsonian text in Baltimore entitled *The Midwife's Practical Directory; or, Woman's Confidential Friend: Comprising Extensive Remarks on the Various Casualties, and Forms of Disease, Preceding, Attending and Following, the Period of Gestation.*

Hersey was fierce in his denunciation of the regular medical profession's obstetrical techniques.

> Many of our men-midwives resort to instruments on every slight emergency, using the forceps to expedite a lingering labor, that would have resulted more favorably, if they had been dead or consigned to Botany Bay, before they raised those instruments of cruelty, merely to evince their scientific skill . . . . The lacerations we have known; the lameness that has been induced, the incontinence of urine, prolapsus uteri, and other disastrous consequences, have been to us matter of solemn warning, to avoid the perforations, the forceps, the lever, the vectis, and the blunt hook, of the scientific accoucheur. The midwife who understands the principles of nature's operation in bringing forth children, will not resort to pincers, tongs nor crowbars, to dig for babies.[64]

Despite the support of Hersey and others from the sects, midwives found their domain of practice shrinking in the late nineteenth century as regular physicians became more involved in obstetrics.

But long after the regulars had begun to gain greater jurisdiction over practice in Maryland, domestic and lay healing remained at the core of most people's medical encounters.[65] Home health guides were printed and distributed widely and in abundance. Women commonly wrote health notes in their recipe books for cooking, and many of the self-help guides intermingled recipes for food, home health advice, and tips on etiquette and craft work. The "cult of domesticity" in the Victorian age left matters of education, religion, and health primarily under the control of women.[66] Men, too, incorporated home health remedies into their daily work, writing occasional health recipes and placing clippings in their letters and account books. They recorded illnesses that had apparently been cured by domestic remedies. On balance, however, domestic medicine remained primarily in the hands of women.

Home health guides continued in heavy use in Maryland. These publications were usually simply printed and relatively inexpensive, offering a wide range of advice on a wide range of domestic topics. In the early nineteenth century, Hannah Williams' recipe book (c. 1819) contained such instructions as how "to cure frozen limbs: A poultice made of yeast and Indian meal, it is equally good for burning."[67] Later in the century, Marylanders could turn to cookbooks from the Sassafrass Beach Company (of Maryland). At the end of one volume are several pages of home remedies, which include the following.

> Cold on the Chest. A flannell dippen in boiling water, and sprinkled with turpentine, laid on the chest, quickly as possible, will relieve a severe cold or hoarseness.

> For Ivy Poisoning. Dissolve a handfull of quick-lime in a pinch of cold water: bathe the parts often and after a few applications they will be quite well.

> Good for Severe Vomiting. 1 Tablespoon black pepper, one of salt, half a thimble full of warm water, and as much good cider vinegar; give of this a tablespoonful (to an adult) every minute or two, stirring well, till the whole glass is taken. The first glassfull may be vomited; if so, repeat the dose; this is good in cholera morbus, and even cholera if taken at the commencement.

The cookbooks could be used to collect clippings of the sort that have found their way into the collections of the Maryland Historical Society (1860–90). Alongside items "about round doilies" are stories about John R. Cox, who claimed to have a new cure for cholera. The author described how the captain of an emigrant ship sailing to the United States from Europe had lost many passengers to the disease. In desperation he had devised his own treatment, which was made by adding one teaspoonful of red pepper and a tablespoon of salt to a half pint of boiling water. Cox maintained that this worked like a charm, curing all the cases on board. He concluded that "this will be worth more to the general common good than all the municipal sanitary measures we can adopt."[68]

In addition to such bogus cures as Cox was offering, Marylanders were deluged with advertisements for patent medicines. Not all of them came from lay persons. In the early nineteenth century, Dr. William Zollickoffer of Carroll County, Maryland, combined a regular practice with the production and distribution of his "Vegetable Purgative and Alternative Pills." His nostrums could be purchased either wholesale or retail from John F. Reese of Westminster and from most apothecaries and storekeepers throughout the state. Later in the century, the business in nostrums burgeoned as industrial growth put cash in the hands of more and more Marylanders and improvements in transportation and communication broadened the market for patent medicines. Advertising became more sophisticated and widespread, and mail-order operations reached out into the small towns and rural areas of the state.[69]

As late as the 1890s, the bulk of the medical care throughout Maryland was still in the home. Fairly typical of conditions outside of Baltimore was Rockville, Maryland, where Dr. Edward Elisha Stonestreet was in practice. Stonestreet had begun his study of medicine under the tutelage of a local physician in Olney and completed it at the University of Maryland medical school, where he received his M.D. degree in 1852. With some financial help from his father, he was able to open an office in Rockville and start a practice that would continue for the next half-century. He was a general practitioner who treated coughs and colds, delivered babies, and performed surgery. He saw patients at his office from 8:00 to 10:00 A.M. and from 4:00 to 6:00 P.M., but he frequently had to journey on horseback into rural Montgomery County to see his patients. When it snowed, he hitched his horse to a sleigh. His patients ranged from the wealthiest to the poorest in the county, and he served for a time as physician for the County Almshouse. Stonestreet, who held several public positions, was active in what became the Montgomery County Medical Society.[70]

Neither the local societies nor any of the other medical organizations in the state had by that time been able to centralize authority over the profession. In the 1890s, medicine in Maryland was still a complex, fiercely contested activity. The regular profession and Med Chi had made substantial progress, but they had not brought medical practice in the state under a single system or theoretical and practical framework. Sectarianism was still vibrant. Self-medication was extremely widespread. Scientific medicine was making inroads, but it still remained unclear how the tensions between the regulars and irregulars would play out in either Baltimore or the state's smaller communities.

Medicine in the Hospital

The Mainstream Institutions,

1799–1940

In Maryland and elsewhere, hospitals arose from a need to care for those who were otherwise left out—sick people who had nowhere else to turn and no one else to care for them. The "left-out" sick came from the socially and economically marginalized parts of the population. Indeed, the social structure within the hospital mirrored that of the society at large. The patients of nineteenth-century hospitals were poor, often immigrants, sometimes unwed or indigent birthing women, and frequently African Americans.[1]

Hospital patients were largely but not entirely city or town dwellers. In a state like Maryland, with a highly mobile population and a rapidly expanding urban center in Baltimore, there were many persons who lacked a network of friends and family to support them in times of illness. Everything that could be done in an early nineteenth-century hospital could be done at home—and was. But if you were unable to afford the services of a physician, you were often left with no choice but to seek hospitalization.

The early development of hospitals and other similar social institutions was constrained by the lack of public capital and the weakness of social values. Nineteenth-century Marylanders were, like Americans in other states, bent upon material progress and suspicious of public authority and the taxes it inevitably entailed. As the state prospered, however, it gradually developed a business elite that could afford philanthropy and recognized the value of helping those who needed hospitalization.[2]

Both the philanthropists and the physicians who founded these institutions stressed the social imperative. As in other states, both men and women were prime movers in establishing hospitals as part of their broader reform activities. Men and women played critical roles in providing seed money and in forming the committees essential to establish support for a new institution. Frequently, these same women would constitute the boards of lady managers and the men would join the board of trustees that commonly controlled nineteenth-century hospitals.

We can, of course, scratch the surface of their statements and find some evidence consistent with a subtle combination of social and self-interest. Urban philanthropists who were connected with commercial and later industrial enterprises were aware of the need to provide treatment for sick workers. As subscribers or trustees, they could give their workers a letter of introduction that would serve as an admission ticket to many voluntary hospitals.

Early to mid–nineteenth-century hospitals also served the needs of elite physicians. Most would-be medical men received no hospital training. But the hospital was crucial to the clinical training of those few, well-connected young men whose ambition guided them toward practices treating the wealthy. During the first half of the nineteenth century, such aspirants frequently went to Europe to gain the training that was offered in Scotland and Paris, where medical education was the most advanced and where infirmary and clinic experience was more readily available. These students learned by seeing large numbers of patients, by matching diagnostic observations with disease histories, and by performing autopsies.[3] But not all who had these aspirations could go to Europe. To them it was of vital importance that Maryland have its own, similar institutions. Hospitals furnished medical students with clinical experience and also provided the social contacts that held the key to elite medical practice.

Thus, the state acquired its teaching hospitals, where the poor were treated free in an implicit exchange for serving as the "clinical material" for medical instruction. In the later nineteenth and early twentieth centuries, hospitals became ever more important centers of education, especially in the emerging specialties.[4] Social need, self-interest, and professional progress thus blended in a characteristically American way to encourage the development of new hospitals in Maryland.

Almshouses

Long before Marylanders had organized their first hospital they had established a number of almshouses that cared for the poor and sick. Those institutions housed people of all ages. Until the late eighteenth century, the impoverished—often tenants in debt, sometimes unable to work because of illness—faced the shame and squalid conditions of debtors' prisons and county jails. Not surprisingly, this treatment frequently worsened the situation for poor families. The state assembly, responding to pressure for change, set out in 1768 to create alms and workhouses for seven counties, and five years later voted four thousand pounds of tobacco for the land they needed.[5] The first workhouse, located on a twenty-acre plot at Biddle and Eutaw Streets in Baltimore, housed and put to work beggars and vagrants while accommodating the sick in its infirmary. By 1814, the growing number of those who were both poor and ill required a full-time physician, seven visiting physicians, a surgeon, a druggist, and a matron. Since the institution's doctors were all on the medical and surgical faculty of the new College of Medicine, the infirmary was performing a dual service. It was providing medical attention to its inmates while giving educational opportunities to the college's medical students.[6]

As Baltimore's population grew, the city's needy overflowed the almshouse. In 1819 Baltimore City and County cooperated in locating a new site, purchasing the Smith family estate for forty-four thousand dollars. After extending the existing house, the new institution was able to take in 533 paupers in 1822. The expanded infirmary quickly became an important part of local medical education. A group of resident students, under the supervision of visiting physicians, attended the sick, oversaw the insane, and assisted in childbirth. For many of the students at the College of Medicine, almshouse patients formed the chief "clinical material" of their training.

Neither the students nor their patients had an easy lot. While attempting to ameliorate the health of the almshouse inmates, the medical students and their supervisors had to struggle against serious public health problems. The institution had been built in an area that suffered from poor sewage disposal and periodically swarmed with mosquitoes. Malaria was not uncommon, and in 1832 a far more frightening disease hit the almshouse—cholera.[7]

Eventually, the city recognized the need to relocate the institution and, after two moves, the establishment was settled at a site on Eastern

Avenue, where it became the Mason F. Lord Chronic Hospital and Nursing Facility. In 1871, the institution was renamed the Bay View Asylum, and with that change inmates were increasingly admitted for medical and psychiatric care, rather than indigency. That year the resident and visiting physicians, medical students, and apothecary treated 1,551 medical and surgical cases and cared for 246 insane patients. The most difficult of the mental patients were sequestered in barred cells in the basement, a common practice in the nineteenth century.

Although the treatment of the insane was traditional, even old-fashioned, Bay View was strongly influenced by modern changes in medicine, in particular by specialization near the end of the century. This development accelerated after 1911, when Dr. Thomas Boggs became the first chief of medicine. Boggs brought with him the spirit of Johns Hopkins, where for ten years he had been a resident under the distinguished physician and teacher William Osler. Boggs oversaw the opening of separate departments for pathology, psychiatry, and tuberculosis. In 1925, the asylum's name was changed to Baltimore City Hospitals, and ten years later a new acute-care hospital was built to house obstetrical, surgical, medical, and pediatric wards. By World War II, Baltimore City Hospitals had a set of extensive buildings housing acute and chronic cases and the institution had largely lost its identification with its almshouse origins.

The evolution from an almshouse to a modern medical hospital was a pattern common to the mainstream institutions in Maryland. Hospitals throughout the state and nation underwent this same social transformation. In the period 1850–1920, they gradually evolved from asylums for the indigent poor to medical centers.[8] Hospitals became institutions for people of all social classes, and they increasingly provided a variety of diagnostics and therapeutics that were not available in a domestic setting.[9] With the emergence of science-based medicine, Maryland's hospitals became important sources of new knowledge and treatment.

The Baltimore General Dispensary

As asylums evolved into medical centers, the need for almshouses did not disappear. It continued well into the twentieth century. As late as 1890, there were still 1,599 paupers in Maryland almshouses, almost 25 percent of whom were African-American and over 40 percent of whom were women.[10] Long before that time, however, it had been clearly recognized that almshouses could not cope with the growing numbers of the indigent sick. The need to separate sick from healthy inmates and provide adequate medical attention had become overwhelming. Even in the early 1800s, all too many of the sick refused to seek treatment. They hung on in their own dwellings, hoping to avoid the shame of charitable asylum.

This was a problem that had already been encountered in several industrializing European countries, and many American physicians and philanthropists saw the English dispensary movement as a model solution.[11] As in the Old World, they sought to separate the "worthy" poor from the "unworthy," the hard-working laborer who had fallen on tough times from the idle vagrant. The worthies, they believed, ought to be spared the humiliation of the almshouse.

In Maryland, the first institutional attempt to ameliorate this problem involved the Baltimore General Dispensary. In 1801, a group of Baltimore philanthropists formed a society, funded entirely by voluntary contributions, "for the purpose of furnishing medical relief to the indigent poor."[12] This endeavor succeeded and by 1807 was incorporated as the Baltimore General Dispensary, making it Maryland's third chartered institution, after the Equitable Fire Insurance Company and the Bank of Baltimore.

Despite the initial support it received from private sources, the dispensary struggled for decades. In an effort to keep it going, the state in 1819 granted it a temporary lottery. These and other efforts kept the dispensary afloat, and its physicians were thus able to continue visiting the city's poor in their residences and supplying them with medicines. The visiting physicians, who served gratis, included a long list of such notable practitioners as Joshua J. Cohen, F. Davidge, and S. C. Chew. From the 1820s through the 1840s, they and their peers provided relief to immigrants and aided in supplying and distributing smallpox vaccine.[13]

Some modern-day commentators have criticized physicians for their insensitivity toward hospital patients, but many of those physicians who visited the sick poor in their homes seem to have been sincerely moved by the "poverty, hunger, and dirt." Dr. William T. Wilson, for instance, remarked to one patient, "It is not medicine you want, but food and fuel." He handed out small sums of money on such visits. In 1852, Wilson left five thousand dollars in his will (a considerable sum for that time) for the dispensary to distribute in the form of "clothing, bedding, fuel, and dietary food."[14] The fact that Wilson did not bequeath his money to the purchase of medicines is informative. He and many of his peers took a broad view of illness, one in which environment was seen as a key element in the maintenance of health.

While the Wilson fund grew in the years that followed, the dispensary clearly could not meet the health needs of all the poor. Dispensary patients, especially those who needed surgery, continued to fall through the cracks. As the institution's managers put it:

> Dispensary patients are not often paupers, and therefore not eligible
> to the Alms House: and many of the other charities are not *all* charity,
> but run for the benefit of Medical Schools, to furnish clinical material;
> whilst others again are hedged about by sectional or sectarian barriers,
> so that by the time the poor patient has been bandied from one to the
> other, he is well nigh dead, ere he finds his credentials of admission
> (if he finds them at all), amply bound with the inevitable red tape.[15]

Seeking to avoid hospitalization, the sick poor turned in growing numbers to the dispensaries.[16]

There was obviously a growing need for this type of institution, but unfortunately, as medical education and treatment improved in the late nineteenth and early twentieth centuries, the dispensary fell further behind. Doctors were unhappy with additional house calls in which they lacked the control provided by a total institution. In Maryland and elsewhere, dispensaries could not provide the clinic setting that existed in hospital wards. They proffered less desirable teaching opportunities and were, therefore, viewed as offering lower status clinical appointments.[17] Little wonder that physicians and medical students alike sought the clinical and professional opportunities available in such institutions as the University of Maryland Hospital.

The University of Maryland Hospital

Baltimore's physicians, acting under the umbrella of the Medical and Chirurgical Faculty of Maryland, had since 1799 been pointing out the need to formalize the training of future generations of physicians. Medical students, they said, should have anatomical demonstrations, as well as a sound grasp of medical literature. With prompting from Med Chi, the state assembly incorporated the College of Medicine of Maryland on December 18, 1807.[18] Then, in 1812, the general assembly transformed the

College of Medicine into a centerpiece of the newly created University of Maryland.

The university's medical school thrived over the next decade, and its faculty increasingly agitated for better clinical opportunities. Of all the early professors, the controversial Scotsman Granville Sharp Pattison most ardently pressed for the founding of a hospital attached to the medical school.[19] In the meantime, however, John Beale Davidge and James Locke attempted to improve clinical training by sending their students to the Maryland Public Hospital, the almshouse, and the dispensary to observe and assist. Dr. Nathaniel Potter delivered clinical lectures to his students at the Maryland Hospital on Joppa Road.[20]

These accommodations, however, were no substitute for having ready access to and control over one's own patients. The situation worsened during the medical school's second decade, when the almshouse moved to Calverton, significantly reducing the accessible "clinical material." Faculty members responded by repeatedly asserting their need to have their own clinical institution. Unable to secure funding from the city or banks, Pattison finally persuaded his faculty colleagues to put up the money themselves. They could hardly have much more control, he argued, than they would achieve by owning their own hospital.[21]

On July 10, 1823, Professors Davidge, Potter, Hall, DeButts, Baker, McDowell, and Pattison signed a ninety-nine-year lease for a site near the corner of Lombard and Greene Streets, opposite the medical school.[22] They modeled this hospital, known as the Baltimore Infirmary, and its relationship to the medical school after the Edinburgh and Glasgow Infirmaries and their links to their famous medical schools. At last, Maryland's medical students could have regular exposure to large numbers of patients in the presence of their teachers.

The foundation for the infirmary was laid in June 1823, and three months later the first patients were admitted. There were four wards (one exclusively for eye injuries and diseases), and the infirmary restricted admission to acute cases. The weekly fee for treatment and care was three dollars, and all patients paid the fee in advance. Upon admission, medical students took patient histories and recited them to the visiting physicians. This provided the kind of experience that the faculty had envisioned. So, too, did the infirmary's operating theater, which, surrounded by elevated seats in the European amphitheater style, permitted several hundred students to observe surgical procedures.[23]

Just as the physicians obtained the clinical access they needed, however, serious problems developed. Trouble broke out between the physicians and the university's administrators. During the late 1820s, in a power struggle between the university's regents and the infirmary's trustees, the regents attempted to control the infirmary, and the state legislature finally transferred the administration of that institution from the regents to a state-appointed Board of Trustees. In most mid–nineteenth-century hospitals, trustees exercised far more control over their establishments than did physicians, and this certainly became the case after the Maryland legislature acted. The medical faculty was distressed. Having just realized their dream, they suddenly discovered that they had lost possession of their property and control of their infirmary to the board. Now the faculty worked both unpaid and unhappy.[24]

Through the 1830s the Baltimore Infirmary continued to struggle just to survive. Supplies were a constant problem, as were inferior medicines and cheap, unpalatable food. There was even a shortage of leeches! Although several lotteries were held to raise money, neither the board nor the faculty was able to solve the organization's economic problems. The infirmary found it difficult to handle its patient population, which included large numbers of sick sailors from the port, many of them with yellow fever.

Finally, in the 1850s and 1860s, the institution began to achieve a degree of stability. State aid helped, as did the impressive accomplishments of the hospital during the Civil War.[25] The war was actually a boom time for the organization, and as a result, the faculty and trustees agreed to expand. In 1866, largely through the efforts of Dr. W. Chew von Bibber, the faculty created an outpatient department, and two years later the board enlarged the dispensary.

Refurbished and renamed, the University of Maryland Hospital was able to obtain thirty thousand dollars in legislative assistance to erect a new Greene Street wing in 1875. This greatly increased the clinical facilities, making it by far the largest hospital of its kind in the state. A new lying-in department followed, as did a special department for the diseases of children. By 1878, the hospital was admitting over twelve hundred patients annually, and the ambulatory sick were paying about fifteen thousand visits to the dispensary each year.[26]

As the hospital flourished, the role of its nursing staff began to change in dramatic ways. These developments were in many regards similar to what was happening in nursing throughout the nation and abroad. Until the second half of the nineteenth century, there had been no formally trained nurses in either the United States or Europe. On the Continent, Catholic orders of nuns had, since medieval times, been the primary nursing work force in hospices for the sick poor and for travelers who became ill away from home. The sick who could remain at home were nursed by their family and friends. When a patient of some means became very ill, the attending physician might recommend a local woman with experience at tending the sick. Such women, however, were not trained. Often noted for their unsavory behavior, they were frequently criticized for being rough mannered, for smoking pipes, and for drinking more alcohol than they should. Even in Protestant and sectarian hospitals in the early nineteenth century, the "nurses" were poorly suited to the task of caring for the sick and dying. Indeed, many were routinely recruited from the transient ranks of convalescents.

When the faculty of the University of Maryland initially considered their options for staffing the infirmary with nurses, they had decided that their best hope lay with an order of Roman Catholic sisters, even though it was a sectarian establishment. This was a reasonable decision. Maryland had a large and well-established Catholic population, as well as long-established religious orders. Recognizing these assets, Dr. Pattison took the initiative and made an approach to the church through Mary Patterson, a Baltimorean of great wealth and influence. Mrs. Patterson contacted Father DuBois, requesting that he send some of the Sisters of Charity from Mount Saint Mary in Emmitsburg, Maryland, to manage the new infirmary. DuBois consented on the understanding that, while serving in the infirmary, the sisters would enforce the standards of behavior ascribed by their order. They would provide nursing care and would have sole control of the daily management of chores. They would appoint the necessary men to carry coal and water, to cut wood, to move the sick, and to act as porters. One sister, in charge of the laundry, was to be "at liberty to hire as many colored women by the day, every week as will be necessary to wash the linen," since it could be done at the infirmary for less than it would cost if they sent it out.[27] The sisters were ready for action when the infirmary opened and continued their work there until 1879.

Then, however, the face of nursing at University Hospital changed suddenly and dramatically. By mutual consent, the nuns and doctors parted ways. The physicians, it seems, had become increasingly annoyed by the assertive sisters, whom they considered insubordinate and not sufficiently frugal in managing the hospital's affairs. The sisters, on the other hand, were tired of being treated like servants. They were particularly disgusted with the medical students who abused them and were, from a Catholic perspective, far too rowdy.[28]

As the Sisters of Charity departed, they left behind a problem that the medical faculty had to solve quickly if they were going to keep their hospital running. Once again they turned to the Catholic Church. This time they worked out an agreement with the Sisters of Mercy. For the next ten years, Mercy nuns ran the hospital, but eventually they, too, were no longer willing to deal with the same conflicts their predecessors had encountered. In 1889 all professional ties between university physicians and the Catholic orders were severed. Nurses, the faculty and board realized, would have to be found elsewhere.[29]

This time, they were able to take advantage of the development of nursing as a profession to staff the University Hospital on a more permanent basis. In the wake of Florence Nightingale's innovations, nursing was being transformed during the late nineteenth century in both Europe and the United States. Nightingale, who had gained her formative experiences in the Crimea, had organized her nurses in a professional manner and set them to work cleaning up hospitals and providing their patients with sound care. She had pressed for the training of respectable women to replace the poor, untrained attendants she had found so wanting in both military and civilian hospitals. In America, the Nightingale movement prompted the establishment of nursing schools affiliated with hospitals and the emergence of nursing as a distinct profession in the last decades of the nineteenth century.[30]

University Hospital doctors recognized this trend and the opportunities it provided. By opening a nursing school adjacent to their hospital, they would have a steady supply of well-trained nurses who would be neither so independent nor so critical of the institution as to make life difficult for the faculty and medical students. Nurses who were being trained on the premises would be far easier to bring into complete harmony with the hospital's routines and values than nuns whose primary orientation was to their church and order.[31]

Looking for a smoothly functioning operation that they could control, they hired Louisa Parsons to superintend the program. They got only half of what they had bargained for. Parsons had been trained by Florence Nightingale at St. Thomas's Hospital's Nightingale Nursing School in London. She had, like her mentor, seen military medicine at work while accompanying a British army detachment into Egypt in 1882.[32] After convalescing from typhoid in England, Parsons was on the move again in 1887. This time she served for two years as a private nurse to an American woman in California and the Carolinas. But this Nightingale nurse knew she could do far more. When in 1889 she was offered the post of temporary first superintendent of the newly founded Johns

Hopkins nursing school, she accepted. In December 1889, when the University of Maryland nursing school was taking shape, Parsons accepted its superintendency.

Although she remained in the post for only two years before wanderlust struck again, Parsons brought to the embryonic school a professionalism and direction that far exceeded the doctors' expectations. The student nurses were, at one level, little more than indentured servants. They signed a two-year contract that entailed long working hours in the hospital, seven days a week, for eight dollars a month and free board. Parsons, though, strove to develop the academic and professional aspects of their training. She taught the students in her off-duty time. She established a uniform designed by Nightingale: a long gray and white chambray dress, white bibbed apron, black shoes and stockings, and the famous flat white Nightingale cap.[33] Armed with a modicum of higher education, distinctive attire, and the esprit de corps that Parsons encouraged, Maryland nursing students formed part of a new breed of nurses and brought to the hospital wards sectarian discipline and skill.

The hospital thus entered the twentieth century with a state-of-the-art nursing staff, and by this time the entire institution and its doctors had also experienced an extended phase of modernization. The medical professors, who also served as physicians to the hospital, increasingly applied the so-called scientific method to their practice and teaching. Successfully raising money, they had developed more up-to-date laboratories suited to the newest approaches to research and training in their profession. They were increasingly specialized. They now had separate clinics in obstetrics, gynecology, and pediatrics, for example, organizations that provided the kinds of clinical opportunities the medical students needed to establish their expertise. The clinics also fostered further specialization among the medical students.

The hospital had acquired facilities capable of sustaining this style of scientific medicine. In 1895, the trustees had turned to the alumni and the Ladies Auxiliary for fund-raising assistance. They achieved their common goal, a new building, in the next two years. After the old hospital was demolished, they replaced it with a neo-Palladian structure. The new 200-bed, five-story hospital was funded by $20,000 from public donations and $70,000 from bonds that the professors sold to themselves. They recognized the necessity of keeping up with other facilities (which were numerous by the turn of the century) and were willing to put their own capital on the line to ensure that the University Hospital would not fall behind its competition.[34]

In the years that followed, the hospital stayed on this course, continuing to expand its research facilities and to develop new specialties. In December 1934, the hospital once again moved into a new building. One of the few skyscraper hospitals in America at the time, the new structure "towered stories into the air." Its staff and trustees boasted of the latest equipment, of its clinics, operating rooms, and modern X-ray department. It was, the press reported, a hospital in which "babies gurgle contentedly in the sunny nurseries, mothers rest in its charming rooms, convalescents grow hourly better under the care of its nurses and doctors, operations are performed in its great amphitheaters and treatments are given to the minute on schedule."[35] As this rosy picture indicated, public relations had by this time spread from private enterprise to medicine.

But even after discounting the puffery, it was apparent that the hospital had become a key medical center for the state. It served a substantial patient population, admitting 5,681 patients in one year (1930). Half of those were boarded and treated gratis. There were 450 maternity cases, 98,657 visits to the outpatient services, and 17,402 visits to the accident department in that same year.[36] University had become a large modern urban hospital, closely tied to government, a relationship that would grow considerably stronger after 1940.

Johns Hopkins and Scientific Medicine

Through much of its modern history, University Hospital developed in friendly competition with another eminent hospital that was affiliated with the Johns Hopkins University. In March 1873, Johns Hopkins wrote to twelve of Baltimore's leaders announcing his intention to establish and endow a hospital that would be directly linked to a medical school that would bear his name. The school but not the hospital, he said, would be part of a new university.[37] Hopkins, who had begun life in a devout Quaker plantation family, had launched his business career in Baltimore at age seventeen. He was a member of a nonconformist religious sect that had already produced many successful businessmen in the New World. Leaving Europe in search of freedom in a new country, Quakers had applied their business acumen to commerce and to many charitable causes. By the time of his death on Christmas Eve, 1873, Hopkins was the wealthiest man in Baltimore; he had amassed about seven million dollars—a great fortune at that time—as a merchant and banker. Childless and single, he bequeathed his fortune in two equal parts to the founding of the hospital and the establishment of a university.[38]

Maryland's new hospital thus stemmed from the substantial economic expansion the state and nation had been experiencing throughout the nineteenth century. The buildup of capital and commerce were remarkable by world standards, as was the rate of population growth. Maryland's population grew from 583,034 in 1850 to 1,042,390 by 1890. Baltimore, the third largest city on the eastern seaboard, also grew rapidly during the nineteenth century, quadrupling its population from 102,313 in 1840 to 434,439 in 1890, according to the U.S. Census. The number of hospitals increased commensurably; there was one general institution in 1840 and, by 1890, another thirty-four hospitals had been opened.[39] In these aggregate terms, Maryland's history was similar to that of the nation and in particular to that of its eastern urban areas.

One of the by-products of the state's economic expansion was a tightly knit elite whose social, business, family, and religious lives were intricately interwoven. Johns Hopkins and Moses Sheppard were both Quaker merchants who founded hospitals as expressions of their religious stewardship. Francis J. King, first president of the board of trustees of the Johns Hopkins Hospital, came from the same social class and was related to Francis King Carey, a key supporter of Provident Hospital. Although women such as Mary Garrett in the case of Johns Hopkins had the wherewithal to found the institutions they supported, the money for Maryland's hospitals usually came from the wealth accumulated by businessmen.

Many societies would have been unable to afford such a dramatic increase in both public and private hospitals, but in nineteenth-century Maryland there was a considerable amount of new money available. Some wealth that had originated on plantations was invested and multiplied through urban mercantile ventures. A diversifying agriculture stimulated Maryland's shipping business, as did major improvements in transportation. Baltimore gradually drew its trade from a broader area of the Chesapeake Bay and beyond, especially after the nation's entrepreneurs began to promote railroad construction. By the 1840s, Baltimore was already at the nexus of a complex set of rail connections—the Baltimore and Ohio (running west through Frederick and Cumberland); the Philadelphia, Wilmington and Baltimore (along the northern seaboard); the Baltimore and Susquehanna (connecting into rural Pennsylvania); and routes to Washington, D.C., and Annapolis.[40] This network and the related expansion of manufacturing spurred the commerce of the city and state, providing a setting in which a shrewd merchant and investor like Johns Hopkins could build what for that time was a magnificent fortune.

Hopkins was not the type of man to leave much to chance. In his instructions to the trustees—and in particular to their president, his close friend Francis T. King—Hopkins stressed the importance of planning the hospital with care. Virtually all voluntary hospitals in the nineteenth century were opened in rented buildings, often ordinary dwelling houses that were not designed to serve that purpose. Many were multistory, overcrowded, and ill-ventilated buildings, in themselves public health hazards.[41] The Johns Hopkins Hospital would be different, a rare exception.

This new institution was a meticulously designed civil hospital that took into consideration current theories of disease transmission. During the Civil War, military hospitals—and the Union had two hundred by the end of the war—had been a revelation to the international medical profession. They were large, temporary facilities that had surprisingly low mortality rates. Physicians concluded from this experience that good ventilation, cleanliness, nutrition, and warmth were at least as crucial to healing as was therapeutics. In the postwar era, this knowledge fueled reform activities and helped shape Baltimore's newest hospital.[42]

Florence Nightingale and the nursing reform movement had urged the adoption of the pavilion plan in hospital architecture, a plan that had won the support of public health reformers and been used in crude form in the Civil War. It involved long, open wards that were spread out to promote ventilation and decrease crowding. In these "units," which often spanned out from a central building, infections were less likely to be transmitted among patients.[43] This was the plan adopted at Hopkins in 1875, after the trustees had solicited plans from five physicians around the country who were considered experts in hospital design. For building design the trustees turned to John Shaw Billings, who proposed the hospital's innovative architecture.[44] Billings, who had served as a military physician, brought to this effort his substantial experience as a physician in wartime hospitals and as a sanitarian in civilian establishments. His scheme for Hopkins involved three-story buildings along Broadway, linked by covered corridors to one-story pavilions behind.[45]

Hopkins had purchased the site for the hospital in the spring before his death. The land in eastern Baltimore (on Loudenschlager's Hill) had been occupied by the Maryland Hospital since 1797. That public institution, later known as the Maryland Hospital for the Insane, had moved to Spring Grove, and Hopkins had been able to buy the old, indebted facility for $150,000. The trustees oversaw the groundbreaking in 1877, but it was not until May 1889 that the hospital was open to receive the first patients. The first, a Cumberland woman with cancer, was admitted the week after the opening.[46]

That same year, in accordance with Hopkins's specifications, the trustees opened a training school for nurses. The school offered "two years of training to women desirous of learning the art of caring for the sick." President Gilman of the Johns Hopkins University appointed Isabel Hampton as the superintendent of nurses and principal of the training school.[47] Hampton, a Canadian trained at the Bellevue Training School for Nurses, stamped a powerful impression during her five-year tenure.[48] She and her successor, M. Adelaide Nutting, were dedicated to the professionalization of nursing and were determined to make their program one of the country's best. The nursing school, which provided a sound education for student nurses, also furnished the hospital with a supply of competent, reliable women to assist the physicians. The student nurses, in their "pale blue gingham, simply made, white apron and cap, and linen collar and cuffs," were on duty from 7:30 A.M. to 7:30 P.M. During their second year, they were on occasion sent out to other hospitals or jobs as private nurses, with the remuneration, of course, returning to the hospital.[49]

While the nursing school helped build the reputation of Hopkins Hospital, the key to its fame lay in the symbiotic relationship between the hospital and the medical school, between clinical and laboratory medicine. This relationship was the embodiment of modern scientific medicine. Whereas the University of Maryland Hospital had been modeled along Scottish didactic lines at a time when Britain led the world in medical training, Hopkins was founded after German laboratory medicine had become the cutting edge in the profession. Hopkins adopted the German model.[50]

The first appointments to the hospital and university reflected the influence of science in medicine and of European training. In 1884, for example, Dr. William H. Welch accepted the post of professor of pathology and immediately went abroad to prepare for his job. When the hospital opened, Welch doubled as a pathologist.[51] By the late nineteenth century, it had become routine for medical school faculty members also to hold hospital positions, but at Johns Hopkins these roles were blended in a new way. In this case, the hospital and school were inextricably intertwined.

Among the other luminaries who boosted the reputation of Hopkins in its early years were William Osler, William Stewart Halsted, and Howard Atwood Kelly. Osler was appointed physician-in-chief and professor of the theory and practice of medicine in 1888. His contributions to the development of scientific medicine, medical education, and hospital organization were of great importance to Hopkins, Maryland, and the international medical community. After some hesitation on the part of Superintendent Dr. Henry M. Hurd, the hospital appointed Halsted surgeon-in-chief and the university's first professor of surgery.[52] As it turned out, Halsted was as remarkable a teacher as he was a surgeon. The third important vacancy, gynecologist and obstetrician to the hospital, was filled by Kelly. Kelly played a crucial role in the development of his practice at Hopkins and of his specialty internationally.[53] Welch, Osler, Halsted, and Kelly carried the hospital and medical school into the twentieth century, putting philanthropist Johns Hopkins's directives into action in ways that even the founder had not been able to anticipate.

From the inception of Hopkins Hospital, the trustees tried to adhere to the benefactor's wishes: "The indigent sick of this city and its environs, without regard to sex, age, or color, who require surgical or medical treatment, and who can be received into the Hospital without peril to the other inmates, and the poor of this city and State, of all races who are stricken down by any casualty, shall be received into the Hospital, without charge." The Quaker ancestors of the Baltimore merchant had suffered from exclusion in the Old World, and he insisted on having an inclusive healing center. The private patients, he wrote, would help defer the cost of treating free patients. When the hospital opened, the maximum fee for a ward patient was two dollars per day; in 1927, it was still only three dollars. Paying and nonpaying patients were assigned to separate wards, and by the late 1930s, in hard economic times, Hopkins was still mainly admitting patients who could not fully pay for their care and treatment. The average daily patient paid approximately two-thirds of the cost to the hospital; the deficit was covered by the endowment and by a "sustaining fund" contributed by Baltimoreans. By 1937, Hopkins was treating an enormous number of the sick, admitting fifteen thousand bed patients annually, seven thousand of whom paid nothing.[54]

In addition to patients treated in hospital beds, many more received treatment in the dispensary clinics. One clinic (Medicine III) began as the Phipps Tuberculosis Dispensary in 1903. At that time, tuberculosis was one of the leading causes of death in the state and nation. There were almost thirty of these specialty clinics by the 1930s. Staffed by graduate physicians and attended by third- and fourth-year medical students, the clinics treated a large number of patients and provided a valuable center for clinical education.[55]

Although well endowed and well organized, the hospital and its staff faced tremendous challenges in the early twentieth century, especially during World War I. Well before the United States began to mobilize in 1917, the director of military relief of the American Red Cross asked Hopkins Hospital to organize an army base hospital. The original unit comprised 24 physicians, who were on the Hopkins staff, 64 nurses, and 153 enlisted men, 32 of whom were third-year medical students. After the United States entered the war, the unit sailed from New York with the first troop convoy and was based at Bazoilles-sur-Meuse, where it remained for the duration. Many more of the Hopkins staff served in other wartime posts in France and on home shores. In total, about seven hundred Hopkins medical graduates had joined the armed services by the armistice in 1918.[56]

Through all of these sudden changes, the hospital continued to conduct its normal functions in treatment, training, and research, but these tasks all had to yield to the emergency created before the war was over by the influenza pandemic of 1918–19. Like other hospitals, Hopkins initially could not cope with the crisis. Few influenza patients could be admitted because of insufficient beds in isolation. As the disease spread, though, hospital staff were stricken and wards had to be given over to their care. Ultimately, at its worst, the flu caused cessation of all general admissions except for emergencies and more than six wards were kept solely for influenza victims.[57]

As the pandemic subsided, the hospital once again entered a phase of growth and redirection. The number of clinics and patients steadily increased in the 1920s and 1930s. In 1925 the Wilmer Eye Institute was founded, and in the following year a new woman's clinic was built according to the wishes of benefactress Lucy Wortham James.[58] Other new structures included the Carnegie Outpatient Building (opened in 1928), the Hampton House Nurses Home, and the Osler, Hurd, and Halsted Buildings, all opened in 1932.[59] As the institution expanded and became more complex, its administration became more professional and its staff ever more specialized. Both developed new capabilities that kept Hopkins at the forefront of scientific medicine in the United States and Europe.

In the years before U.S. involvement in World War II, Hopkins reached beyond its own institutional walls, developing an affiliation with the Baltimore City Hospitals. City Hospital patients received treatment from Hopkins physicians, and Hopkins medical students gained additional clinical experience by patrolling City Hospital wards. Drawing heavily upon funds from the U.S. Public Health Service, City Hospital substantially expanded its Social Service Department (established in 1907) during the difficult years of the 1930s. With an unemployment rate of 25 percent, Marylanders badly needed this kind of medical assistance in the worst years of the Great Depression.

Long before the Depression hit Maryland, Hopkins had established its reputation as one of the leading centers of medical innovation in the United States. Examples abound. As early as 1893, Dr. James Brown had performed the first catheterization of the male ureter, and his colleague, Dr. Howard Kelly, successfully completed catheterizations of the female ureter that same year. William Welch, who became the first editor of the *Journal of Experimental Medicine,* discovered the gas bacillus in 1891, when the germ theory of disease was just beginning to make deep inroads in American medical science. Between 1910 and the 1940s, Hopkins neurosurgeon Walter E. Dandy made a number of groundbreaking discoveries, including the first use of ventriculography in palliative brain surgery. Meanwhile, several Hopkins scientists were making important contributions to the development of tissue culture techniques and to an improved understanding of sickle cell anemia. In cardiovascular research, chemotherapy, and studies of the thyroid gland, Hopkins was widely recognized as an institution at the forefront of American medical advances.[60]

When the United States entered World War II in 1941, Hopkins was a vital medical center that had in just fifty years gained international renown for its teaching as well as its research. More so than any other Maryland hospital, it was committed to scientific medicine and the development of new medical knowledge. Every aspect of the institution was permeated by this ideology and by the values and activities it sustained.[61]

Patterns of Change

So progressive was Hopkins, and so renowned, that in some societies it might well have absorbed all of the state's resources and become the only hospital serving Baltimore and Maryland. But the state wisely opted for diversity. Maryland kept an array of medical institutions, decentralized, partly private and partly public, and over the long term this system served the people well by promoting innovation in therapies as well as research. But that outcome was not at all evident as late as 1940.

By 1940, there was clearly much that could be done in the hospital that could no longer be done in the home. Patients no longer avoided hospitals, which had lost their social as well as their medical stigma. With the widespread acceptance and application of antisepsis and asepsis, "hospitalism" was no longer a leading cause of mortality and morbidity. Infections still could be spread between patients—sometimes by the unclean hands of medical attendants—but substantial progress had been made in preventing conditions such as erysipelas (a severe streptococcal skin disease) and puerperal fever, which had once added greatly to the fear of childbirth among strangers.[62] The introduction of ether, chloroform, diethyl ether, and other anesthetics had reduced the shock associated with surgery and enabled surgeons to perform a greater number and range of procedures.

By 1940, therapeutics in mainstream hospitals like Johns Hopkins and University Hospital had caught up with diagnostics. Hospitals now had X-ray equipment and laboratories where recent developments in microbiology and biochemistry could be applied in clinical diagnosis. The germ theory of disease was in the throne, and surgeons had long ago swapped their street clothes for white coats. At Hopkins, Halsted had introduced surgical gloves, and at both institutions attention to cleanliness had taken on new dimensions in operating rooms and on the wards. Surgical procedures, too, had advanced. Abdominal surgery, for instance, which had entailed horrendous death rates in the mid–nineteenth century, was greatly improved.

This was one of the two distinctive patterns of change that can be discerned in Maryland. Driven by a new ideology of science, a new professionalism, and new patterns of therapeutic control, hospitals in Maryland and the rest of the nation were coalescing around a new, less variegated model of operations and development. Specialization had become a driving force. Struggles over hierarchy had ensued and the advocates of medical modernism were usually the victors. Diversity became harder to tolerate when the hospitals and their patients were benefiting from the new understanding of disease and the means of controlling it. By 1940, the state's mainstream hospitals stood marshaled and relatively unified, ready to take hold of the first dramatic breakthroughs of the therapeutic revolution.

Paradoxically, there was another, contrasting pattern in Maryland—a pattern that has received less attention than it deserves from historians of medicine. This pattern involved a gradual extension of hospital care to different parts of the population, some of which had been poorly served. Women began to receive specialized attention, as did the members of various religious groups and others in the population whose special needs were not always accommodated by the mainstream institutions. In the following chapter, we look to the institutional decentralization that also characterized the history of hospitals in Maryland.

THREE

Medicine on the Margins

A Complex Array of Institutions,
1799–1940

Rapid expansion of the population and economy encouraged experiments with new hospitals in Maryland and throughout the United States. In 1873, the first survey identified 178 "regular" hospitals in the nation; fifty years later, the figure was 4,978.[1] The growth rate for Maryland was comparable, and by 1890 the state's population was being served by 34 separate institutions, each of which developed its own approach to treatment and its client base.[2] This chapter looks briefly at the early history of this array of Maryland hospitals—those that were not mainstream institutions. Frequently, as we will see, they served Marylanders who were themselves outside of the mainstream in terms of their wealth, power, and standing in society.

Despite the impressive figures on hospital growth, many of these less fortunate residents of the state could not be certain to receive care under conditions their physicians desired. In June 1908, for example, Dr. H. F. Hill wrote to Dr. R. Dorsey Coale, who was dean of the faculty of medicine at the University of Maryland. Hill asked that the institution's hospital admit his "colored male patients." He explained that, in his extensive practice throughout the Baltimore community, he had to struggle to find hospital beds for all his needy patients. While the Hebrew Hospital would accept his poor white patients, he had nowhere to send African-American men. Hill was disturbed about their fate and sought permis-

sion to attend them himself at the University Hospital. He even offered
the payment of one dollar a day for each man. The medical faculty re-
plied that it was willing to accept Hill's African-American male patients
into the hospital, but he would have to relinquish their treatment to
the hospital's appointed medical and surgical staff.[3] As this vignette suggests, access and control were as important to hospital practice then as
they are today, and we will explore these themes in this chapter.[4]

As Baltimore grew in population and diversity, various communities
of patients and practitioners identified their needs as separate and particular. Pregnant women, African Americans, and immigrant patients
were sometimes excluded from hospitals, and when they were included
they were often treated in ways that left them and their physicians dissatisfied. Catholics and Jews objected to the Protestant religious ethos
that permeated several of the hospitals, and patients who sought medical care from other types of medical systems could not find alternative
therapies in the existing "regular" hospitals.

Practitioners who belonged to minorities also found cause for dis-
content with the emerging system of hospitals in Maryland. Women and
African Americans were excluded from medical education for much of
the nineteenth century. Even when finally admitted, they encountered
daunting obstacles in gaining hospital appointments. Their only option,
in many instances, was to found hospitals of their own.

A Hospital for the Jewish Community

While the University of Maryland Hospital admitted the sick regardless
of religion, it paid little regard to its patient's religious needs, especially
if they were not of the Christian faith. This created particular difficulties
for the Jewish population. "Many of us know," said Dr. Joshua J. Cohen,
"the instances, in which our poor co-religionists, stricken down upon the
bed of sickness, in the hands of strangers, have been greatly annoyed and
their last moments embittered, by the obtrusion of sentiments in the vain
attempt to throw them away from the God of their Fathers."[5] Indeed,
Jews at University Hospital or other general institutions could not obtain
the food required by their religious laws unless it was privately supplied.
In death, they were rarely attended by members of their own faith.

Baltimore's Jewish matrons, who were the first to seek a solution to
this problem, pleaded for a hospital of their own.[6] The Hebrew Benevolent Society (forerunner of Associated Jewish Charities) responded to

their pleas and set out to acquire an appropriate facility. Local Jewish philanthropists purchased the land on which the city poorhouse stood, and in 1866 they laid the cornerstone for a new hospital. As the extant pewter plaque from that stone indicates, Baltimore's mayor, John Lee Chapman; Maryland's governor, Thomas Swann; and the president of the United States, Andrew Johnson, all supported this successful local effort.[7]

In 1868, the Hebrew Hospital and Asylum opened its doors and was immediately inundated with patients, receiving forty-eight in the first year and experiencing overcrowding throughout the 1870s. During the 1880s, the Hebrew Hospital was able to add new buildings, but it still encountered some of the problems that beset many other hospitals of the period, insufficient numbers of nurses and insufficient funds. The financial strains were in part a product of the fact that the hospital accepted both free and paying patients. Private patients paid according to means on a sliding scale, with the lowest charge at four dollars per week and the top bill set in the mid-1870s at ten dollars.[8] But the free patients continued to outnumber those who could pay. In cooperation with the Hebrew Benevolent Society, the hospital also cared for "outdoor cases," sending doctors and medicines to the sick in their homes. Later, this outreach program was formalized when the hospital established a Department of Social Services. This department, based in the dispensary, largely used volunteers and also ran an ambulance service in cooperation with the Jewish convalescent home.[9] In an effort to deal with the staffing problem, the hospital opened its own school of nursing in 1907, and the school's corps of student nurses significantly improved conditions in the wards.[10]

The Hebrew Hospital, which clearly filled an important gap in the state's medical facilities, continued to expand. In 1895, a ward was devoted entirely to the treatment of children, and efforts began to separate the aged from the sick. At the Hebrew Hospital, like other general hospitals of the time, "no applicant with a contagious or infectious disease [was] admitted." Such persons were "excluded for the sake of the safety of the other inmates." The institution set aside a room for religious services for the patients and gave special care to diet, allocating funds for Passover bread and building a Kosher kitchen in 1922.[11]

Despite its constitutional provision prohibiting contagious disease cases, the hospital was flexible when confronted with a public health crisis. In the early twentieth century, for instance, it treated large numbers of typhoid patients. From October 1908 to December 1909, the hospital's physicians treated seventy-six such patients, six of whom died.[12]

The only extant case history of a patient from the years before World War I details the progress of that disease and the treatment. Ezra W. Jones, a thirty-three-year-old, single man, who was the manager of a light company in Baltimore, was admitted on April 20, 1911. His symptoms included severe headaches, fever, delirium, incontinence, coughing, sore throat, and depression. After a physical examination, Dr. Perkins, the attending physician, diagnosed typhoid.

Jones, who was a private patient, stayed in the hospital for over five weeks, receiving the type of treatment generally applied at this time, a combination of medicines, careful diet, and physical care. He was treated with urotropin, morphia, whiskey, enemas, turpentine, aromatic spirits, throat sprays, and Veronal. His largely liquid diet was gradually supplemented with crackers, soft-boiled eggs, gruel, and custards. Apparently blessed with a hardy constitution, Jones made a slow, painful, but full recovery and by early June was spending many hours on the hospital porch.[13]

In the years that followed World War I, the hospital continued to expand its services, but Rabbi William Rosenau, among others, became convinced that the word *Hebrew* served to turn away patients who were not Jewish. He was concerned that this affected applicants to the nursing school as well as patients. As Rosenau wrote, "I might call your attention to the fact that the Catholics do not call their hospital *Catholic* Hospital, but Mercy, Saint Joseph's and Saint Agnes; that Episcopalians, Presbyterians, etc., do not designate their hospital as *Protestant* Hospital, but rather now as Union Memorial; and that the Methodists do not designate their hospital as *Methodist* Hospital but rather as Maryland General." In July 1926, the hospital's governing committee decided that Rabbi Rosenau was right and paid a fee of ten dollars to the Maryland State Tax Commission, which legally changed the name to Sinai Hospital of Baltimore, Incorporated.[14]

A Hospital for Women

Local physicians mounted several early efforts to found hospitals for women in Baltimore. In 1876, for example, Dr. Bennet Bernard Browne opened the Women's Hospital for Medical and Surgical Treatment of Diseases Peculiar to Women, the first of its kind in Maryland. His four-bed establishment at 211 Eutaw Street (which had a dispensary) permitted Browne to attend his own gynecological cases. Also, Dr. A. F. Erich

organized the Maryland Women's Hospital (at Maternité), which provided clinical opportunities in gynecology and obstetrics through its affiliation with the College of Physicians and Surgeons.[15] Neither of these
small hospitals could, however, satisfy the needs that were becoming evident in the state's female population.

Although these innovators emphasized the opportunities rather than
the dangers of what they were doing, their institutions were risky undertakings for physicians at that time. Specialization was still scorned by
many of the practitioners in the more conservative medical ranks in
Maryland and elsewhere. Indeed, some physicians were reluctant to accept faculty and hospital posts for fear of losing social and professional
standing.[16]

Over time, more physicians thought that the opportunities seemed to
outweigh the dangers. As a result, specialization became an increasingly
popular strategy, spreading to the United States from London, where
hospitals along these lines had existed since the 1840s. This style of
medical institution had subsequently spread to Britain's provincial urban
centers, and groups in New York and Philadelphia had followed, establishing hospitals exclusively for women in their cities.

Baltimore followed the lead of Philadelphia and New York. Ambitious practitioners who lacked the social and professional connections
associated with appointments to the large teaching hospitals could see
that special hospitals for women offered opportunities for advancement,
both their own and that of the profession. Such hospitals provided a
clinic environment in which large numbers of women suffering from
similar ailments could be treated and in which physicians and students
could learn in a more intense, focused fashion. Outside the hierarchy of
the large teaching hospitals, these physicians had control over their own
patients and enjoyed much more freedom to innovate. They could provide their patients with a more congenial atmosphere than that of the
large wards of general hospitals. In the special hospitals, patients were
also less subject to problems of cross-infection, and they benefited from
nursing staffs that were especially trained for gynecological care.[17]

In addition to the physicians, Baltimore's philanthropic women became increasingly interested during the last quarter of the nineteenth
century in founding a hospital exclusively for women. As they already
knew, the establishments in other cities were popular with female patients
and physicians alike. Patients often preferred them because they were
staffed with a far higher proportion of women doctors and students than
the mainstream general hospitals. Patients more readily submitted to em-

barrassing physical examinations when performed by another woman. The patients also appreciated the gentler regimes that ruled in hospitals exclusively for women. For aspiring and practicing women doctors, these hospitals furnished the clinical training they needed. Moreover, they provided an oasis of professional and emotional support in what women frequently experienced as a desert of male-dominated medicine.[18]

Convinced of the need for a general hospital for women in Maryland, but lacking any real sense of what such an establishment should be, the Mrs. John Gill, O. A. Parker, and Pembroke Thom undertook in the early 1880s a scouting trip to New York. There they inspected several hospitals for women. After returning, they reported to their fellow philanthropists, who promptly selected a governing board, obtained a charter, and formed a corporation under the title the Hospital for Women of Maryland, of the City of Baltimore. Having already gathered the financial support they needed, they were able to open their hospital at 25 McCullogh Street in April 1882.[19]

This specialized institution, like the Hebrew Hospital, was an instant success. Because the state legislature contributed two thousand dollars biennially, the hospital was able to accommodate many sick women who could not afford to pay for special treatment. Demand for its services was so strong that, after four years, the hospital moved to new quarters on John and Townsend Streets (later Lafayette Avenue). Here, the patients and practitioners had an establishment that was designed for the purpose. In this new setting, they could give attention to cleanliness, ventilation, and pleasant grounds, all of which were seen as beneficial to patients' recoveries and staff morale. By 1888, the facility was outgrown again, and the trustees found it necessary to add a new wing with a dispensary and two free wards.[20]

The Hospital for Women was a successful institution with a broad base of support. Although it was launched by Baltimore's benevolent women, the hospital was substantially backed by several influential parties in the medical profession. Although Bennet Bernard Browne, for instance, had his own hospital, he was anxious to develop the new specialty of gynecology in his home state. As he recognized, his little institution had barely scratched the surface of new opportunities for treatment and training. The Hospital for Women also benefited from its cooperation with the Women's Medical College in Baltimore.[21]

Throughout the state's medical profession, specialization was now steadily becoming more common. During this same period, ophthalmology, psychiatry, and neurology were also developing their own professional identities and institutions, including special hospitals.[22] This setting favored increasing acceptance of the emerging specialty of gynecology and the hospitals in which it was taught and practiced. By 1892, Maryland's special hospital for women was treating well over one hundred patients a year; there were, as well, more than six hundred visits to its dispensary. Among those hospitalized, seventeen underwent oophorectomies, one had a hysterectomy, and two had exploratory laparotomies. Other procedures and treatments included cutting the hymen, dilation of the uterine cervix, and removal of breast masses. In 1904, practitioners performed 180 operations in the hospital, and there were 1,466 visits to the dispensary. There was a waiting list for the free wards, which were constantly full, and the private rooms, at three to six dollars a week, were also well used.[23]

As in other voluntary hospitals, strict rules applied to patients and their visitors and to the cases admitted and excluded. Patients could not leave the hospital without permission; they were barred from consuming alcohol except as directed. Free patients, when deemed able, were required to assist in nursing. Visitors were permitted singly from 3:00 to 5:00 P.M. and were forbidden to bring any food or drink for the patients.[24] The women's hospital was even more rigorous in its admissions policy than most general hospitals. Men were, of course, excluded, and so, too, were patients with "contagious diseases, specific, chronic, incurable, or mental diseases."[25]

As medical science changed and the state's population grew, the Hospital for Women continued to expand and develop. In 1911, the hospital extended its facilities to accommodate 69 patients and opened a pathological laboratory. The hospital now had its own training school for nurses, and by the early 1920s, Edith Cushing Marshall, president of the board of managers, was happy to announce that the nursing school was running close to full capacity. By that time, the hospital was able to admit 2,300 patients in one year, and over 450 babies were born there in 1921 alone.[26]

This volume of patients made the hospital a major institution in the city and state. The majority of cases were private, with the daily average of free patients at 9.1 percent, partly free patients at 14.3 percent, and full-pay patients at 69.9 percent.[27] During the Great Depression of the 1930s, both patients and staff experienced economic hardships. The hospital accepted more free and part-pay patients and made substantially less use of its more expensive rooms. In 1932, the organization, like many in Maryland and the rest of the country, was operating at a deficit, which it handed down to the entire hospital staff in the form of a 10 percent salary cut. Subsequently, nurses throughout the city were forced to take similar reductions because of the economic crisis.[28]

The Depression was long, and its effects were felt throughout the state and its medical establishments. With almost a quarter of the work force unemployed, local and state welfare organizations were overwhelmed. The complex relationships between Maryland's economic situation and its medical maladies were apparent to many practitioners, including those associated with the Hospital for Women. In response to this dire situation, the hospital created a new social science office under the supervision of Miss Emily Randall.[29] The hospital's managers also found it necessary to reshape their building plans. In 1928, they had launched a major building program aimed at providing a much larger, more modern structure. Two years later, the managers used $203,024 of subscription money to buy a new site at University Parkway and Saint Paul Street.[30] As the Depression cut deeply into the state's economy, however, they decided that the move was impractical. After considering the hospital's needs and the available funds, they decided to sell the new lot and channel the resources into extending the existing building.[31]

The hospital finally launched this expansion plan in 1938 and was able to open the additional facilities the following year. With increased patient capacity, the institution was able to treat over 3,000 women in 1940, when there were also 7,500 visits to the dispensary. This represented a total increase of 2,500 over the previous year.[32] The new facilities were physically and medically modernized: air conditioning was installed in the labor and delivery rooms; the nursery facilities were duplicated so that, if infection broke out in one, it could be closed to prevent the disease from spreading; the patients' rooms were improved and they had private lavatories for the first time.[33] A new pharmacy and modernized laboratory and X-ray departments improved working conditions for the staff.[34] Now a modern institution with substantial expertise in the treatment of women, the hospital continued to be primarily oriented to therapy, rather than research. In that sense, it was a good complement to Johns Hopkins and University Hospital.

Provident Hospital

During the latter part of the nineteenth century, African Americans in Maryland continued to suffer from marginalization and alienation in education, in the work force, and in politics. The state was not as harshly racist as the Deep South, but neither did it open the doors of economic and social opportunity as swiftly as did the more northern states. In this border state, African Americans found it necessary to foster their own institutions for professional advancement.[35]

By the mid-1880s, African-American educators had formed their own schools and teachers' associations, but physicians still had no hospital of their own. They lacked access to and the professional opportunities associated with admitting privileges and with adequate clinical material.[36] They could not hold hospital positions in the white establishments. This meant that African-American patients found themselves attended by white doctors and nurses; the patients were third-class citizens and were inevitably relegated to the worst hospital wards.

For many years, African Americans had been practicing medicine. James McCune Smith (1811–65) was apparently the first African American in this country to have received a medical degree (1837). For that degree, however, he had to travel to Glasgow, Scotland — an extremely unusual scenario for the antebellum son of a freed slave.[37] At that time, African Americans could not gain admission to medical schools in their homeland. Nurses were similarly restricted. Their opportunities were largely domestic and informal; they were something akin to house servants.

In postbellum America, more and more African Americans began to receive training as physicians, but still they were frustrated by the limitations of a European American–controlled medical world. In Baltimore, six African-American physicians finally decided to change that situation, and in 1894 they rented a little house on Orchard Street in the northwest part of the city. This became America's "first private colored hospital."[38] Acting as both trustees and attending physicians, these men installed ten beds and other basic hospital equipment. Drs. William T. Carr, William H. Thompson, and their colleagues had three explicit goals: to have a place where people of color could be treated by physicians of their own race, to provide a hospital where African-American physicians could develop themselves professionally along specialty lines, and to organize a training school for African-American nurses.[39] Within the first year, Carr had founded a training school for nurses under the direction of superintending nurse Lena V. Ashton, who had graduated from Freedman's Hospital in Washington, D.C. This was Maryland's only African-American nursing school.[40]

Provident Hospital and Free Dispensary struggled financially, but it clearly met the needs of a significant number of Baltimore's citizens. The hospital grew rapidly, and after only eighteen months its staff moved to larger premises on West Biddle Street. There, twenty and later forty beds could be accommodated.[41] Still, few of the patients could pay much, and they pressed hard on the hospital's severely limited resources. Efforts to build and renovate failed for lack of funds. Although America was prosperous and Baltimore's economy was expanding by the 1920s, the prospects for Provident Hospital were gloomy. In 1925, the hospital was teetering on the brink of closure. Dr. Carr, the only remaining member of the original hospital staff, acted as superintendent, overseeing just a few patients and two nurses (who, in addition to nursing, performed virtually all other chores).[42]

Then, when all seemed lost, an African-American maid and her employer launched a fund-raising campaign. Anita R. Williams was a maid to the Carey family and a supervisor of the Bureau of Catholic Charities. She persuaded Francis King Carey and Dr. John M. T. Finney of Johns Hopkins to extend a campaign across racial lines. After nine years of spluttering, the drive raised $423,703 in 1927. John D. Rockefeller Jr. and Julius Rosenwald contributed about 20 percent of this sum, but the remainder was donated primarily by 759 whites ($149,000) and 6,496 African Americans ($165,000).[43] Many of the whites subscribed in the names of longstanding family servants. This enabled the purchase in 1928 of the old premises of the Union Protestant Infirmary (the original Union Memorial Hospital) on Division Street, which increased the institution's bed capacity to 130.[44]

The new facilities and funding helped move Provident into the era of modern medicine and the modern hospital. At this time, Dr. A. J. Lomas, superintendent of the University of Maryland Hospital, served also as consultant superintendent to the new Provident. He helped arrange for the training of the administrative, laboratory, and ancillary teams at University Hospital.[45] This kind of interaction, once barred by racial prejudice, helped the physicians and staff at Provident draw on a broader medical base than the hospital itself could provide.

The hospital, it seems, had providentially changed in the nick of time; only one year later the Great Depression hit. In its previous situation, the hospital would almost certainly have been forced to close. But now Provident was able to endure economic hardships. Indeed, through the 1930s, it continued to modernize and expand. In 1937, the superintendent (Betty Jenkins Phillips, R.N.) oversaw the purchase of an oxygen tent and a portable X-ray machine. During the following year, Phillips reported that the hospital treated 1,727 bed patients, the emergency service treated a further 5,932, and the outpatient department treated 7,605. Although the hospital's trustees welcomed the income from paying patients, 77 percent of the sick were attended free. By this time, the state of Maryland and the Department of Welfare together were contributing the bulk of the hospital's operating expenses, $20,000 and $28,000, respectively. With public support in hand, Provident was able to look beyond the problems of the Depression and actually lay plans for an expansion that seemed inevitable during the late 1930s.[46]

The Sheppard and Enoch Pratt Hospital

While ill African Americans were institutionally neglected for most of the nineteenth century, the insane of all races were both neglected and abused. Efforts to change that situation led to the organization of the Sheppard and Enoch Pratt Hospital, Maryland's second institution specifically for the insane and the first that was private. Conceived by a Baltimore philanthropist, it was organized along the lines of European facilities that had begun to employ "moral treatment." Moses Sheppard (1775–1857), a wealthy merchant, was the archetypical early nineteenth-century humanitarian; he used his money to express a religious commitment to improving social conditions in his community. An active member of the Religious Society of Friends, he was involved in assisting freed slaves to emigrate to Africa. He was also a warden of the city poor and a prison commissioner.[47] In these capacities, he had direct knowledge of the appalling conditions under which the insane were often kept. Wealthy families frequently sequestered their mad relatives in attics or basements; poorer families left them to be brutalized in almshouses or the state asylum.

Europe's mentally ill had suffered similarly until Philippe Pinel at Bicêtre and Salpêtrière Hospitals in Paris and William Tuke at the York Retreat in England literally and figuratively replaced chains with kindness.[48] Their so-called moral treatment emphasized the curability of insanity. To achieve this end, they established a setting that mimicked a large, functional family. Within this institutional "family," the mentally ill were encouraged to perform the duties deemed appropriate for their gender, age, and socioeconomic standing. Ideally, asylum keepers attempted to replace externally imposed physical restraint with the inmates' internally imposed moral self-restraint.[49]

Moses Sheppard had learned about these new ways to treat the in-

sane both from European sources and from persons familiar with the
highly touted work of Thomas Kirkbride at the Pennsylvania Hospital
for the Insane.[50] Sheppard could not bear the thought of poor, mentally
ill Quakers being interned at the Maryland Hospital for the Insane. This
convinced him to establish a special private hospital for their treatment
and for as many of the general public as space permitted. In 1853, Sheppard obtained an act of incorporation for the hospital to bear his name,
and upon his death four years later he bequeathed $567,632 to that end.[51]
His appointed trustees purchased a 340-acre farm, known as Mount
Airy, between York Road and Charles Street, and promptly began construction. Building was slow, however, since Sheppard, like Hopkins,
had directed use of only the interest on his endowment. Gradually, during the Civil War and over the following two decades, the grounds were
landscaped and buildings erected in such a manner as not to give the
impression of a hospital. In this pleasant retreat, the entrance itself resembles a Swiss chalet.[52]

In the 1890s, as the hospital finally neared completion, the trustees
employed Dr. Edward N. Brush as superintendent and physician-in-
chief. Brush, who had been assistant superintendent of the Pennsylvania
Hospital for the Insane, worked at the Sheppard Asylum until his retire-
ment in 1919. He had a strong reputation in the psychiatric community
and served as president of the Medico-Psychiatric Association (the forerunner of the American Psychiatric Association). He visited European
mental institutions and followed the principles of the York Retreat; with
kindness and gentle occupation, he believed, the insane could be cured
or at least improved.[53]

Many, indeed, were pronounced cured or improved. The first patient,
a forty-six-year-old woman with dementia, was received in December
1891. During its first full year (1892), the hospital admitted fifty-three
patients and discharged twenty-seven. Of those discharged, four were
pronounced recovered, three much improved, and six improved; four
had died while under treatment. This was not a high cure rate, but Brush
was satisfied that it marked an improvement over older facilities. Seeking
to use as little physical restraint as possible, Brush administered mor-
phine and its compounds instead. The other drugs he employed included
stramonium for mania, digitalis or conium for melancholia, and chloral
hydrate as a sedative.[54]

Hoping, in the spirit of Moses Sheppard, to get away from the popular image of institutions for the insane, Brush was pleased to change
the name from *asylum* to *hospital* in 1896. He was also pleased, we can
assume, to have greater resources. In September of that year, Enoch

Pratt, another wealthy Baltimore merchant, died, leaving $1,631,493 to the Sheppard Asylum, on condition that additional buildings be erected, that more of the indigent insane be accommodated, and that the institution's name be changed to the Sheppard and Enoch Pratt Hospital. After this expansion and the related infusion of capital, the hospital moved away from custodial care toward the kind of medical care characteristic of the leading national institutions in the twentieth century.[55]

Pratt's and Sheppard's endowments continued to allow the hospital to expand its physical plant. In the asylum days, the entire medical staff, including the Brush family, resided in the main buildings. This was in keeping with the theory of moral treatment; the insane, they hoped, would learn to readjust to normal family life by observing functioning, healthy families. The patients were encouraged to believe that every member of the hospital community—from gardener to superintendent to patient—was part of one extended family. Nevertheless, Brush must have been relieved when the endowment funds proved to be sufficient to pay for his own attractive house (completed in 1904) on the institution grounds. Other structures followed, including a new service building with larger kitchens (1908). During the 1920s, the trustees and medical staff were able to add another eighty beds. They also opened a special reception building that housed newly admitted patients for observation and diagnosis.[56]

Therapy, too, was expanding. Dr. Meyer, director of the Phipps Psychiatric Clinic at Johns Hopkins, maintained close association with Sheppard Pratt, periodically visiting the patients and delivering lectures to the medical staff in the 1910s and 1920s. When Dr. Ross Mc. Chapman became the institution's second medical director in 1920, he continued to foster these ties. Chapman maintained substantial professional contacts with Meyer and Johns Hopkins. By the 1930s, the therapies they used included rest and medicine, but also massage, hydrotherapy, light treatment, exercises, electric treatment, and psychotherapy. This array of treatments—all that modern medicine had to offer—was well established by the beginning of the Great Depression, when the hospital was forced to go into a holding pattern until World War II.[57]

A Homeopathic Hospital

Initially, homeopaths and their followers played no role in the development of Maryland's hospitals. Patients who desired homeopathic treatment could not receive it in allopathic institutions. This left two other

groups of people dissatisfied and seeking access to hospitals: would-
be homeopaths (many of whom were women) and homeopaths who
sought training in the specialties. Since, however, the differences between the "regulars" and the "irregulars" were at this time irreconcilable,
no progress was made in reaching an accommodation. This brought
some homeopaths to the conclusion that, if they were to have control
over their patients and if patients were to receive homeopathic care in
hospitals, they would have to develop separate facilities.

Other states had already taken this path. By 1880, there were thirty-
eight homeopathic hospitals in the United States, as well as twenty-three
state societies, thirty dispensaries, and eleven colleges. Homeopathy was
most popular in the northern states. New York, in particular, had a
strong homeopathic following and had several hospitals and insane asylums that were run according to homeopathic principles. Some were
even state-funded.[58]

In Maryland, the number of homeopathic physicians had steadily increased in the nineteenth century. Baltimore's first infinitesimal-prescrib-
ing physician was Dr. F. R. McManus, who began practice in 1837. There
were fifteen or sixteen such doctors by 1865 and thirty-eight by 1880. In
1874 they formed a city society and from that came the initiative three
years later to establish the Baltimore Homeopathic Free Dispensary.[59]
Soon, however, they began to feel the need for a residential facility
for the sick, and in 1890 twenty-six Baltimoreans, fourteen of whom
were physicians, joined forces to incorporate the Southern Homeopathic
Medical College and Hospital of Baltimore. They also organized a Homeopathic Dispensary and Hospital at 323 North Paca Street, and they
closed the old free dispensary. The hospital physicians, all with M.D.
degrees, constituted the faculty at the college, and now at last they had
access to and control of clinical cases and were able to train the next generation of homeopaths.[60]

The hospital had private rooms to accommodate up to fifteen paying patients, as well as forty-three free beds. Thirty of the "charity beds"
were maintained by the city in a separate part of the building. This wing
of the hospital was always crowded and provided abundant opportunities for clinical teaching. The hospital also had a nurses training school,
and the wards were staffed by student nurses. In addition, the college
dispensary operated as a polyclinic in which there were a pharmacy and
separate departments for the eye and ear, gynecology, surgery, diseases
of children, orthopedic surgery, diseases of the throat and chest, skin
diseases, those of the genitourinary organs, and those of the nervous sys-

tem.[61] These clinics enabled students and faculty to gain experience in the specialties just as did the practitioners and students in the regular medical profession.

As Maryland's homeopaths entered the twentieth century, they had every reason to be optimistic about the future of their institutions. Working with state, city, and private support, the hospital was highly successful and by 1894 had moved to a larger building at North Mount Street and Riggs Avenue. By 1898, further expansion had increased the bed capacity to sixty-five.[62] In 1912, the state's homeopaths celebrated the opening at the hospital of a new cancer center, which they hailed as "the first in the South to be devoted to the study and treatment of cancer and the only institution in the city, with the exception of Bay View, where indigent persons suffering from the disease will be admitted."[63] Cancer patients, like those with infectious or incurable diseases, had generally been excluded from hospitals, but the homeopaths instituted alternatives in this practice, as in other aspects of medicine.

As it turned out, however, homeopathy's confidence in the new century's professional potential was misplaced. In the wake of the Flexner Report in 1910, homeopathic practice and institutions went into a steady decline. The Flexner Report was sponsored by advocates of the new scientific medicine and used Johns Hopkins as a "model" institution, as we will see in chapter 5. The decline of homeopathy, however, should not be laid at Abraham Flexner's feet. The seeds of decline had already been planted in the late nineteenth century with the rise of modern scientific medicine. Whereas regular medicine had all too frequently been helpless and sometimes harmful, by the century's end, diagnostics, therapeutics, and surgery had begun to improve significantly the results and the image of orthodox treatments.[64] Although such prominent figures as John D. Rockefeller clung to homeopathy into the second decade of the twentieth century, younger Americans turned to the new science. Homeopathy could not, in their view, compete with scientific medicine.[65] According to Dr. Maurice E. Shamer, looking back on the decline of his discipline in Maryland, "new remedies that came along had something to do with it. For instance, way back when the mortality from diphtheria was about 50 per cent, homeopathic treatment had better results than any other. When antitoxins came along and then immunization, the mortality rate dropped and so did the popularity of homeopathy. The same thing happened with treatment for pneumonia."[66]

As homeopathy lost ground in therapeutics, it began sliding economically, too. Even before Flexner's findings, many homeopathic medical schools were struggling or closing their doors. Rising tuition fees and longer training decreased the number of students enrolling, just when modern standards were calling for greater expenditure on equipment and facilities.[67] The homeopathic medical college in Maryland suffered from these pressures, faltered, and then closed in 1910, a victim not of the Flexner Report but of its scientific creed.[68] The Maryland Homeopathic Hospital continued to operate for another eleven years. It was, however, doomed by its inability to compete with modern, scientifically organized hospitals and by the lack of homeopathic students.

Peninsula General Hospital

As the number and variety of hospitals in Baltimore increased, these institutions served more of the patient population and satisfied more of the medical profession's needs. But the rural areas away from the city still had little access to hospitals. For much of the nineteenth century, the distance to Baltimore presented serious problems to patients, their families, and their physicians. It was difficult for many to make the journey, and going to Baltimore meant being attended by strangers.

Physicians in rural areas faced a dilemma. To treat patients who required daily visits, they had to travel many miles by horse. Whole days could be occupied visiting a handful of the sick. If, however, doctors sent their patients to a city hospital—even if that were feasible—they lost control of their cases and forfeited potential fees. This was particularly a problem for those parts of the state, especially the Eastern Shore, that were least accessible to Baltimore.

In the years after the Civil War, the Eastern Shore experienced substantial economic and demographic growth. In the 1870s, the army corps of engineers, funded by federal rivers and harbors money, turned its considerable energies to the task of improving America's waterways. Better harbors and deeper channels permitted passage and shelter to larger vessels. In 1882 the Maryland Steamboat Company began shipping locally grown produce from the Eastern Shore to Baltimore markets. Salisbury thrived. From the 1880s on, the town's mostly native-born population steadily increased as this trade grew.[69]

One Salisbury physician, George W. Todd, who was still trying to call on his patients in their homes, found himself overly extended. He decided to remedy his situation by having patients come to him instead. Todd was a young man, imbued with the concepts of hospital medicine and specialization. In 1897 he opened a simple yellow and white frame house on the corner of Fitzwater and West Main Streets as the town's — indeed, the Eastern Shore's — first hospital. The following year, Todd took on J. McFadden Dick as the hospital surgeon.[70]

The new institution was an instant success in the Delmarva community and drew support from the area's philanthropists. A board of lady managers and a county auxiliary ladies board held bazaars and donated furniture, bedding, food, and flowers. Seventy patients — labeled the "diseases treated" persons — were listed as cured or improved during the establishment's first year.[71]

Dr. Todd and his managers quickly expanded the Peninsula General Hospital. The original building, a little dwelling house, was overflowing, so they purchased an adjoining house and doubled the bed capacity from seven to fourteen. This, too, proved insufficient, and local good will and philanthropy came to the rescue. William H. Jackson, a lumber manufacturer and former First District congressman, donated fifty thousand dollars to erect a new hospital on the corner of South Division and Locust Streets. By 1904, the building that would be the central unit of the hospital was completed. In the years that followed, the Jackson family continued to support the hospital, and William's son, Senator William P. Jackson, largely funded the erection of the hospital's nurses home.

Peninsula General played a key role in the health care of the entire Eastern Shore and, despite the Great Depression of the 1930s, was able by 1939 to launch another expansion campaign. By that time, overcrowding had become so severe that extra beds filled hallways and in the middle of the night the not-too-sick were frequently asked to sleep in wheelchairs, giving up their beds for emergency cases. The hospital appeal, which drew support from Virginia and Delaware as well as Maryland, raised $153,000 for a new wing. When it opened in early 1941, it added 77 beds, bringing the capacity to 174.[72]

Peninsula's history was a success story, stemming in part from its unique location. It was close enough to a city and to research hospitals to benefit from their medical expertise and influence. Yet it was far enough away not to share the medical problems of Baltimore. Blessed with substantial political and financial support, it was able to provide its patient population with better medical care than they could otherwise have received, all at a reasonable cost to society.

Allegany Hospital

A story similar to that of Salisbury can be told about Cumberland, in
far western Maryland. A flourishing nineteenth-century town, Cumberland's chiefly white, native-born population increased from 2,428 to
39,463 in the century following 1840 (U.S. Census figures). In those years,
Cumberland had a thriving business and industrial economy. In the early
twentieth century, improved rail and road connections linked the city
with other urban centers and also provided local commercial links to the
rural and mountain areas. By 1916, Cumberland was able to attract the
Kelly-Springfield Tire Company, which built a three-thousand-worker
plant there.[73]

Urbanization and industrialization placed new demands on the local
medical community, which had also been steadily growing. There were
frequent industrial accidents, and the businessmen needed somewhere
to send their injured and sick workers. Local physicians also wanted
a centralized facility where they could efficiently attend relatively large
numbers of patients with the aid of modern technology. The business
and medical communities, headed by Dr. Erwin B. Claybrook, collaborated in 1905 to found an area hospital in Cumberland, a twenty-five-bed
facility at 215 Decatur Street named Allegany Hospital.[74]

Although the business community was a prime force in establishing
Allegany Hospital, its members did not want the responsibility of managing the institution. Neither did the medical community. Dr. C. H.
Brace, representing the medical profession, and William E. Walsh, an
attorney who represented the business interests, urged the Mother Superior of the Sisters of Charity in Emmitsburg, Maryland, to take charge
of the hospital. By 1911, this Catholic order (the Daughters of Charity
of Saint Vincent de Paul), whose mission was to serve the poor, had accepted this challenge and assumed complete responsibility for running
the organization.

Sister Florence was the first administrator, and in a letter to the
Mother House in her first year she explained some of her joys and problems. The sisters struggled with the unfortunate structure of the building; the arrangement of the kitchen, boiler room, and refectory was im-
practical, and the smell of food permeated the establishment. This could
not easily be remedied. On the other hand, as Sister Florence wrote,
"We decided to have the maternity department on the same floor as the
operating room so we should have a small room for nursery also a small
room to give the anesthetic to patient. Dear Mother, you can't imagine

what it means to patients to receive the anesthetic in the O.R. it is so much better to have the patient asleep in a quiet room outside and then bring them to O.R." [75]

Like Peninsula, this rural hospital soon ran out of space. Companies throughout the region sought admission for their injured, keeping the sisters busy with accident cases. Indeed, the hospital had to run an ambulance service to collect the patients. When, in Sister Florence's first year, the ambulance man discovered that two such injured workers were "colored," he telephoned her to determine whether or not to bring them. The sister consented and said she would find space for them somewhere. In her letter, she explained that "Sister A. and I moved some patients about and put them in a ward with two Polish men the only way we know they do not like to be with them is they make faces at them and say 'black men don't like.' This is the best we could do, as every other ward was full." [76] As in other hospitals, immigrants and African Americans were not infrequently housed together, grouped in the dominant mind as third-class citizens.

Sister Florence acted swiftly to solve the space problem, and she received the support she sought. The following year more buildings were incorporated, and by 1912 the bed capacity was tripled to seventy-five. The sisters and student nurses lived in neighboring houses, adding to the sense that this was a cooperative, community enterprise. [77] Growth continued in Cumberland, and by 1920 the city had fifty-nine physicians (four of them women), three osteopaths, and eighty-six trained nurses (U.S. Census, 1920). By the 1930s, the hospital had again become overcrowded, but despite the depression the controlling board was able to finance additions. Once more, the business, medical, and religious communities collaborated to raise funds, and in 1936 construction began on a five-story annex. Archbishop Michael J. Curley opened this new $150,000 wing the following year.

Like Peninsula, Allegany met an obvious need, benefited from its location, and mustered strong community support. Unlike Peninsula, it drew a significant element of its ideology, leadership, and labor from a religious order that was committed to particular patterns of caring. If the Sisters were less dedicated to scientific medicine than the staff at Johns Hopkins, the effects were barely discernible as late as 1940; they were perhaps concealed by the staff's overwhelming devotion and service to others. For that there was a great demand in Western Maryland, and everywhere else as well.

By that time Maryland had a full range of hospitals. They provided a wide variety of services, and each had experienced the transition to modern medical science in a somewhat different fashion, as did their patients. Their variety was their long-run strength because they drew support from many different parts of the state's population. They also kept alive some medical traditions and practices that seemed outdated to the most advanced institutions and their leaders, but in the decades that followed, the profession would on occasion return to older knowledge and be grateful—as were many patients—that a single, central hospital model had not been adopted in Maryland.

FOUR

Medical Education

Diversity, Expansion,
and Decentralization,
1799–1876

To do justice to the development of medical education in Maryland, we must again jump back in time, into the eighteenth century, where we can meet John Archer (1741–1810). Archer was born in
Churchville, Maryland, received his bachelor's and master's degrees from
Princeton, and became in the early 1760s a Presbyterian minister. Alas,
he had an unprepossessing voice that handicapped his ministry in an age
that expected a reverend to hold the attention of his parishioners, as well
as to instruct them. Archer decided to try again, this time as a physician,
a profession in which his voice might soothe his patients and thus be an
advantage. He returned to the academy, this time to the College of Medicine of Philadelphia. The college, which had been organized in 1765 by
European-educated John Morgan, was the first such school in America.[1]

Philadelphia offered instruction in anatomy, formal classroom education, and clinical experience. Ambitious students regularly attached
themselves as pupils to well-known physicians in that city. Some attended lectures at the College of Medicine. Many did not complete the
course, often because of insufficient funds, but in America at that time
they could launch their medical practices without a degree. The wealthier
students, who were more likely to stay the course, spent the year going
to two sessions of up to four months each (the second being merely a re-
peat of the first) and departed with medical credentials.[2] The advantages

of studying at the medical school, in addition to private pupilage with a physician affiliated with the institution, were manifest. Students obtained access to the hospital, the workhouse, and the dispensary, all of which were visited by the professors. Thus, students witnessed operations and gained experience with relatively large numbers of patients. This was an expensive undertaking. In 1790, the matriculation fee was eighty pounds, which must have seemed considerable, since room and board for the year was just forty pounds.[3] But for one intending to practice as a "regular" in an urban setting, the cost was doubtless in line with the benefits of this superior education.

By the end of the eighteenth century, three more "medical institutes" had been founded, in New York, at Harvard, and at Dartmouth College. But John Archer made the practical decision to stay close to home. His ability to move as easily as he did from the ministry to medicine was symptomatic of a society in which the boundaries of the professions were far less distinct than they are today. In colonial America, the distinction between religion and medicine was especially vague; the preacher-physician symbolized the common belief that illness and sin were inseparably connected.[4]

Archer may have failed as a preacher, but he soon became a medical pacesetter. Because of his alphabetical position in the initial graduating class of ten, he became the first person to receive a medical diploma in America. His diploma still hangs at the Medical and Chirurgical Faculty in Baltimore, an organization of which he became one of the founding fathers. In Harford County, where he settled, Archer was a pillar of his community. He was also a tireless builder in his profession. He established a small school, a "Medical Hall," in which, between 1786 and 1800, he passed on the medical knowledge he had gained in Philadelphia to about fifty pupils.[5] This was one of the first attempts in Maryland to provide some semblance of institutional medical education.

For centuries, learning by doing, by way of apprenticeship, had been the primary educational setting for the profession. Despite the efforts of Archer and others, apprenticeship did not give way quickly to medical schools. Older patterns of training persisted long after the modern institutions that eventually dominated the profession—and the history of medicine—were organized. In such related professions as dentistry and pharmacy, both of which have had a substantial history in Maryland, training was also usually informal, frequently by means of apprenticeship.

Certainly, at the end of the eighteenth century and during the early

nineteenth century the vast majority of Maryland's aspiring doctors received their education as apprentices. The quality of that education varied
widely. Students could supplement it by reading in their spare time,
but practical experience and structured learning were only as good as
the master. Some physicians accepted pupils' fees and gave little in return besides a signature attesting to the qualifications of the young,
still uneducated men. Others, however, organized informal lectures for
their students and permitted them to shadow their masters in daily practice. Some students assisted in minor surgical procedures and occasional
birthings. They usually had access to a few standard texts, which they
may or may not have perused. In short, while some pupils left their masters reasonably well prepared for practice, many more were doubtless
inexperienced and ill educated.[6]

Archer, who was attempting to change that situation, included among
his students his four sons. The eldest, Thomas (1768–1821; also a founder
of the Medical and Chirurgical Faculty) practiced in Harford County,
but his activities were restricted by chronic illness. Neither he nor his
brother Robert earned a medical degree. Robert Harris Archer (1775–
1857), the second son, also remained in Maryland to practice medicine,
moving around the state to various positions. He was, among other
things, physician to the City Hospital and surgeon to the Twenty-seventh
Regiment of the Maryland Militia. Returning to practice at home in Harford County, Robert became a prominent member of that community.
The two younger sons ventured farther afield for their education. After
their paternal pupilage, John Jr. (1777–1830) and James (1779–1815) traveled to Philadelphia and studied at the University of Pennsylvania.[7]

John Archer Jr. (and probably his brother as well) attended the lectures
of the famous Dr. Philip Syng Physick, who was then professor of surgery at the university. John Jr.'s lecture notes provide us with a glimpse
of what the top of the line in American surgical education was in 1804.
The lectures covered more than sixty subjects and treatments. These included various fractures, dislocations, wounds, cataracts, cancer, ulcers,
hernias, amputations, and lithotomy. Given surgeons' capabilities at the
time and the traditional realm of their work, it is not surprising that
Physick dealt primarily with the body's exterior and touched very little
on internal maladies. As he observed, opening the peritoneal cavity was
almost always fatal.[8] It was essentially impossible (as well as virtually un-
ethical) for a surgeon to try to penetrate the body cavity successfully.
Physick, like his peers, mainly confined himself to troubles that were
potentially treatable.

John Archer Jr. learned in detail about ulcers of the skin, irritations that Physick categorized into eight groups. Fractures and their treatments also featured prominently in his notes. Physick recommended immediate amputation in all cases that involved compound fractures of the "large heads of bones." He advised removing all accessible foreign materials from the wound, but "without laborious search, for the great and painful operation does more injury to the patient than the extraneous matter." Should inflammation follow, Physick prescribed bloodletting and milk poultices. Bloodletting in all its forms was the most frequently recommended treatment for inflammation, which in the late eighteenth and early nineteenth centuries was the catchall sign of disease. Venesection, purging, rest, and "low diet" were all suggested for inflammation of the external cerebral membranes resulting from head trauma.[9] The treatments of the period were of limited variety—mercurials, botanicals, and alcohol rounded out the therapeutic repertoire—and were largely aimed at restoring bodily balance. It was this body of knowledge that John Archer Jr. took with him when he returned to Maryland to practice medicine.

In the decades that followed, the system of medical education in the state, as in the nation, experienced more rapid growth than did the profession's body of knowledge. During the nineteenth century, Americans created an unprecedented number of new colleges and universities. In part, this expansion was a consequence of rapid economic growth; in part, it reflected the society's belief in progress; in part, too, it reflected deep-set ideas, many of them religiously based, about the need for an educated populace. "Betterment" was more often sought and respected along practical and material rather than intellectual lines, and this encouraged the leaders of numerous occupations to seek professional status. Certification, which proffered material proof of practical learning, became increasingly important, and one of the most popular means of acquiring credentials was through schooling.

This setting shaped medical education in Maryland, as it did elsewhere in the United States. Maryland established its first medical school, the College of Medicine (later the University of Maryland School of Medicine) in 1807. In the thirty years after 1810, the College of Medicine acquired twenty-six new rivals throughout the nation and another forty-seven between 1840 and 1876.[10] In Baltimore alone, various parties launched eleven new medical schools between 1807 and 1912. As early as 1877, America's schools were turning out as many as 2,313 doctors in one year.[11] The graduates of these various institutions held quite different credentials. The schools accurately reflected America's intense dedication to betterment and its matching disdain for regulation of any sort. The schools' programs were almost as varied as the apprenticeships they were steadily supplanting. While the practitioners they were producing were all prima facie equally qualified, in practice they possessed widely differing skills. At the University of Maryland and its sister institutions in Philadelphia and Boston, there were serious and sustained efforts in the first half of the century to develop sound curriculae, but other programs operated simply as diploma mills. Moreover, numerous medical men did not even bother to enroll in a diploma mill; instead, they manufactured fictitious medical degrees, and apparently few knew the difference, especially in rural areas.[12]

While the dominant theme in Maryland and the rest of the nation was expansion in practice rather than improvement in therapies, there were some encouraging developments. Gradually, the apprenticeship system became more standardized. Between the 1820s and the 1840s, pupils usually apprenticed for about three years at a cost of around one hundred dollars annually (including room and board). They prepared drugs, assisted the physician, cleaned, and tidied; they also read their preceptor's books and were frequently quizzed on the contents.[13] Once in a while, often illegally, physicians obtained corpses and, with the pupils, performed dissections to teach gross anatomy and surgery.

An Anatomical School for Maryland

After completing apprenticeships, the privileged few who could sustain the expense traveled to Europe, most often to Great Britain during the late 1700s and early 1800s.[14] Those who desired certification but had only moderate funds followed John Archer's path to Philadelphia, where there was a private anatomical school in which pupils could learn by direct experience with dissection. There, as elsewhere, such establishments were opened by physicians who had spent time in British anatomical schools. Perhaps the most famous of these establishments was that of the entrepreneurial surgeon William Hunter (1718–83) in London. Hunter had amassed the city's largest collection of models and preparations, which he used as teaching aids. But, as historian Roy Porter has indicated, Hunter's chief lure was his unusual ability to procure corpses for medical students to dissect.[15] Unable to obtain that experience in other settings, students paid for the privilege of gaining the firsthand anatomical knowledge that was becoming increasingly necessary for a successful career in surgery.

In America, as in Britain, there was fierce opposition to human dissection. At times it was forcefully expressed, as it was in late December 1788, when a crowd of impassioned Marylanders stormed Dr. Charles Frederick Wiesenthal's anatomical school. Wiesenthal (1727–89) was a Prussian immigrant who had served as Frederick the Great's physician. Upon arriving in Baltimore, he had quickly became a prominent figure in local medical circles and within the community at large. Finding the city wanting in medical education, he opened a small anatomical school behind his residence on Fayette Street.[16] Like many foresighted Europeans, he believed that medical students needed to develop a sound knowledge of human anatomy and, thus, should perform direct work on the human body. Wiesenthal had in mind the type of school (on a more modest scale) that Hunter had established in London and that William Shippen had imported to Philadelphia. Wiesenthal was successful enough to encounter much the same opposition that his British counterparts had met.

The mob that attacked his school in 1788 destroyed the furniture and, from under the eyes of the assembled medical students, snatched the corpse of executed murderer Patrick Cassiday.[17] Public opinion and medical opinion clashed and, in this instance, the public won, putting this particular training session on hold. This violent scene, involving Maryland's first dissection mob, occurred in response to the earnest efforts of a distinguished medical man to promote professional understanding, an effort in which education was a key element. To the gathered lay persons, however, this was just another example of the nefarious activities of a profession many of them already held in ill repute.

Medical practitioners and medical students had long had a reputation in Britain for obtaining human cadavers illegally, by graverobbing or even by burking (murder for dissection).[18] Rumors of such behavior echoed in America, and with good reason. Within medical corridors, it was well known that bodysnatching took place during the greater part of the nineteenth century.[19] This frequently incited religious opposition to dismantling the dead. Much of the lay fear was, however, aroused within the lower class because it was the unclaimed poor and the executed criminal who were legally dispatched to the dissection table. Doubtless, bodysnatching and burking victims also hailed from the same class. Since a decent funeral was a way of showing respect for the deceased as well as the remaining relatives, dissection was considered a repulsive practice.

General public antagonism to the regular medical profession added to the suspicions engendered by dissection. Poorer people, in particular, were antagonized by what they saw as efforts by a professional elite to erode their medical choices. They voiced complaints about the high price of medicines provided by physicians; Native Americans and other informally trained healers offered more reasonably priced remedies. The same was true of medical practice; midwives charged substantially less than physicians practicing obstetrics. These resentments came into play when medical leaders promoted dissection and when they pressed for licensing.[20]

This hostile environment influenced medical education. Doctors in this era who were concerned about public opinion instructed their pupils in basic professional and medical ethics, teaching them how to work effectively with other physicians and within their communities.[21] After completing their education, these young men frequently remained close to home and practiced near the communities in which they had trained. Some joined their preceptors' practices, so practical considerations alone suggested that they should remain attentive to the local culture.

Dr. Wiesenthal, however, was a senior professional cut from a European cloth. Undeterred by either the mob or the charges that his profession was undemocratic and monopolistic, he pushed ahead with his efforts to educate young medical men through a relatively formal adaptation of the apprenticeship system. His program was strengthened by the commitment of other local doctors and by his son, Andrew. Baltimore-born Andrew Wiesenthal (1762–98) benefited from the best medical education of his day. He attended lectures in Philadelphia before studying medicine for three years in Britain. Upon returning home, young Wiesenthal took over his father's anatomy school. He joined forces with George Buchanan (1763–1808), who had apprenticed with the senior Wiesenthal before also continuing his education in Philadelphia and Britain.[22] Back in Baltimore, these young men again started using corpses for anatomical instruction. They persevered with the type of teaching that would eventually blossom into the University of Maryland School of Medicine.[23]

The University of Maryland School of Medicine

The University of Maryland sprouted from humble roots. It evolved from the private classes conducted by Drs. John Beale Davidge and James Cocke in 1802–7.[24] Davidge (1768–1829) was a native of Annapolis, where he apprenticed with local doctors James and William Murray. After obtaining his A.B. degree at Saint John's College, Davidge attended lectures in Philadelphia and Edinburgh, ultimately earning his M.D. degree from Glasgow University in 1793. He practiced medicine for a time in Birmingham, England, but then returned to Maryland, where he became an attending physician to the Baltimore General Dispensary in 1801. He started teaching medicine the following year.[25]

Numerous other American medical students were following this same pattern. After gaining experience abroad and returning to America, they attempted to organize facilities similar to those in Europe and to offer new courses in the "medical sciences."[26] In 1807, Davidge, who was determined to improve medical training in Baltimore, built a small anatomical school on some land he owned on Liberty Street. Joining forces with Cocke, he announced his purpose in the local newspapers. What followed was a virtual replay of events at Wiesenthal's school. Having obtained a corpse, Davidge and Cocke began a practical lesson with a group of students. Suddenly an antidissection mob burst in and wrecked the building and its contents.

This time, however, the profession was well enough organized to turn the situation to its advantage. Davidge and Cocke and four other Baltimore practitioners proposed founding a formally incorporated medical college and rallied their colleagues in support of the innovation. On December 18, 1807, within a month of the riot, the state assembly approved a charter of incorporation for the College of Medicine of Maryland, giving the faculty permission to grant medical degrees. Recognizing that it would be inappropriate to have uncredentialed faculty members, the legislators bestowed medical degrees on those three of the six petitioning practitioners who did not hold M.D. degrees.[27] The first faculty comprised John B. Davidge and James Cocke as joint professors of anatomy, surgery, and physiology; Nathaniel Potter, professor of the theory and practice of medicine; John Shaw, professor of chemistry (replaced, after his death the following year, by Elisha DeButts); and Samuel Baker, professor of materia medica.[28]

Initially, the faculty and the act of incorporation were the only assets the college had. It had no money, no equipment, and no building. As a result, the professors conducted small, private classes in their homes, working under the title of the college. In this regard, it was typical of many other American institutions at a time when the entire nation was capital poor and its citizens were frequently hard pressed to pay their debts. Despite its lack of resources, the school attracted a trickle of students, who began to work toward degrees under this rudimentary program. Although it was a proprietary institution that later channeled students' fees into the professors' pockets, initially, all of the revenue was applied to apparatus and the faculty worked gratis. Until the University of Maryland was established in 1812, the Medical and Chirurgical Faculty retained complete control of the examinations of prospective physicians.[29]

Despite its slender resources, the new college survived. It appealed to students who did not want to incur the difficulties attendant to traveling far afield for formal medical studies. The faculty, looking to draw students from surrounding states, proclaimed their institution to be the first medical school in the South. To their advantage, Baltimore was on a main East Coast axis of travel and communication. In addition, board and lodging were cheaper than in Philadelphia or New York and professional training was far less expensive than it would be on a European sojourn.

Although Baltimore could be advertised as southern, it was temperate enough to avoid some of the climatic disadvantages that would affect medical training in the Deep South. In Baltimore from fall through spring, dissections could be performed before the heat accelerated decomposition to an intolerable degree. As more southerly medical schools began to open, their faculties attested to the revolting conditions in their dissecting rooms.[30] Flies, maggots, and the stench discouraged all but those students with the strongest stomachs and soundest health.

As it began to appear that the new school would succeed, the need for a suitable building became more pressing. The faculty wanted a grand structure in keeping with their lofty educational goals. But they were not wealthy men, and some of them were still quite young. Since this was a proprietary school, they were unable to raise money through private donations, so they resorted to selling lottery tickets. The proceeds came in slowly, however, forcing them to turn to the banks for loans. Successful in obtaining credit, they purchased, for a token sum, a lot on the corner of Lombard and Greene Streets from the hero of the American Revolution and former governor, John Eager Howard.[31] Construction began in May 1812 and was sufficiently far along by that fall for the main building, later known as Davidge Hall, to be opened.[32]

Now a part of the University of Maryland, the medical school occupied the centerpiece of the institution. Davidge Hall was classically designed, with a special feature added by the architect, R. C. Long. Externally, the building resembles a Greco-Roman edifice, and inside there were two magnificent amphitheaters, as well as laboratories and offices. Behind and beneath all these areas, however, were a set of small, half-hidden rooms, separate little staircases, and concealed storage spaces and trapdoors. Here corpses could be stored (commonly in whiskey barrels) in secret places. In the event of a raid from antidissectionists, the bodies might not be found, and meanwhile the faculty and students could use the passages to escape.[33]

Instruction in practical anatomy was just one of the ways in which the faculty tried from the beginning to raise educational standards. Among the ten students who graduated in 1813 was John D. Sinnott, who was the first recipient of a gold medal for the best thesis in Latin. (The school discontinued the medal in 1837.) His educators wanted to encourage classical fluency and were willing to dispense with a graduation fee for any student who already held a degree in the arts or sciences.[34] The faculty made substantial efforts to obtain sufficient clinical material to educate their students, and they occasionally took their students to see patients at the various small charitable institutions throughout the city.

For a student of means, his degree from the University of Maryland's medical school was still likely to be followed by a pilgrimage to Europe in pursuit of postgraduate education. One of these was David Sterett Gittings, who traveled to Britain in the summer of 1818 to gain clinical experience. Gittings (1797–1887) was the son of Richard Gittings, a Baltimore merchant.[35] Rather than joining the family business, young David aimed for a professional life and graduated in medicine from the University of Maryland. Then he set sail for the postgraduate adventure that would place him among the elite of his profession.

This was not an easy or luxurious trip. During a voyage that took about a month, Gittings initially suffered from severe seasickness. Once clear of the Chesapeake Bay and into the Atlantic, the weather tamed and so did his stomach. With appetite restored, however, he was dismayed to discover how crude the victuals were—much cruder than those he was accustomed to consuming at his parent's home in Berry Hill. He was concerned especially about the lack of cool water and dairy products.[36] Arriving finally at the English coast, Gittings survived a terrifying landing in a small boat navigated by sailors who had been drinking whiskey and were, he thought, totally drunk.

Things were not much better when he reached London. Lodging at a Piccadilly inn, he felt "completely at a loss what to do" in a strange place where he knew no one. After buying a hat and a pair of boots, however, he felt "completely Londonized" and used his letters of introduction to meet some physicians and see the sights. Still, he did not particularly like London and soon headed for his primary destination of Edinburgh.

The Scottish capital was just as he had hoped. In letters home, Gittings expounded upon the educational opportunities available at what was then one of the world's leading medical schools. The clinical wards at the Edinburgh Infirmary were not opened until late October, when lectures commenced, but until then Gittings was able to visit the hospital daily. He was aware of the need to gain clinical experience, an experience that was not regularly available to students at the University of Maryland before the proprietary infirmary was opened in 1823.

> "Though a Doctor by title I feel myself but ill qualified to enter on the responsibilities attached to the practice of medicine. Though Doctor Davidge is a man of the first talents, and deservedly holds the highest rank among his professional brethren in Baltimore, and though I am confident I would not exchange the medical opinions he has taught me for any the world can offer, yet do students of his labour under one of the greatest disadvantages: they see nothing of the practice of medicine."[37]

In Edinburgh, by contrast, each day at noon students toured the wards with the attending physician and his clerk. They had access to case histories and could thus follow the treatment and outcome of diseases. Understandably, young men, including many other Americans, were flocking to Edinburgh for training. During the winter season, Gittings reported that there were four or five hundred students crowding around the various patients' beds.[38] After over a year of this kind of experience, Gittings returned to Maryland confident in his clinical abilities. Settling in Baltimore County, he established a thriving practice and became an important figure in his community as well as his profession.[39]

While students continued in subsequent years to make postgraduate voyages to the Old World, they were able after 1823 to receive their clinical training in Baltimore. After the University of Maryland opened its new infirmary that year, the school could at last meet its students' basic clinical needs. Indeed, one of the school's greatest strengths became its faculty's commitment to clinical teaching. With the program, faculty, and facilities it needed to be successful, the school's popularity soared. Word got out quickly. By 1825 over three hundred students were registered and the faculty had grown commensurately.[40]

Just as success was being achieved, however, the faculty and the university administrators entered into a bitter and protracted struggle that cast a pall over the medical school for more than a decade. The trouble, which continues to confound many universities today, stemmed from tension between the school's administrators and its practitioners. In 1825, the state legislature replaced the regents with a board of trustees.[41] This created a serious problem for the medical faculty. The professors had, after all, founded the medical school, and they owned it. They had strong opinions about how the school should be run and resented interference. The board of trustees, on the other hand, had been selected from among the city's most respected and successful business and legal figures, and they felt confident about their ability to run the school.

A clash was inevitable and not long in coming. The trustees made the first move, wresting control of the infirmary from the doctors and attempting to abolish tenure. Granville Sharp Pattison, one of the most prominent and more volatile professors, promptly resigned in disgust. The conflict then spread beyond the medical faculty. In sympathy with Pattison and Davidge, the eminent law professor David Hoffman also quit. It seemed that the young university was losing its best professors, just as the medical school was facing direct competition in Baltimore for the first time.[42]

Horatio Gates Jameson opened Washington Medical in 1827, just as relationships at the University of Maryland seemed to be reaching a disastrous state. The new school was essentially a diploma mill. In view of the conflict at the University of Maryland and the lower fees and standards at Baltimore's second medical college, however, Washington Medical posed a real threat.[43] The competition started a downward spiral at the university. As some students began to matriculate at Washington Medical, enrollment fees at Maryland declined; this reduced professors' incomes, leading to an ever more disgruntled faculty.

The tedious struggle within the University of Maryland continued until 1837, when the old faculty resigned *en masse*. The trustees, after confiscating the university and infirmary, had refused either to make a monetary settlement that the faculty deemed fair or to provide the professors with salaries that compared with the income they had previously earned from fees (which in 1826 was about four thousand dollars each annually). In a society as litigious as the United States, it was inevitable that the embroilment would be carried over into the courts; appeals were launched, decisions reversed, and lawyers' wallets plumped. Finally, the Court of Appeals returned the university to the faculty and reassigned its management to the regents.[44] While this decision was a severe blow to the state, which had lost control of this important educational institution, the court's intervention was a blessing to the University of Maryland School of Medicine.

Once again, the faculty could concentrate on medical education and the job of attracting large numbers of students from Maryland and other states. During the 1840s and 1850s, as young men increasingly sought training in professional schools, Maryland was able to offer thorough training and effective credentialing to substantial numbers of physicians. From 1845 until the Civil War, about two hundred students enrolled each year in the medical school, with about sixty-five graduating annually. The old faculty was gradually replaced by fresh, if not such blue blood. Perhaps the most eminent among the new generation of professors was Nathan Ryno Smith, who became a powerful leader within the institution and a prominent surgeon in the state. The younger faculty members increasingly emphasized practical experience not just in the clinical wards but in the basic sciences, too. They encouraged laboratory experimentation. To graduate, students were required to complete a thesis and pass a final examination; gradually, the thesis became less significant as the examination grew in importance.[45]

By the end of the 1850s, the medical school's future seemed assured, but then the conflict over slavery posed a new challenge to the institution. When travel between North and South became almost impossible and potential students began to go to battle instead of school, enrollment suddenly plummeted. The university successfully limped through these years, despite the fact that some faculty as well as many students enlisted. From the sampling that George Callcott carried out, more aligned with the Confederate than the Union forces.[46] Several members of the faculty, as well as some alumni and students, played significant roles in the war. William A. Hammond, professor of anatomy and physiology and a unionist, left a lasting mark on the history of military medicine. He had been a surgeon in the U.S. Army before joining the University of Maryland faculty, and in 1860 he resigned his chair to take up a military post again. Two years later, he was appointed surgeon-general to the U.S. Army.[47] Meanwhile, Nathan Ryno Smith, who held the Chair of Surgery at the university from 1827 to 1869, had developed an anterior splint for fractures of the femur, an innovation that proved invaluable for treating the fractures of this sort caused by gunshots.[48]

Not all of the Civil War experiences cast such a favorable light on the quality of America's medicine and medical education. During the war, the armies found a great many of the practitioners they recruited woefully ill educated, in some cases illiterate. The need for reform became evident, and after 1865 the University of Maryland School of Medicine began to play a substantial role in the efforts to improve medical education.[49] One aspect of this reform movement was greater emphasis on specialization, a process of change that in part reflected the improved state of knowledge stemming from the war. At Maryland, for example, William T. Howard occupied a newly created chair in the diseases of women and children (1867). During the following academic year, the school held its first clinics on diseases of the eye.[50]

In the postbellum years, medical school faculty members also sought out new clinical opportunities and made special efforts to expand their students' practical work. Experience in the emergent specialties was vital for both the school and its students' careers. One of the faculty members most active in this field was J. J. Chisolm, professor of ophthalmology. In 1870, he received sufficient financial backing from the university to open an eye and ear infirmary.[51] This twenty-bed facility functioned as a specialty clinic for Chisolm's teaching. In 1879, when the infirmary's maintenance overreached the university's budget, the Presbyterian Church took it over and transformed it into the Presbyterian Charity Eye, Ear and Throat Hospital. The hospital continued to provide medical students with substantial specialty training, which in turn helped promote ophthalmology and otology as separate disciplines. By the 1870s, the University of Maryland had thus begun to turn forcefully toward the type of specialization and research that would, in the decades that followed, recast medical education in the state and the nation.

Dentistry Enters the College

Medicine was not the only division of the University of Maryland to enhance its position in the state's growing system of professional education during the nineteenth century. Dentistry, which over the span of half a century was transformed from a low-status trade into a scientific profession, also acquired an important place in the university and in the state.

Since ancient times, dentistry had been practiced throughout the world, with varied degrees of skill and knowledge. During the colonial era, the itinerant toothpuller was a familiar part of the social landscape in Maryland and the rest of America. Carrying a few implements — chiefly dental keys and other extractors, perhaps a wooden dental chair — he traveled around the country's many small settlements. This was not a glamorous job, but a secure one. Since treatments for mouths were restricted to herbal remedies, alcohol, and narcotics, ailing teeth and gums usually resulted in extractions. Blacksmiths often doubled as dentists. They possessed the necessary tools, and they, like itinerant toothpullers, sometimes provided artificial replacements. There was, in fact, quite a business in false teeth. Probably the most famous sets in America belonged to George Washington, and one pair used by the Father of the Country now (appropriately) resides at the University of Maryland. Personal appearance, as well as the ability to speak coherently, has long been important to public figures.

By the turn of the eighteenth century, prosthetics, operative dentistry, and oral surgery were growing areas of protoprofessional expertise. Dentists, like physicians, were broadening their intellectual domain, and immigrant colleagues from Europe frequently accelerated the progress by introducing new techniques. In an effort to foster further improvement and elevate the status of their occupation, Maryland dentists became interested in improved education and licensing regulations. In 1805, they sought to achieve both goals by moving underneath what they interpreted as the umbrella licensing of the Medical and Chirurgical Faculty. Hence, anyone who wanted "legally" to practice dentistry in the state had to appear before the Faculty examination board. As with physicians, enforcement was sketchy, especially in the more remote regions. Nevertheless, a trial run with licensing had begun.[52]

One of Maryland's first and most influential dental licentiates was Horace H. Hayden (1769–1844), who was a prime mover behind the foundation of the world's first dental school, the Baltimore College of Dental Surgery. Hayden, who was born in Connecticut, had as a youth followed in his father's footsteps and learned carpentry and architecture. But his career underwent a marked change in the 1790s after he had a tooth pulled in New York by John Greenwood, who was one of George Washington's dentists. Hayden was so impressed with Greenwood's skill that he immediately signed up as the dentist's apprentice. After practicing for a few years in the North, Hayden headed south and around 1804 opened his dental practice in Baltimore.[53]

From an early point in his career, Hayden was committed to elevating dentistry from a trade to a reputable profession. He sought to transform the social perception of its practitioners from illiterate artisans to scientific gentlemen. He was, in short, adopting the pattern of change that seemed to be succeeding with the state's medical men. Their efforts frequently revolved around education, and Hayden gave to improvements in training a key role in his campaign. He began holding evening classes by tallow light in his office. A gentlemanly figure, Hayden gained the respect of the state's physicians as well as its dentists. He developed sound working relations with medical professors at the University of Maryland

and with physicians at the Medical and Chirurgical Faculty, which he joined in 1810. In fact, this dental reformer encouraged some of his students also to study medicine at the University of Maryland.[54]

Hayden began delivering occasional lectures on dentistry to medical students at the university in the early 1820s.[55] By 1837, these lectures had become more regular and formalized; as Hayden's reputation as a skillful practitioner, educator, and intellectual spread, more young men came to study with him.[56] One was Chapin A. Harris (1806–60), whom George Callcott has characterized as an ambitious fellow in a hurry. Evidently, he had already hurried into medical credentials, which he had purchased from an Illinois diploma mill, before deciding that his true and probably more profitable calling was dentistry.[57] With this change of course came a change of heart; Harris decided that, in order to succeed, he needed to earn his dental degree legitimately in the best setting possible. Around 1830 he arrived in Baltimore to study with Hayden.

The teacher and his pupil were quite different in personality and in their approaches to professional advancement. But after the younger man had properly earned his way into dentistry, Hayden and Harris became partners in a collaborative effort to place dental education in Maryland on a firm institutional footing. Harris had begun to promote professional dentistry as well as his own work in 1839, when he launched the *American Journal of Dental Surgery*. The following year, the two men organized the American College of Dental Surgeons. Increasingly frustrated by the inadequacies of apprenticeship and medical schooling, they pressed for separate, formal, scientific education. In 1839, they tried to persuade the University of Maryland to open a dental school, but the university, which was then in a shaky position, refused.[58] Undeterred, they decided to go it alone and open an autonomous proprietary college.

In February 1840, the General Assembly granted them a charter for the Baltimore College of Dental Surgery. The faculty consisted of Hayden as professor of dental physiology and pathology, Harris as professor of practical dentistry, H. Willis Baxley as professor of anatomy and physiology, and Thomas E. Bond as professor of special pathology and therapeutics. Baxley and Hayden brought to the dental school their respective anatomical and pathological cabinet collections, which they used to illustrate their lectures.[59] In November 1840, the new faculty advertised that they would deliver introductory lectures on Tuesday, November 3, at 7:30 P.M. in the Baptist Church on Calvert Street, between Lexington and Saratoga Streets. They placed the announcement in numerous newspapers and journals on the East Coast, as far south as Charleston, South Carolina, and as far north as New York City.[60]

As it turned out, they had been wise to spread their advertising net so widely. Five students were drawn to the opening class—two from New York City, two from Baltimore, and one from Norfolk, Virginia. Candidates for the degree "Doctor of Dental Surgery," or D.D.S. (a title devised by Hayden and Harris), were required to attend two courses of lectures at the college. Those who had already completed a session at a medical school were expected to study dentistry for only one year. Before they could graduate, all candidates were examined by the faculty, were required to defend a thesis, and had to present at least one specimen demonstrating the preparation and setting of false teeth. The professors charged thirty dollars for each annual set of lectures. To this was added a matriculation fee of five dollars and a diploma fee of thirty dollars.[61] Although the diploma fee seems relatively high, it was a price the market would bear. Thirty dollars gave the graduates an all-important item that could be prominently displayed to both patients and colleagues, attesting to their professional training and knowledge. This aspect of professional behavior changed very little, if at all, in the next century and a half.

In reality, many practitioners obtained the diploma and title without spending two full years in the lecture halls or, indeed, in some cases, without even setting foot in a classroom. This was a proprietary institution with no endowment. The faculty relied entirely on student fees for maintenance. As members of an emerging profession, they recognized the value of offering credentials to any student or practitioner who seemed to merit them. Hence, anyone who could meet all of the graduation requirements and pay the thirty-dollar diploma fee could become a Doctor of Dental Surgery. Along the same vein, the college awarded honorary degrees to established practitioners whose work was sound and who had already contributed to the advancement of dentistry.[62]

Though no great moneymaker, the policy of bestowing honorary degrees was a clever strategy on the part of the college faculty. It fostered collegiality and good will in dentistry, and since these honors were widely distributed throughout America and parts of northern Europe, they drew attention to the college and helped attract students.[63] This discreet form of professional advertising, and others as well, helped the college grow. By 1850, its graduates numbered 82, and they hailed from eighteen states in America, the District of Columbia, and northern Europe. By 1874, 738 persons (including one woman) held D.D.S. diplomas from Baltimore.[64]

By that time, the faculty had broadened the program as well as advertising it. They opened their first dental clinic in 1846, when they moved to larger premises on Lexington Street.[65] They treated the clinic patients free in exchange for their patience with dental students who were still honing their skills. Their new operating room contained ten chairs. In small, separate classes, students were each assigned a chair upon whose occupants they worked all morning under supervision. In the laboratory, too, students had individual places in the eighty-foot-long room where they learned to assemble prosthetics.[66] As clinical teaching received more and more attention, the college's managers hired more demonstrators, and in 1872 they appointed James H. Harris, M.D., D.D.S., to a new professorship in clinical dentistry.[67]

The success of the expanding Baltimore College of Dental Surgery encouraged other dental entrepreneurs to enter the market. Professional education was becoming a new frontier for ambitious young men in Maryland and elsewhere in the United States in the aftermath of the Civil War. In the two decades following the war, aspiring American dental educators founded twenty-two new schools, two of them in Baltimore.[68] Expansion and increasing diversity were keynotes of this era of rapid urbanization, industrialization, and population growth.

The first new competitor was the Maryland Dental College, which was chartered in 1873. Its first dean, Richard Bayly Winder, had served as a major in the Confederate Army and after the war had graduated from the Baltimore College of Dental Surgery (1869). He established his new school at 42 North Calvert Street, and while it was smaller than the Baltimore College, it was modeled along similar lines. Winder, who granted various credits for prior experience, offered a basic course consisting of two years of lectures and practical work. He set fees that were identical with those being charged at that time by his senior competitor:[69]

Professor's and demonstrator's fees	$120 annually
Matriculation fee	$5
Diploma fee	$30

Unwilling to undercut the prices charged by its established rival, Maryland Dental had trouble attracting students. During the next five years, Winder struggled along, unable to find an angle that would give his small institution a competitive edge. Finally, the little college collapsed in 1878 and was absorbed by the Baltimore Dental College. This was more a merger than a hostile takeover, since some of the faculty stayed on and Winder later became dean of the Baltimore College.[70] The Baltimore College of Dental Surgery was again unrivaled in Maryland, but it would not be able to enjoy that situation very long. The next competitive threat would be far more serious than the one mounted by Maryland Dental.

A School of Pharmacy

Like dentists, pharmacists in America succeeded in opening their own colleges in the nineteenth century, placing their occupation on a more professional footing. They, too, sought autonomy from physicians, and in 1839—the same year that the Baltimore College of Dental Surgery was created—Maryland's pharmacists began organizing a campaign to launch a special college to train their practitioners.

Though an ancient occupation, pharmacy had long been regarded as a trade that straddled medicine and magic, blending legitimate therapies with quack remedies. In Maryland, pharmacy was molded along English lines, with some important additions drawn from Native American customs. In Baltimore, as in other American cities, this mixture had also acquired a lacquer of French "higher pharmacy."[71] In the practice of pharmacy, America was clearly a melting pot.

During the colonial era, training had been largely informal and individual, with apprenticeship as the most organized system of education. In the early nineteenth century, however, urban pharmacists in the seaboard cities began to press for more formal training in professional colleges. The first such institution was founded in Philadelphia in 1821, followed by two more in Boston and New York.

In each of these cities—and then in Baltimore—the pharmacists (or, as they were commonly known, druggists) had to fight harder than dentists to gain professional stature. In England, the work of apothecaries and doctors had been separated and regulated, but in America physicians and druggists were often in direct competition. People who could not afford a physician's fees or simply preferred to avoid doctors frequently sought the advice of druggists. Druggists provided "informal" diagnoses and then prepared and sold the remedies they recommended. This infuriated the medical profession. Meanwhile, druggists felt cheated by those physicians who dispensed their own medications.[72] With the two groups competing in this manner, it was inevitable that the druggists would find that every step toward full professionalization was a battle involving jurisdiction and money.[73]

In Maryland, the conflict turned out to be less acute than it had been in New York and Boston. Fortunately for pharmacy, medicine, and the state's people, the medical men at the University of Maryland decided that cooperation was preferable to an all-out war. Important members of the medical faculty actually rallied in support of formalized pharmaceutical education. Early on, William E. A. Aiken (1807–88), professor of chemistry at the University of Maryland, eased the path to cooperation by inviting pharmacists and their apprentices to his lectures.[74] Another chemistry professor at the university, William R. Fisher (1808–42), promoted the idea of bringing pharmacists together at the Medical and Chirurgical Faculty to plan a college for their profession.

With the physicians' backing, the pharmacists were able to obtain a charter for the Maryland College of Pharmacy in January 1841. Actually, *college* is a rather grand term for the single rented room they occupied at Baltimore and Gay Streets, but at least they had a formal establishment.[75] In the early years, the college's program matched the physical setting, and both were matched by the public's unenthusiastic response to this educational innovation. Indeed, the little college was failing when, in 1844, some of the faculty at the university provided assistance. They offered space at the University of Maryland and opened their chemistry lectures gratis to the pharmacy students. This assistance enabled the institution to avoid collapse.

David Stewart, who had received his M.D. degree from the University of Maryland and served as inspector of drugs for the Port of Baltimore, began to offer lectures at the college in 1844.[76]

The course, which was intensely practical, was designed to provide pharmacists with the training they needed to elevate their trade to a profession. Because some in the Maryland public considered druggists moneygrubbers who frequently cheated their customers and often sold tainted, dangerous products, the college program emphasized weights, measures, and careful chemical and botanical processing. Stewart was shortly joined by W. S. Reese, who became professor of materia medica, and by six of the city's druggists, who served on a voluntary basis.[77]

Practical as the curriculum seems, the venture was still slow to gather steam or students. Although the students paid only ten dollars for the course, only fifteen enrolled for the 1844–45 session. Just a handful graduated, and, indeed, the college remained little more than a name and a lecture series until 1856. Then, a few of Baltimore's pharmacists called a meeting with the board of trustees and demanded a rigorous reorganization. Under the leadership of druggist Israel Graham, the local pharmacy association and the college came to one another's aid. At this time, the board added thirty-one new members, broadening the school's base of support in Baltimore.[78]

After these changes in the governing body, the College of Pharmacy began to gain importance as its faculty and trustees increasingly followed the example of the medical school and the proprietary system. The professors, who relied on students' fees, reduced the number of classes and the expense to eight dollars per lecture course. The training consisted of lectures and practical work in the fields of botany and materia medica, pharmacy, chemistry, and analytical chemistry. In 1858, the faculty and the city's pharmacists cooperated to launch the *Journal and Transactions of the Maryland College of Pharmacy,* which presented lectures that were given at the college on everything from "syrup of rhubarb" to "the preparation of savin cerate." The *Journal* also published the new code of ethics that the pharmacists, like other professionalizing groups, had drafted.[79]

The pharmacy faculty was realistic about the relationship of their discipline to medicine in Maryland.[80] Their basic strategy was to make pharmacists indispensable rather than independent. They stressed contacts with wholesale pharmaceutical companies, including those specializing in homeopathic preparations. Recognizing that their credential was worth less than either a medical or a dental degree, they kept their fees lower than those in the medical school. As late as the mid-1870s, they were still charging only the following fees:[81]

matriculation fee	$4
analytical chemistry	$15
tickets to lectures	$12 (for each session)
graduation fee	$10

The pharmacists encouraged foreign students, who bolstered both the reputation and income of the school, to attend and were always willing to make special arrangements for them.[82] By the 1870s, pharmacy's role in the state's system of medical education was not as well developed as that of medicine or dentistry, but Maryland's pharmacists had at least laid down an institutional foundation on which subsequent generations of professionals would be able to build a modern, science-based program.

In education, as in hospital development and therapy, Maryland's experience during the century after American independence was characterized more by diversity than unity, more by differences of opinion than consensus, more by expansion than consolidation. The state had, nevertheless, acquired by 1876 a significant cadre of leaders and a substantial array of institutions dedicated to training the next generation of physicians, dentists, and pharmacists. These institutions and their staffs were still in flux, but so, too, was the state's economy, its population, and, for that matter, the entire medical establishment. Shortly, that establishment would be turned on its head by new ideas flowing from the Old World to the New, ideas that would eventually revolutionize the practice of medicine in Maryland.

FIVE

Medical Education

Science and Centralization,
1876–1940

In the late nineteenth century, a new Maryland institution moved quickly to the forefront of medical training in this country. The Johns Hopkins School of Medicine, as historian Richard Shryock has noted, exerted a unique influence on medical practice in America and became a model for the society's rapidly changing system of medical education.[1] From its inception, the school was dedicated to the scientific method and to the development of new medical knowledge through meticulous scientific research.

The school's advances did not stop there; Hopkins accepted female medical students at a time when few leading programs were open to women. Four powerful young Baltimoreans were responsible for that particular, rather startling policy. M. Carey Thomas, Mary Elizabeth Garrett, Mary Gwinn, and Elizabeth King were all daughters of Johns Hopkins University trustees and all aware of the educational and professional bias against women throughout the United States.[2] When Hopkins encountered a financial crisis due to the decline in income from the endowment's investment in the struggling Baltimore and Ohio Railroad, these women saw an opportunity to exert some influence upon the institution. These financial difficulties, which arose in 1888, just as the hospital was nearing completion, jeopardized the proposed medical school.

Into the breach stepped the four women, who in May 1890 established the Women's Fund Committee. They set out to raise the money needed to open the School of Medicine in exchange for the admission of women on equal terms with men. The committee approached such prominent female physicians as Elizabeth Blackwell and such prominent social figures as First Lady Mrs. Benjamin Harrison. Once they had raised $100,000 (including $47,787 from Elizabeth Garrett), the committee went to the university's trustees. As Caroline Bedell Thomas explained, they were helped by the fact that the majority of the trustees were Quaker and hence accustomed to the concept of equality between the sexes.[3] Still, University President Gilman and others were not thrilled about admitting women.

Gilman and the university were, however, in a tight corner. Hopkins's trustees had stipulated that $500,000 was needed to proceed with the medical school. With his back against the wall, Gilman looked to the Women's Committee for help, but initially even the committee's enthusiastic campaign fell short of the mark. Then, finally, on Christmas Eve 1892, the wealthy Miss Garrett contributed the additional $306,977 they needed to attain their goal. Tough-minded as well as generous, she attached a new string to the gift. Garrett insisted that, as well as opening the school to women, the trustees would have to require all of the incoming students to have the equivalent of a Johns Hopkins bachelor's degree.

This was a bold proviso and one that initially distressed the medical faculty. The new school needed to attract students, and William Welch, among others, was concerned that the stiffest admission requirements in the country would drive off potential candidates. He had good reason to suspect that this would happen. When several of the academically sounder medical schools, including Harvard and Pennsylvania, had raised their standards in the 1870s and 1880s, admissions had suffered, and they had been forced to retrench.[4] Fortunately for Hopkins, by the time its School of Medicine opened in 1893, it was able to attract enough qualified applicants. The new school had several powerful attractions. It was purpose-built, it had its own hospital, and it was staffed by eminent teachers well versed in the scientific method.

To ensure that the faculty would have time both to teach and to do research, Johns Hopkins appointed its preclinical teachers to full-time positions. It was the first American medical school to do so on a regular basis. The idea was not new. In 1871, Henry Pickering Bowditch, who had studied with Carl Ludwig in Germany, had become professor of physiology at Harvard Medical School.[5] His full-time, salaried appointment was the nation's first and marked the start of a new era in medical education, an era characterized by a growing emphasis on professionalization and specialization of function. As late as 1893, however, none of the country's other medical schools had made as abrupt a break with past practice as did Hopkins.

Full-time appointments were a source of economic tension between professors and practitioners, and that tension in part explains why other schools had not adopted this practice in the two decades before 1893.[6] Traditionally, medical school faculties had divided their time between teaching and medical practice. Not surprisingly, then, when German and Austrian-influenced physicians began seeking full-time professorships, they aroused opposition. Practitioners realized that their access to hospitals and patients—and, hence, income—might well be curtailed by this new, school-based elite.

This professional rift widened in the years that followed. The practitioners and professors had different intellectual, economic, social, and political interests. Practitioners at this time worried a great deal about the encroachment of "irregulars" and lobbied against homeopaths. Since homeopaths did not affect the day-to-day activities or livelihood of full-time academics, however, they posed little threat to the medical school community. Antivivisectionists, on the other hand, were the bane of the educators as they threatened to inhibit the practices of both scientific teaching and research. To most practitioners, by contrast, antivivisection was not a salient political or social issue.[7]

Ignoring these tensions and low academic salaries, scientifically trained doctors increasingly pressed for full-time appointments.[8] Many, it seems, were influenced by their educational experiences in Europe. Thomas Bonner estimated that, between 1870 and 1914, at least fifteen thousand American medical students and physicians studied in German, Austrian, or Swiss universities, getting training that ranged from six weeks in a specialty course to three years of laboratory research.[9] Gradually, those medical men and women intellectually superseded an older generation of practitioners primarily influenced by British and French clinical medicine. In the German style of medicine, higher learning was linked with the type of original research that normally required an academic setting.[10] These ideas had a dramatic influence on Hopkins. While there were, as Gert Brieger has explained, some important domestic influences, Daniel Coit Gilman imported most of his ideas from the European universities he had visited. The continental influence, particularly that of Germany, was manifest throughout the new institution.[11]

Before 1893, German concepts had made an impression on several of America's better medical schools. In the 1870s and 1880s, the faculties at Harvard, Michigan, Pennsylvania, and Syracuse had attempted to remodel along German lines. Most of these efforts had been blighted, however, by the forces of tradition. At Hopkins, a new school in a new university, the organizers could pay less heed to tradition and innovate more freely and more completely. Hopkins had the benefit of a fresh start.[12]

William Welch, President Gilman, and the trustees took full advantage of that situation to establish a pioneering program based largely on the German model. When they were hiring the faculty, they staffed all of the preclinical departments—anatomy, bacteriology, pathology, pharmacology, physiology, and physiological chemistry—with full-timers who would thus be able to devote themselves entirely to teaching and research.[13]

Gilman also broke with American tradition in his search for the core professors. Instead of appointing local physicians, he cast his net widely, looking for the best across America and even in Europe. His search for talent put some noses out of joint. Baltimore physicians and professors at the University of Maryland were offended when none was invited to join the new faculty.[14] They had good reason to be surprised by such a novel concept. Even twenty years later, only a handful of schools in the entire United States went "outside the local profession to procure clinical teachers."[15] But by doing so, Gilman and the trustees were able to furnish their medical school with one of its greatest strengths, an outstanding faculty.

Gilman built his new medical faculty around a pathologist, as pathology was then regarded as the key science in medical education. After his European travels in the summer of 1883, he had consulted with Julius Cohnheim, with whom William Welch had studied in Breslau. Cohnheim recommended Welch for the position, and on April 7, 1884, the trustees appointed him professor of pathology in the university.[16] Welch (1850–1934) had already established America's first experimental pathology laboratory at Bellevue Hospital Medical College in New York, but Hopkins was able to lure him away from New York with the offer of a full-time, salaried post. Welch, the first of the so-called Big Four, brought to Hopkins a strong conviction that the university hospital should be committed to scientific investigation as well as the treatment of disease. Toward that end, he insisted that the new Pathology Building be located near the wards. In his laboratories, Welch gave his students the latitude to follow their own investigative noses, and the results included a wide range of important scientific studies and significant discoveries.[17]

Welch played a forceful role in securing the appointments of the rest of the Big Four. As the hospital moved closer to opening, Gilman and Billings were on the lookout for a surgeon-in-chief and professor of surgery, as well as a physician-in-chief and professor of medicine. Welch strongly supported William S. Halsted (1852–1922) for the first of these posts. He had worked with Halsted in New York and had taken the surgeon into his home and laboratory in 1886, after Halsted had spent a year in a sanatorium recovering from a cocaine addiction acquired while experimenting with local anesthesia. Accepting Welch's strong recommendation, the trustees appointed Halsted as associate professor of surgery in 1889 and the next year as surgeon-in-chief of the hospital and professor of surgery at the medical school. In his clinic, Halsted began at once to conduct the type of work that embodied the conjunction between science and medicine, research and teaching that Gilman and Billings had envisioned.[18]

In 1888, with Welch's encouragement, the trustees appointed William Osler (1849–1919) physician-in-chief and professor of medicine. Born and educated in Canada, Osler was professor of medicine at the University of Pennsylvania before accepting a comparable but more extensive role at Hopkins. Like Welch and Halsted, he had studied in Europe but, although they were profoundly influenced by the German-Austrian system, Osler still preferred British notions of medical education.

The fourth member of the Big Four was also the youngest. Howard Kelly (1858–1943), unlike the other three, was imbued with American medicine. He had received his medical degree from the University of Pennsylvania and taught gynecology at that university's medical school. Gilman had not planned to appoint a gynecologist, but in late 1889 the trustees decided to open a search for a professor in this branch of medicine.[19] Kelly's appointment reflected the growing importance of specialization in medical education and the pioneering role of gynecology in that movement.[20]

The Big Four—Welch, Osler, Halsted, and Kelly—have acquired almost mythical standing in the history of the institution. Although their roles in the institution's early development were certainly outstanding, there were other crucial contributors, most notably, at first, Martin, Remsen, and Billings. A joint committee of the hospital and university trustees had appointed these three when it was initially planning to open the new school in the 1880s. John Shaw Billings became professor of hygiene; Ira Remsen, professor of chemistry; and Henry Newell Martin, professor of physiology. Remsen stationed himself on the arts and science campus, but Martin focused his substantial energy on the emergent medical school. His own training in England had bridged medicine and science, and he brought to Hopkins a commitment to experimental physiology, à la Claude Bernard. Martin launched a graduate program as well as a premedical course. He resigned just before the medical school opened (and subsequently collapsed into alcoholism), but two of his students joined the first medical school faculty: John Jacob Abel became professor of pharmacology, and William Henry Howell, professor of physiology.[21]

Another important, although less visible, faculty member was Franklin Paine Mall. After receiving his medical degree from the University of Michigan in 1885, Mall spent three years as a fellow and assistant in Welch's laboratory at Hopkins. He then held positions at Clark University and the University of Chicago before he was enticed back to Hopkins by the offer of a professorship in anatomy (1893).[22]

With the faculty in place, the hospital in full operation, and the medical school's buildings completed, Hopkins admitted its first class in the fall of 1893. There were eighteen students, five of whom had been Hopkins undergraduates and three of whom were women. Word about this modern medical school had traveled fast, and the majority of the students, like the faculty, came from institutions outside the state.[23] Several of the female matriculates from the early days considered Hopkins already to be the best school for women in the country.

Admissions requirements were stiff. Until 1901, when Harvard adopted the baccalaureate requirement, Hopkins was the only medical school in the United States to demand a bachelor's degree in addition to substantial scientific and language preparation.[24] As one student, Mabel Glover, was pleased to discover, however, few students in the initial years were able to meet every detail of the admissions requirements. Glover, for example, had taken neither organic chemistry nor advanced physics. But she was otherwise qualified, and the faculty and administration were willing to display a modicum of flexibility.[25]

The curriculum was initially in flux. Before students were introduced to human dissection, they received instruction (October 9 to November 15) from 9:00 A.M. to 5:00 P.M., five days a week, in osteology, histology, physiology, and physiological chemistry. When some of the students complained to Welch about the poor quality of the histology and osteology course, the professor acknowledged that he was still ironing out the kinks in this part of the program. He moved quickly to correct the problem, and during the following term the course was said to be both bigger and better.

During the remaining three-quarters of the first academic year, the faculty featured anatomy while introducing the students to bacteriology and embryology.[26] In the second preclinical year, the students began their studies in pathology. Welch supervised them as they attended autopsies in the hospital and examined specimens and microscopic preparations in the laboratory. The medical school instruction in this setting was no longer ad hoc, as it had been through most of the nineteenth century. The professors presented well-organized lectures that were part of a curriculum carefully designed to build knowledge of the complementary fields in a cumulative manner. The faculty members conducting this training were all involved in original medical research. Thus, they were able to introduce the students to knowledge from the forefront of medical science and were determined to teach each student to think and act scientifically. This was echoed to the sixty-three members of the entering class in 1898 by T. Clifford Allbutt (Regius Professor of Physic at Cambridge University, England), who said that not "every physician shall be a man of science" but all "shall have the scientific habit of mind."[27]

The same ideology inspired the hospital-oriented faculty who guided the students through their third and fourth years of clinical training. During the third year, the students were divided into four groups, each of which spent two months rotating through medicine, surgery, obstetrics, and gynecology. Hopkins Hospital played a central role in this program, one in which the clinic, the laboratory, and the classroom were inseparable. Little wonder that this quickly became the dominant model in American medical education.[28]

The school and its influence continued to expand. At the turn of the century and with greater urgency after the Flexner Report in 1910, medical school faculties and administrators throughout the country attempted to improve clinical training in their institutions. Following Hopkins's lead, they increasingly established formal unions with hospitals in an effort to promote teaching and research. The training hospitals found these arrangements desirable because they could then provide the most up-to-date patient care and could attract patients on the basis of the teaching and research conducted at their institution.[29] In Baltimore during the early twentieth century, other local hospitals, including the City Hospital and Sheppard Pratt, adopted the Hopkins model and fostered academic ties.

The Hopkins influence extended far beyond Maryland and the rise of the American teaching hospital. The Hopkins faculty helped reform medical education and strengthen their various academic disciplines.[30] They pioneered new operative techniques, introduced curricular innovations, conducted pathbreaking research, and helped to launch new scientific societies and journals. Their individual contributions were far too numerous to list here. Suffice it to say that they were leaders in the reformation of medical education, medical science, and therapeutics.

During the first generation at the school, Osler's clinics were the most popular with students, and he soon acquired an international reputation as a great bedside teacher. While Welch was importing German techniques in laboratory science, Osler was modifying the English and Scottish system to fit the new Hopkins style of clinical education. He introduced the clinical clerkship, an innovation that ultimately influenced every medical school, teaching hospital, and student in the country.[31] Clerkships in the hospital were for third- and fourth-year students; Hopkins broke with the English system, in which only the cream of the student crop received them, and threw the clerkships open to all.[32] In clerkships the learning was active, not passive; students were assigned five or six of their own patients. Under supervision, they took case histories, performed physical examinations, carried out routine technical procedures, and followed their patients to recovery or autopsy. The hospital clerkship did for clinical education what the laboratory did for scientific education.[33]

There were problematic aspects of the clerkships. Only so much could be learned from performing a simple task, such as drawing blood, again and again. Students understandably complained of the boredom stemming from repetitive routines. Patients, too, sometimes complained that they felt like objects or educational tools, and indeed their best interests were at times in conflict with those of the medical educators. Faculties attempted, with limited success, to reduce these tensions, but whether they were successful or not the system thrived.[34] Despite the boredom, clerkships were on balance beneficial to the students, and they guaranteed to the hospitals a valuable source of talented yet inexpensive labor, much like that of the nursing students. The system's advantages for the medical schools, the hospitals, and the students outweighed all other considerations, and the new program spread throughout the country.

Some relief from boredom was provided at Hopkins by organizations like the Pithotomy Club. The club provides us with a rare window on some of the things the school's students were doing when they were not engaged with their lectures, laboratory work, and clerkships. The Pithotomy Club had its origins in the house of William G. MacCallum (later chair of the Department of Pathology) and his fellow senior classmate, Joseph L. Nichols. They rented the house for the academic year

1896–97, bought a keg of beer, and invited students, friends, and the faculty to their housewarming party at 1200 Guilford Avenue. The event proved so enjoyable that their classmates helped organize further gatherings under the name of the Peanut Club. Seeking a more medically inspired name, MacCallum came up with Pithotomy from the Greek *pithos,* meaning "vessel," and *otomos,* meaning "to open." In short, "to tap a keg."[35]

This was a male drinking society, intended "to further the sense of brotherhood between the students themselves and between students and faculty." As the club's founders stated in the constitution, "The object of this society is the promotion of vice among the virtuous, virtue among the vicious, and good fellowship among all."[36] The Johns Hopkins School of Medicine had begun with a relatively small faculty that was highly conscious of its pedagogic imperative and a small student body that was highly qualified but doubtless awed by some of faculty members and by the school's demanding program. The club's atmosphere enabled the faculty and students to cross barriers of intellect, professional standing, and age, and some of the professors, including in particular Welch and Osler, were regular guests at the Pithotomy Club.

Around 1905, the club launched a student review, the Pithotomy Show, in which the faculty and the school were the subjects of mirth. The faculty received the presentations jovially and took the opportunity "to spend an informal evening with their colleagues, drink a little too much, sing a little too loudly, [and] urinate in the alley." While women (including female medical students) were excluded from membership, they were permitted to attend certain functions as guests. But the Pithotomy Show was off-limits and, judging from the contents, one can see why. At a show in the late 1920s, for instance, two scenes depicted examinations of women, and in one—a parody of Dr. Cullen performing a gynecological examination—an offstage trio sang such ditties as "I know a girl from Asia Minor, she's got warts on her labia minor."[37]

The pranks and drunkenness of the students in the Pithotomy Club— now on North Broadway—regularly offended their neighbors, and some of the complaints reached the faculty. C. L. C. Horn wrote to Henry Hurd in 1907: "I am sorry to complain but the behaviour of the Doctors Club at 510 N. Broadway is scandalous their beer parties lasting all night up until 2 o'clock in the morning keeping us up not getting any sleep with their screaming and running and playing the piano."[38] If Hurd and his fellow faculty members took any action to improve town-gown relations in this matter, they seem to have left no record for the historian to consider. Given the circumstances, one doubts that radical changes ensued.

While women were spared from the Pithotomists' most bawdy behavior, they were very welcome at the club's dances. Held in the fall, these social occasions were regarded as important events in Baltimore. The medical students and young physicians were eminently marriageable, as were the area's debutantes. Many suitable matches apparently originated at such social events.[39]

In addition to promoting social alliances, the club played an important role in furthering its young members' professional lives. It was not just a drinking group; it was an elitist honorary society. New members were invited by unanimous election and were initially selected from top members of the senior class. Around 1908 membership was opened to all classes, but it was still restricted to forty-five students.[40] During Hopkins Hospital's early years, the house staff was picked from the medical students on the basis of their class ranking. The top six graduating students were offered internships in medicine, and the next six were offered surgical posts. Most of these students were Pithotomists and were accustomed to socializing with influential Hopkins figures. As Pithotomy historian Robert Harrell put it, "Many positions were traded at the Club itself, and thus careers shaped."[41]

This avenue of professional advancement was closed to Hopkins women. Though not explicitly barred by the Pithotomy constitution, women were never elected to membership.[42] Mary Elizabeth Garrett had pried open the doors of the medical school for women, but even her wealth could not break down the social barriers to professional advancement that women still faced at an institution that was far more advanced in this regard than any other medical school in the United States. The sexist atmosphere at the institution affected some women more than others. According to Dorothy Reed Mendenhall, a Hopkins student at the turn of the century, Osler went out of his way to discourage her from studying medicine purely on the basis of her sex. But she persevered and came to hold the famous clinician in the greatest respect. Hardened to prejudice, she nevertheless loathed the prurience that regularly accompanied extracurricular activities. She recalled being profoundly shaken by the proceedings of a student monthly meeting at which Simon Flexner presided and where Dr. Mackenzie contrived to turn a one-hour lecture on nasal pathology into a quasi-pornographic "defilement."[43]

Not everyone agreed. Yes, they were excluded from the social and professional advantages of the Pithotomy Club. But women such as Caroline

Bedell Thomas maintained that Johns Hopkins nevertheless provided a setting that was conducive to success for female medical students. Thomas, who became professor of medicine at Hopkins, graduated in the class of 1930. Among the seventy-one students in 1926 who had entered that class, there were eight women. They were joined by another four in advanced standing, and all twelve graduated. Moreover, they all went on to work actively in medicine, with five becoming academics. Thomas, who had married into a fourth-generation Baltimore medical family, maintained that, from World War I through the 1920s, "women entered medical schools with feelings of eagerness and freedom rather than a sense of inferiority."[44]

In the early years at Hopkins, men as well as women had good cause to worry about aspects of their lives that transcended gender and professional standing. So, too, did the faculty. As Dr. Thomas B. Futcher reported in 1909 to Dr. Remsen, "Whether justly or unjustly, the Medical School has obtained an unfortunate reputation for the prevalence of pulmonary tuberculosis among the students."[45] Although a few medical students lived and dined at the Pithotomy Club—relocated in the hospital's vicinity—most put up in boardinghouses. The medical school faculty and administrators became concerned that the conditions in those establishments might be endangering the health of students, placing them at increased risk of developing tuberculosis. Already, in 1904, Remsen (who was by then the university's president) had arranged for a committee of physicians to investigate the conditions under which students lived and worked. The students answered survey forms that inquired into their living conditions. Several complained of inadequate heating and lighting and of cramped quarters. The greater number objected to the poor food and the lack of athletic facilities. Since the faculty and administrators took seriously the problem of tuberculosis, they acted along the lines of prophylaxis and detection. Of the 568 students registered in 1904, 32 were "compelled to leave their class on account of health," and 19 of them never returned. Of the 24 with tuberculosis, half had TB in their family history and half had been exposed to the disease in Baltimore.[46] The school mounted a program to inspect and improve student accommodations in an effort to ensure that they would have sufficient heat, light, ventilation, and food; the institution also sought to minimize domestic exposure to tuberculous persons.[47]

An even more serious threat to the school's future came from the Great Fire of 1904, which engulfed over sixty of the buildings bequeathed by Johns Hopkins. This dealt a harsh financial blow to the hospital and to clinical instruction at the medical school. In an effort to meet the crisis, Welch approached John D. Rockefeller's financial advisor, Frederick T. Gates. These negotiations led to a grant of $500,000 to get the school through this devastating situation. The state granted another $40,000, which, given the calls upon public money for rebuilding, constituted a serious vote of confidence.[48] Although the hospital's trustees continued to place a high premium on accepting patients regardless of economic status (as stipulated by the founder, Johns Hopkins), they were tempted during this period of fiscal difficulty to favor those wealthy patients who could easily contribute to the institution's revenues.[49] Shortly, though, the medical school had recovered from the fire and was able to stay on a course that stressed scientific and medical, rather than commercial, advances.[50]

When educator Abraham Flexner inspected Hopkins in December 1909, he was immensely impressed by what he found. Flexner was a spokesman for the effort to push medical education in the entire country to yet another, higher level. With support from the Carnegie Foundation, Flexner was able to make a vigorous tour of all 155 American and Canadian medical schools and to compare their facilities and programs. As a professional educator who had received his bachelor's degree from Hopkins, he was prejudiced in favor of the school. But his findings could not be explained by simple favoritism. Flexner waxed eloquent in praise of "the first medical school in America of genuine university type." He found the laboratory and clinical facilities exemplary and financially secure. As he explained, "The Johns Hopkins most nearly represents desirable conditions; for there a teaching hospital belonging to the medical school is supported by adequate and separate endowment, so that clinical facilities impose no burden on the funds of the medical school proper. Moreover, there from the first clinical teachers have been salaried and, in a measure, withdrawn from general practice."[51]

At the time of Flexner's visit, there were 297 students in the school and 112 members on the teaching staff, 23 of whom were professors. Instructors, whose full-time employment was teaching and research, conducted the laboratory classes. The facilities in the laboratories were, Flexner said, "in every respect unexcelled." And the Johns Hopkins Hospital and Dispensary provided "practically ideal opportunities. The medical staff of the hospital and the clinical faculty of the medical school are identical." Flexner admired the flexibility of the program and noted with approval the lengthy period of anatomical training that the students received. Seven hundred hours of anatomical instruction were offered, of which four hundred were compulsory. This, he said, compared with 427 at Harvard and 265 at Cornell.[52]

The emphasis on firsthand experience in anatomical dissection—something that Mall had started—continued to characterize the program for many years. As alumnus Mark Ravitch noted, during the 1930s "dissecting manuals were disdained, and never used." Embalming fluid impregnated the students' ungloved hands, leaving Ravitch with visceral memories of the program and the inescapable smells. "The sight of several dozen cadavers embalmed, vaselined, and wrapped like mummies suspended from their ears by tongs on an overhead trolley in Hartley's [the custodian's] domain was never to be forgotten."[53]

By that time, Hopkins had survived the Great Fire and was making its way through the difficult years of the Great Depression. The school had managed to keep its momentum during the transition from the first to the second generation of faculty members and administrators. Osler had been the first of the core faculty to go. He had taken over the deanship from Welch in 1904, and by the following year he was burned out by the responsibilities of his position. Determined to leave, he accepted the Regius Professorship of Medicine at Oxford University in England.[54] Osler was succeeded by Lewellys F. Barker, who clearly represented a new generation of clinical teachers. Barker established three new research laboratories (hence "Divisions") in the Department of Medicine: Physiology, Biology, and Chemistry.[55] Unlike Osler, who left scientific experimentation to the preclinical departments, Barker wanted laboratory investigation to be thoroughly integrated into clinical work; he spearheaded this innovation.[56]

Barker (supported by Welch) pressed for the adoption of full-time appointments in the clinical fields. If clinical professors could rely on their salaries, he contended, they would not have to concern themselves with sustaining private practices. This would eliminate the gap that had developed between the clinical and the preclinical faculties as a result of the time clinicians devoted to paying patients. Under Barker's plan, clinical faculty would devote more time to research as well as teaching. In 1913, with a $1.5 million grant from the General Education Board, Hopkins placed the Departments of Medicine, Surgery, and Pediatrics on the full-time system and added some full professors to the payroll. When he had guided the institution through that significant transformation, Barker resigned as director of the Department of Medicine, handing the job over to Theodore Caldwell Janeway.[57]

Hopkins was thriving and continuing to evolve in 1917, when America entered World War I on the side of the Allies. The national effort suddenly supplanted individual efforts at the medical school and other American institutions. The school's faculty and graduates participated in a variety of capacities. Janeway acted as a consultant to the surgeon general; Welch served as president of the National Academy of Sciences.[58] Although Welch was sixty-seven, he took a very active role, offering to serve in any capacity his former student Surgeon General William C. Gorgas deemed useful. With a major's commission in the Medical Section of the Officers' Reserve Corps, he toured the country inspecting military camps.[59] By 1918, a third of the faculty was on active duty at home and abroad.

During and shortly after World War I, the transition to the new generation of leaders accelerated. Mall died in 1917. Two years later Kelly retired, followed by Halsted in 1922. By that time, Welch and Howell had already transferred from the School of Medicine to the School of Hygiene and Public Health. The consequences of this turnover could have been catastrophic, but in fact the medical institutions entered a period of substantial growth. New financial support was forthcoming, and the trustees were able to expand the faculty and the programs. Between 1916 and 1927, the school appointed new department heads in anatomy, gynecology, medicine, pathology, pediatrics, physiology, physiological chemistry, and surgery.

Hopkins continued to grow and improve. The school opened the Wilmer Ophthalmological Institute in 1925 and established the Institute of the History of Medicine four years later. These departments enlisted new faculty members. Following the hiring policy used to acquire the original faculty, the trustees, administrators, and faculty harvested another crop of outstanding researcher-teachers from across the nation. In several instances, the best person for the job was an alumnus. Among the second generation who had trained at Hopkins were Lewis H. Weed as head of the Department of Anatomy; William G. MacCallum, who joined Welch's staff; and William M. Clark as head of the Department of Physiological Chemistry. These men and a greatly improved physical plant kept Hopkins on top of medical education in the United States through the twenties and the depression years of the 1930s. In fact, because of the shrewd financial management of new Dean Alan Mason Chesney, it was possible for Hopkins to launch a new phase of expansion.[60]

The University of Maryland Medical School

While Hopkins was attracting a great deal of well-deserved attention in Baltimore and around the nation, the University of Maryland's Medical School was also continuing to develop new programs. In 1887, the university faculty had contributed to a fund set up by some of Baltimore's women's clubs to found a free lying-in hospital. This new institution provided obstetrical care for poor women and offered a setting for specialty training in obstetrics.[61]

The school had every reason to promote improvements because it was operating in a fiercely competitive and rapidly changing market. In the prosperous post–Civil War era, new medical colleges had popped up like mushrooms after a week of rain. Standards varied widely and, unfortunately, the worst schools undercut the reputations of the better ones. Many were proprietary institutions that turned out poorly trained doctors; some were nothing more than diploma mills.[62] Some, however, were institutions that met the special needs of groups that the older establishments had long neglected. All of the new schools, whatever their quality, threatened to deprive institutions like the University of Maryland of students, income, and public support.

In an attempt to deal with this problem, professors from established schools, including Maryland, urged the formation of a national association that could oversee accreditation. This was neither a new nor an entirely popular idea. Poorer schools feared for their futures, and many a proprietary school's faculty resented any hint of external interference. In fact, Maryland's Professor Eugene F. Cordell, who urged such reform, received a cool response from his own colleagues. He was, however, determined to promote accreditation, and in 1889, with the assistance of a group of Johns Hopkins professors, he organized a meeting of representatives from six Baltimore medical schools. Little accord was reached, but the representatives agreed to launch an effort to establish a national society of medical colleges. That effort succeeded. In Nashville in 1890, delegates from 134 colleges formed the Association of American Medical Colleges (AAMC).[63]

Although the association initially lacked the power to confer accreditation, its very organization was an important first step toward setting standards in medical education. Like the American Medical Association, the AAMC would become an advocate of scientific medicine and would work toward disenfranchising the sects and increasing the regular profession's political and economic power.

The main course of change was clear to many medical leaders, and in the next two decades Maryland's school of medicine would follow that lead, change decisively, and develop the ability to teach and promote scientific medicine. In 1892, the school launched a new three-year, graded curriculum. Ten years later, the trustees increased the school term from five and a half months to seven; in 1916 they opted for an eight-month term. Now, too, the school required entrance examinations. While these new standards were hard on the poorer students who could not afford longer courses, they succeeded in producing better-educated doctors. As a result, the school—like most others—experienced substantial declines in enrollment; at Maryland the fall-off was from 111 students in 1890 to 50 in 1895.[64] Fortunately for the university, enrollments began to increase again after 1900.

Promising as these developments were, they did not satisfy Abraham Flexner. He concluded, among many other things, that the state government should close the University of Maryland School of Medicine. Indeed, he thought that all but one of the state's schools should be closed. Hopkins, he said, should be allowed to continue training doctors. This expert evaluation flew in the face of those in the state who thought that the University of Maryland School of Medicine was making steady progress. Not Flexner. Examining the school a hundred years after its birth, he concluded that, "with the foundation early in the nineteenth century at Baltimore of a proprietary school, the so-called medical department of the so-called University of Maryland, a harmful precedent was established."[65] He based this cutting conclusion on firsthand information, acquired on the grounds. When Flexner visited in March 1909, Maryland had 61 members on its teaching staff, 24 of whom were professors. There were 316 attending students, and, as Flexner noted with disapproval, they were able to get into the school with less than a high school education.

Flexner approved of Maryland's clinical facilities. The school controlled its own hospital, which housed 140 teaching beds, and those senior students who could "pay for the privilege" served as clinical assistants. The dispensary, Flexner wrote, was "large, properly equipped, and well kept." But other aspects of the school, including the laboratory facilities, were found wanting. "Good undergraduate laboratories adequate to routine teaching are provided in two poorly kept buildings for the following subjects: chemistry, physiology, including physiological chemistry and histology, pathology and bacteriology. Anatomy is poor.

There is a small museum. In a separate building is a large and interesting library, but it is open only two hours each day." [66]

With Hopkins as his ideal, Flexner could see no point in permitting any of the other six Maryland schools to remain open. He found the Atlantic Medical College and the Maryland Medical College "unconscionable concerns." He was disturbed by the ease with which students who had failed at other establishments were advanced to graduation in some of these schools. The upper classes at Atlantic Medical and Maryland Medical were "largely recruited by emigration from other schools." [67] The College of Physicians and Surgeons and the University of Maryland School of Medicine, he said, were "large commercial enterprises, whose financial responsibilities are far too expensive for their capital or fee income."

Flexner was concerned about efficiency, a popular subject in an era enamored of so-called scientific management. It was extremely inefficient, he said, for the state to provide financial aid to six medical schools and their hospitals. "Should the state ever conduct its philanthropic business intelligently, these irresponsible methods would stop; and with them, the medical schools which they have helped to float. The Johns Hopkins Medical School, for which neither the state nor the city of Baltimore has ever done anything, is thus the only medical school in Maryland that either ought to or can live, and to its development greatly increased means should be freely devoted." [68]

Elitist to the core, Flexner, like many other American professionals, was dedicated to high scholastic standards, to the scientific method, and to the same sort of concentration that was taking place in the economy. This came out most clearly in his proposed solution to Maryland's problems. He suggested that all the other medical schools' hospitals be turned over to Hopkins "to strengthen its clinical resources." After a couple of decades, the state could determine whether this experiment with public monopoly had worked. While concentration in this style would substantially decrease the number of doctors the state produced, Flexner thought that was a reasonable outcome; to his mind, there were far too many already. Nor was he buying into the "poor boy" argument. To the tough-minded Flexner, if a poor boy were earnest in his desire to follow a medical career, "he need only take thought in good season, lay his plans, be prudent, and stick to his purpose." Flexner was a belligerent, outspoken advocate of the kind of planning and expertise that Americans were trying to develop in their independent regulatory commissions during the Progressive Era. He did not believe in "equivalents" to give "poor boys" a leg up. He was more concerned about lowering standards than he was about keeping entry open to those talented youths who had started out behind.[69]

Flexner's 1910 report to the Carnegie Foundation created a crisis for the University of Maryland School of Medicine. While Flexner did not actually cause the crisis—the problems he identified had long been accumulating—he was the whistle blower, or, as Robert Hudson put it, the catalyst for change.[70] Maryland's faculty knew they had to listen to Flexner's whistle and effect changes if they were going to keep their school growing. With business interests becoming increasingly involved in medical philanthropy, a report of this kind could well cut off their access to research funds.[71] It also threatened to cut into state aid for the medical school. In that event, the school might be unable to provide the clinical training essential to medical education. There was no doubt that Flexner's report touched on real problems. The proprietary schools lowered the standards of medical education in Maryland; they could not afford the expensive new equipment necessary to train students in the sciences. Some of the poorer schools needed to close, and they did.

But Flexner's proposal to consolidate all of Maryland's medical education under the control of Hopkins smacked too much of monopoly and of elitism to garner widespread political support. American values favored competing centers of power and the "poor boy" argument resonated with a legislature that did not think it was necessarily lowering standards in Maryland by keeping open more than one avenue to professional preferment. That was especially true after some of the managers of proprietary schools decided to consolidate their operations. In 1913, the Baltimore Medical College merged with the University of Maryland, and two years later the College of Physicians and Surgeons followed suit.[72] This combination of resources substantially strengthened the university and gave it an opportunity to realize its full potential.

From our perspective today, the state's decision to favor competing institutions seems wise. Competition, decentralization, and diversity worked to the advantage of innovation in medicine, as they did in other parts of American society. In the years that followed, the university's School of Medicine continued to grow, to incorporate the modern sciences in its programs, and to become more of a teaching-research school and less of a proprietary institution. Enrollments increased from 278 in 1919–20 to 371 by 1926–27. These were prosperous times and, although Maryland students were rarely wealthy, they were able to afford the increase in fees from approximately $350 in 1920 to over $500 toward the decade's end.[73]

The 1930s were trying years for the university, as they were for the entire state. Because the school continued to attract lower income students, enrollment dropped off during the Great Depression. But the institution weathered that storm, too, and even managed to expand its physical plant. At the end of the decade, the school opened the Frank C. Bressler Research Laboratory, and many of the preclinical departments moved into this modern, six-story building. The departments of gross anatomy, embryology, histology, pharmacology, and physiology were now all housed in spacious, well-equipped facilities. The fifth floor contained the research divisions of the clinical departments, as well as the students' laboratory for clinical research. The top floor housed the animal research and cadaver facilities.[74] By this time, even a Flexner could not have condemned the school for its lack of research facilities or original scientific work. Maryland had indeed become a modern medical school.

University Dentistry

By the end of the 1930s, the University of Maryland included a thriving dental program. In the late 1870s and early 1880s, there had been rumblings within the Maryland dental profession to the effect that dentistry should enter the university, foster stronger ties with a medical department, and broaden its educational system. In response to this movement, the state legislature chartered the Dental Department of the University of Maryland in 1882. Two important Baltimore Dental College figures promptly transferred to the new program: Ferdinand J. S. Gorgas, who became the new dean, and James Harris, who occupied a new chair of operative and clinical dentistry.[75]

The faculty had to be pleased with its facilities in the new Dental Infirmary and Laboratory Building on Greene Street. The infirmary provided ample clinical material, and the laboratory was state of the art. Students could also attend certain clinics and operations in the hospital infirmary, particularly those involving oral surgery. The faculty and students had access to the university's museum, which contained many specimens of significance to their profession.[76]

The Dental Department adopted a fee plan comparable with those of the proprietary schools. The department required students to attend two years of lectures and to work in the laboratory and clinic before they could graduate. Of the sixty-six students who registered for the first session (1882–83), twenty had already completed one year at another dental college. Sixteen of the transfers came from the Baltimore College of Dental Surgery.[77] The university's new venture put competitive pressure on the Baltimore Dental College's faculty, and relationships were far from friendly. Faculty, students, and alumni from the two schools displayed "flagrant rivalry." The problems of the Baltimore College were multiplied by the fact that university dental students had the option of taking an extra year and also graduating with a medical degree.[78]

The situation became even more tense after a third school entered the competition. In 1895, the Baltimore Medical College opened a Dental Department. It was yet another graduate of the Baltimore College of Dental Surgery who launched this new project and became its first dean. J. William Smith had received his degree in 1888 and was actually helped by Gorgas in obtaining a charter.[79]

Gorgas apparently thought he had little reason to worry. The University of Maryland's Dental Department was thriving, with students flocking to it from all over the country. As a result, the department repeatedly expanded its physical plant, making four additions to the original structure. Finally, in 1903, the university demolished that building, and in 1904 it opened a new facility on the corner of Lombard and Greene Streets.[80]

As it turned out, Gorgas was right: in 1913, Baltimore Medical College, including its dental operations, merged with the University of Maryland School of Medicine.[81] Ten years later, the competition in Maryland ended when the university also took over the Baltimore College of Dental Surgery. The old proprietary school had long been struggling, caught between rising costs and demands for curricular expansion. By the early 1920s, the dental program at the University of Maryland was four years long and the students were being offered extensive clinical and laboratory experiences. Universities could provide sound training in modern scientific subjects, and their faculties and trustees were well aware of the power that gave them vis-á-vis private competitors. As Gardner Foley noted, state boards of dental examiners and dental organizations at the local and national levels were increasingly mandating this longer, more scientific program. Lacking endowments or state support, proprietary schools like the Baltimore College of Dental Surgery could no longer compete effectively. Rather than just closing their shop, its owners decided to merge with the university and preserve the BCDS identity while turning over all of its laboratory and clinical equipment.[82]

The merger was difficult to consummate. Dean J. Ben Robinson had to deal with the tensions generated by differing approaches to professional training and by institutional pride. The fact that a university department had absorbed the world's oldest dental college was painful for some faculty members to accept. Gradually, however, Robinson was able to relieve these tensions, build new facilities, and give the department's students the hands-on clinical and laboratory training they needed. The department emerged from World War II with a strong faculty and a modern program.[83]

Pharmacy

Pharmacy in Maryland, like dentistry and medicine, experienced a major transformation in the later nineteenth and early twentieth centuries. European developments in organic chemistry were transforming practice and product in this profession. In an effort to keep up with the expansion of knowledge in the field, the trustees of the Maryland College of Pharmacy lengthened the term of instruction to six months in 1889. To graduate at the highest level, students now had to complete two graded, three-month courses. Still concerned to attract as many students as possible, the trustees hedged their bets: they combined this innovation with a less demanding alternative. The faculty offered both a "short course" (from October 7 to November 27) and a "long course" (from October 7 to January 22).[84]

After the college merged (1904) with the University of Maryland, the faculty further extended the term of instruction (1910) but, once again, they compromised. They lengthened the courses to eight months each, but depending upon the amount of study time students had available, they were allowed to obtain the Doctor of Pharmacy degree (Pharm. D.) in either two or three years. The university's Department of Pharmacy also expanded the curriculum to cover modern scientific topics such as plant histology and toxicology.[85]

Formalization and specialization continued in the ensuing years, and by 1940 the Department of Pharmacy had, with state aid, come to occupy a purpose-built site consisting of ample laboratory and classroom space "especially designed to house the work of pharmacy." The degree had become a Bachelor of Science in Pharmacy, which required three years' attendance. Pharmacy was, like other branches of medicine, being transformed by the therapeutic revolution and by new government regulations. As the older style of pharmacy gave way, the department's program continued to evolve. By completing a fourth year, students could now earn a master's degree. In addition, the faculty had by that time developed a doctoral program.[86] These new dimensions were indicative of the stature pharmacy had acquired by World War II. It had undoubtedly become a profession.

The Woman's Medical College of Baltimore

Despite the strides made by the University of Maryland's faculty in the nineteenth century, its members long denied access to women on the grounds that such training would be "indelicate."[87] By the later decades of the century, however, such exclusion was being strongly challenged both in medical circles and among women in the community. Some men began to support the notion of a separate school solely for female medical students, and that sentiment was nurtured by the philanthropic matrons of Baltimore. In January 1882 they convened a meeting to establish a medical college exclusively for women.

These women belonged to the city's social elite. Some were doctors' wives, and they collaborated with several local physicians to found the college. Mrs. Charles E. Waters, Mrs. John K. Carven, Mrs. Eugene F. Cordell, and University of Maryland Drs. Randolph Winslow and Thomas A. Ashby, among other prominent citizens, believed that a triadic assembly of institutions was needed.[88] A medical school and a training school for nurses, complemented by a hospital, would provide special care for women and special training for female medical students and nurses. All would provide new occupational opportunities for women.

Women had been seeking such opportunities in growing numbers during the nineteenth century. Urbanization and industrialization were changing America and its work force. By the time of the Civil War, about half of America's women would at some time in their lives, usually before marriage, undertake waged work.[89] For those women who did not need or desire waged employment, other new roles were being defined. Middle- and upper-class women were entering the political arena and playing vital parts in reform movements, fighting for temperance and for the rights of women. In the post–Civil War period, the "woman question" gathered momentum and fueled debates about a "woman's proper place."[90]

One "proper place" for nineteenth-century women was in the home, acting as domestic manager, caretaker, and moral arbiter. For middle-class, urban women, the elements of such activities were codified in the so-called cult of domesticity.[91] As medical historian Regina Morantz-Sanchez has convincingly demonstrated, this cultural and social construct legitimized women's entry into the caring professions. Teaching, in particular, had become a well-established profession for women by the second half of the nineteenth century. But women continued to be virtually excluded from the medical profession, except in nursing. A few women with enough courage, determination, and money had traveled to continental Europe to study medicine, but they were rare exceptions.[92]

In 1882, when local luminaries officially launched their drive, there were just four other women's medical colleges in the United States. New York had two, and Philadelphia boasted the Woman's Medical College of Pennsylvania.[93] Chicago's school, the Woman's Medical College, was the first in the Midwest.[94] So Baltimore's activists had models to emulate, models that they studied as they set out to organize the first such teaching institution in the South. By February 1882, seven prominent local physicians had adopted the cause, enabling the trustees to incorporate the Woman's Medical College of Baltimore.

Unlike the colleges in New York and Philadelphia, Baltimore's organization began with an all-male faculty, several of whom held their primary positions at the University of Maryland. John S. Lynch became professor of principles and practice of medicine; B. Bernard Browne, professor of diseases of women; Thomas A. Ashby, professor of obstetrics; Randolph Winslow, professor of surgery; Eugene F. Cordell, professor of materia medica and therapeutics; William D. Booker, professor of physiology; Richard Henry Thomas, professor of diseases of throat and chest; John G. Jay, professor of anatomy and operative surgery; Cameron Piggot, professor of chemistry.[95] While this may have created some tension, it allowed the founders to open the doors of the college at 126 North Eutaw Street on October 1, 1882.[96]

The initial two-year course consisted of seven-month, graded sessions with written and oral examinations. Each session of lectures cost seventy-five dollars, plus an extra ten dollars for the required practical anatomy. Although the school remained relatively small, it was instantly successful. Of the twenty-two matriculates in 1884–85, five were graduating from various institutions.[97] In 1887, the course of instruction was extended to three years.[98] First-year students covered anatomy, physiology, chemistry, materia medica, pharmacy, and histology—taught by lectures, laboratory work, dissections, and textbook recitations. Anatomy, physiology, chemistry, and materia medica were also part of the second-year instruction, but in that year the students received more clinical teaching in surgery, obstetrics, diseases of women, diseases of children, diseases of the throat and chest, dissections, and clinics. The senior year was devoted largely to reinforcing and supplementing second-year clinical work. Students attended parturient women in the patients' homes. They also developed their clinical skills across the street from the college at the Good Samaritan Hospital.[99] Originally, the college's organizers had planned to conduct the primary clinical teaching at the Hospital for Women, but they had changed their minds. Claribel Cone explained, "It was soon realized that medical education for women should differ in no respect from that of men, and that if woman was to be a success as a physician, she must be subjected to the same course of study and requirements as men."[100]

In subsequent years, the college expanded, both physically and intellectually. The school came to occupy a set of buildings on the corner of McCulloh and Hoffman Streets. In 1895 the faculty and managers lengthened the curriculum to four years so that they could expand and isolate preclinical work during the first two years. Subjects such as embryology and bacteriology now received more attention. During the final two years of clinical instruction, there was a similar increase in subjects; orthopedics, dermatology, and neurology, for instance, gained ground. By 1896, there were thirty-four faculty members (virtually all part-time), including six women, some of whom had graduated from the college.[101]

A number of the alumni remained close to the college. Some practiced in Baltimore and served as demonstrators and lecturers. Claribel Cone came to hold a prominent position at the college and its hospital. A Baltimore native, she graduated from Western Female High School. In 1890, she graduated from Woman's Medical and, after an internship at the Blockley Hospital in Philadelphia, was appointed as lecturer on hygiene at her old college (1893). Two years later, she became professor of pathology and pathologist at the Good Samaritan Hospital. Another graduate (1891) and fellow intern of Cone's at Blockley, Flora Pollack, also settled in her home town. She served as lecturer on embryology and associate professor of embryology and physical diagnosis at Woman's Medical in 1896 and 1897. Pollack studied for a while in Berlin before returning to Baltimore. She worked as an attending physician in two of the city's institutions and was finally appointed as assistant in gynecology at Johns Hopkins Dispensary.[102]

By the early 1900s, the college was well established.[103] The faculty and trustees had successfully broadened the clinical opportunities available to students, but Abraham Flexner was not terribly impressed.[104] He noted that Woman's Medical, while not among the worst schools in terms of testing students, was far from the best. He found their work was "only partially graded." Flexner acknowledged that the college's small laboratories were "scrupulously well kept" and that the staff obviously tried hard "to do the best possible with meager resources: pathology, bacteriology, embryology, chemistry, and anatomy [were] thus taught." But the clinical facilities, he said, were "quite insufficient." Lacking any endowment, the little school was maintained on the mere two thousand dollars annually provided by fees. Like the University of Maryland School of Medicine, its faculty required less than a high school education for admission.[105]

Flexner's judgments were not, however, the chief threat to the college; its success was.[106] As Woman's Medical College and other similar schools cracked the gender barrier, the leading medical schools in Maryland and elsewhere began to see the advantage of accepting women. In effect, the need for a school for women began to evaporate just when it was becoming clear that the college could not afford the superior facilities of schools like Johns Hopkins. As a result, the May 1910 commencement exercises at Woman's Medical were the last such ceremony.[107] The forces of centralization were powerful, and they were recasting medical education in Maryland in the early twentieth century.

The Southern Homoeopathic Medical College —
Atlantic Medical College

Women were not the only ones excluded from the larger schools. The "irregular" sects also had no place at the University of Maryland or, for that matter, at the Woman's Medical College. But, like the regular medical profession, the irregulars realized that formal training was increasingly necessary for survival.[108] By the 1870s and 1880s, the most prominent of these irregular sects was homeopathy.[109] Homeopaths could practice and promote their profession in much of late nineteenth-century America.[110] By 1880, there were already eleven homeopathic medical colleges in the United States.[111]

Understandably, Baltimore's homeopathic physicians and patrons thought the time was ripe for establishing a school in their city. There was enough local support. Baltimore was relatively inexpensive and would serve as a gateway to the South, where homeopathy was beginning to make inroads.[112] Their efforts bore fruit on May 15, 1890, when four-teen homeopathic physicians and twelve other interested Marylanders received the articles of incorporation for the Southern Homoeopathic Medical College. Under the charter, they were permitted to open medi-cal, dentistry, pharmacy, and veterinary science departments and to ad-mit male and female students. The homeopathic college, like the Uni-versity of Maryland School of Medicine, was a proprietary institution in which the faculty purchased shares and served as physicians in the hospi-tal and dispensary. It was a relatively small school.[113] The college faculty apparently recognized the need to provide for the students' well-being after classes, as they opened a reading and amusement room and fostered a close relationship with a branch of Baltimore's Young Men's Christian Association (YMCA).[114]

At the turn of the century, homeopathy seemed to be in a powerful position in Maryland and the rest of the nation. In 1905, there were al-most fifteen thousand homeopaths, including many women, who had trained in the nation's twenty colleges. Throughout the country, home-opathy's holistic approach to health was popular, and homeopaths had organized 143 professional societies.[115]

But, in fact, this was the crest of a wave that was just beginning to break. As scientific medical education swept to the forefront across the United States, homeopathic schools, including Baltimore's, headed into a steep decline. Baltimore's Southern Homoeopathic Medical College struggled financially, especially with the increasing demand for up-to-date laboratory equipment. The state legislature provided $2,500 in both 1902 and 1903 and $5,000 in 1905. This helped the faculty purchase equip-ment, but the state funds ran dry after the Great Fire of 1904 consumed all of the available money for rebuilding. The Southern Homoeopathic was already foundering before Abraham Flexner issued his devastating report.

Flexner excoriated homeopathic schools throughout the country, and he ranked Baltimore's college among the poorest. None of the fifteen homeopathic institutions operating in 1908 required more than a high school education for admission, and eleven accepted even less. "The Louisville, Kansas City, and Baltimore schools cannot be said to have admission standards in any strict sense at all," Flexner wrote. He was also dismayed by the standards of scientific teaching, noting that, although homeopaths paid lip service to the importance of "the scientific posi-tion," their actions betrayed them. Most of the homeopathic schools had

weak science departments and ill-equipped laboratories. Baltimore's homeopathic college was, in Flexner's view, one of the country's six worst.
It was, he declared, "utterly hopeless," with dirty, neglected buildings
and confused "so-called" laboratories. Indeed, in the Southern Homoeopathic lecture room he found but half a skeleton, some damaged physiological apparatus, a few frogs, and a small collection of old, useless
books. Even more insidious was the fact that the Baltimore institution had dropped "homoeopathic" from its title, presenting itself as the
"Atlantic Medical College" and admitting students who had been dismissed from other medical schools in the city.[116]

Flexner, who considered homeopathy dogmatic and unscientific, issued a report that delivered a stiff blow to a set of schools, Baltimore's
included, that were already in decline. Enrollment was dropping off
as students turned instead to the "scientific" schools. By 1908, Atlantic Medical was operating on a budget of $3,905 a year, compared with
$44,530 at the University of Maryland. At that time, the homeopathic
college had forty-three students registered, thirty-one of them seniors.
There was only one student in the freshman class. As Flexner noted, almost all of the graduates in the class of 1908 had failed at other medical
schools or at the state board examination.[117] In 1910, the Atlantic Medical, penniless and studentless, closed its doors.

The Medical and Surgical School of Christ's Institution:
An African-American Venture

The African-American community was even less successful than the homeopaths in establishing a medical school in Maryland. In the aftermath
of the Civil War, many freedmen, freedwomen, and emancipated slaves
hoped for new occupational opportunities, but their access to business,
skilled trades, and the professions was severely limited by their lack of
capital and education, as well as by racism. In the South, many became sharecroppers. The avenues to social mobility were a little broader
in the North, where the ministry and teaching offered openings. Across
the nation, however, access to the medical profession was extremely limited for African Americans. A few northern and midwestern schools,
including the University of Pennsylvania, Woman's Medical College of
Pennsylvania, the University of Illinois, and the University of Michigan,
admitted African Americans in the late nineteenth century. But southern medical schools tenaciously clung to their traditional, white-only

policies. Howard University was the first southern institution to grant equal access after its trustees founded a medical school in 1869. Gradually, others followed (many under religious auspices), and momentum gathered, as it had for women. The more African-American medical graduates there were, the more the impetus to promote opportunities for future generations. As Todd Savitt noted, several of the first cohort of African-American physicians established proprietary medical colleges in which they could transmit their knowledge to the next generation. Between 1869 and 1907, fourteen such proprietary or religious medical colleges were organized in the South.[118]

Most of these colleges were short-lived, and Baltimore's had the shortest existence of all. In May 1900 at the Superior Court of Baltimore City, George W. Kennard, William M. West, John F. Brown, James E. Smith, William M. A. Cole, and Thomas H. Brown incorporated a new college, the Medical and Surgical School of Christ's Institution of Baltimore City. They were, however, unable to open their institution, and a second attempt in 1906 also failed. Marylanders never were able to establish an African-American medical school.[119] There had been sufficient support to found and expand Provident Hospital but not to sustain a college. Although Maryland had in Johns Hopkins University the most modern medical school in the country, Hopkins admitted no African Americans until well after World War II.[120]

In a little over a century, Maryland had experienced tremendous shifts in medical education. Apprenticeship had given way to medical school education and to a phase of institutional expansion. The state saw eleven schools organized, schools with widely differing aims and characteristics. Some were designed to meet specific needs; some, for profit. For a time, most operated in a relatively unregulated environment that encouraged innovation—for better or worse.

Near the end of the nineteenth century, however, as national organizations and government began to be involved more actively, medical education began the slow process of standardization and centralization. As a consensus emerged around the central ideas of scientific medicine, many of the weaker and "irregular" schools began to founder. As a result, Maryland ended up with just two—the University of Maryland and Johns Hopkins—both medical schools with large hospitals and university affiliations. The process of centralization was far more advanced in education than it was in therapeutics or hospital care, a situation that would persist for many decades. But the state had wisely resisted the advice of Abraham Flexner and kept two different centers of education. The wisdom of that choice would become clear in the years after World War II.

Even in medical education, some aspects of the institutional setting remained virtually unchanged. Long after scientific medicine became firmly ensconced in the schools, the general population still showed substantial fear of human dissection. The problem of obtaining a sufficient supply of cadavers had by no means been resolved by the end of the nineteenth century. Even at Johns Hopkins, more than half of the corpses arrived illegally at the end of the 1890s.[121] In subsequent years, access to cadavers improved somewhat (usually by way of tuberculosis sanatoria), but as late as World War II, the donation act was still a thing of the future.

As this revealed, there was a gap in understanding between the professional educators and the public. The leaders of the medical profession had a tendency to believe that reform in education would necessarily benefit the lay population. In this assumption, physicians differed little from other professionals. Of course, the nonmedical population frequently saw things differently, hence the public objection to increasing access to human dissections and hence, too, the reluctance of many to enter teaching hospitals for their treatment. This tension may also have been expressed in the stubborn resistance to scientific medicine and the continued resort to "irregular" medical practice and to self-medication.

Within the medical schools, however, there was by the eve of World War II little concern about this gap. The leaders of the two major institutions in Maryland were self-confident and justifiably proud of what had been accomplished. Students from overseas were coming to Maryland to study. It was beginning to seem that the cutting edge in medical education might actually be crossing the Atlantic.[122]

SIX

Public Health

A New Mission in
an Urbanizing Society,
1832–1899

One of the most important social dimensions of health care in Maryland has long been provided by the activities and institutions associated with public health. Historian John Duffy provides a good working definition of public health: "Essentially it means . . . community action to avoid disease and other threats to the health and welfare of individuals and the community at large. To this may be added the current view, which emphasizes a more positive approach — that public health policy should actively promote health rather than simply maintain it." [1] Through the end of the nineteenth century, however, public health's primary functions were more reactive than positive and were largely focused on threats to the community at large.

Maryland's responses to public health hazards tell us much about the society, its perceptions, and its material and social conditions. In the nineteenth century, for instance, tuberculosis was one of the chief killers, but the disease was largely perceived as a constant presence, a blunt instrument about which little could be done. By contrast, many epidemics — cholera and typhoid, for instance — that resulted in lower mortality rates prompted substantially more terror. In fact, until about the 1870s, tuberculosis was frequently romanticized in art and literature, an image that finally began to change after Robert Koch's discovery of the tubercle bacillus in 1882. [2] The same situation had pertained with smallpox and yellow fever in colonial times. Although these two epidemic diseases posed less serious threats than endemic illnesses such as malaria and enteric disorders, they were more feared. Perceptions such as these had important effects on the way communities responded to health hazards, as they still do today.

Within Maryland, threats to the public health affected different populations in different ways, and the public responses had much to do with which groups wielded power and how they perceived the state's many hazards. With this in mind, I have tried to draw out elements of diversity—to examine what I regard as the archaeology and the geography of public health in this state. Socioeconomic, racial, religious, and sex differences, as well as urban-rural dynamics, have shaped the nature of public health in Maryland. So, too, has age, and many public health workers have been especially motivated by the problems that affect children. This was especially true in regard to diphtheria, but it was also pertinent where other epidemics were concerned, including smallpox and cholera.

The Ad Hoc Era of Public Health, 1832–1861

During the winter of 1831–32, many Baltimoreans lived in fear. Like the citizens of other ports, they dreaded the arrival of Asiatic cholera. The epidemic, which had swept from Asia through Russia and Poland, was devastating in terms of its symptoms and mortality rates. Patients sometimes died within hours of taking to their beds. Usually, the disease took a few days to carry off its victims, but its rapidity was still shocking to behold. Given its mortality rate of 47 to 90 percent, cholera left little room for hope.[3] The disease produced acute diarrhea, vomiting, cramps, and eventually severe dehydration and collapse; the invalid's body became cold, with the pulse sometimes imperceptible, and the skin shriveled. The dying sometimes seemed already dead, and there were stories of sufferers actually being buried alive. Cholera could wipe out entire families in a matter of days.[4]

Anticipating cholera's advance across northern Europe, the English had established rigid quarantine controls, including an armed *cordon sanitaire*. But the disease sneaked through, causing terror in its path. The Canadian and American medical communities watched carefully, tracking the deadly cholera as it moved steadily westward. Although quarantine efforts had failed in England, health officers and physicians in the United States hoped that the Atlantic Ocean would provide protection.

Not willing to take any chances, they also established specific quarantine procedures. During the fall of 1831, Baltimore, Boston, Philadelphia, and Charleston followed New York's example and organized quarantines for all passengers and products from Russia, the Baltic, and eventually from Britain.[5] Cholera attacks were not limited to the warmer months (as yellow fever was), so quarantine action was sustained throughout the 1831–32 winter season.

In Baltimore, the City Board of Health, which had existed since 1793, was in charge of that effort. Like the boards elsewhere, Baltimore's tiny agency responded to specific health threats as they occurred. It did not attempt to maintain any ongoing restrictions or activities. As some scholars have observed, the authorities' unwillingness to seek permanent reforms was in part a reflection of the popularly held notion that Americans were the naturally tougher, healthier hybrids of their inbred, confined European ancestors.[6] Healthy and hearty Americans needed protection, this line of reasoning went, only when something unusual happened, like an encounter with yellow fever.

The Baltimore board was accustomed to organizing ad hoc quarantine restrictions in response to yellow fever outbreaks. Until the turn of the nineteenth century, that disease had been assumed to be contagious. John B. Davidge had asserted, in the *Federal Gazette of Baltimore* of 1797, that yellow fever was not contagious but mosquito-transmitted.[7] The veracity of this statement was not, however, immediately accepted, and debate continued well into the early nineteenth century about whether or not yellow fever was an infectious disease. It was only in 1830 that Horatio Jameson, consulting physician to the Baltimore Board of Health and a respected member of the Medical and Chirurgical Faculty, was able to persuade the City Council to abandon yellow fever quarantines.[8]

Since, however, the Board of Health was quite familiar with quarantine measures, the members of the Medical and Chirurgical Faculty thought no further action on their part necessary when the threat of cholera loomed.[9] In addition to quarantine restrictions, the city of Baltimore gave high priority to street cleaning. The Board of Health, in accordance with a new ordinance of July 7, 1831, substantially revamped street cleaning efforts in the hope of reducing the onslaught of cholera.[10] The city spent more than fourteen thousand dollars repairing gutters, and a "great number of additional hands [were] employed for the purpose of keeping the streets, lanes, alleys, &c. in the cleanest possible condition."[11]

Marylanders had every reason to be anxious. By June 6, 1832, the

Atlantic barrier had been breached; cholera was reported in Montreal, Canada. Eight days later the disease appeared in New York State. By rail, boat, and road, along all of America's new transportation links, cholera fanned out along the eastern seaboard.[12] On August 4, the Maryland Hospital admitted Baltimore's first reported case.[13]

After the fact, Baltimoreans moved quickly and more forcefully to deal with this new threat. The City Council appropriated forty thousand dollars to the Board of Health to open public hospitals as soon as possible. By July 10, the Maryland Hospital was receiving a steady flow of victims. The city established and equipped two other makeshift hospitals, one in the old almshouse and another in the Tunker Church.

There remained, though, the problem of finding people to care for these patients. Given the fear associated with cholera, the city did not find it easy to acquire a nursing staff. Initially, the Board of Health found "it impossible to procure suitable persons to attend upon the sick" at the two temporary facilities. Local priests mediated and found help from two traditional sources, the Sisters of Charity and the Sisterhood of Saint Joseph's. The nuns began work on August 25, with their ranks supplemented by all of the Sisters of the Orphans' Asylum. Together they performed extremely arduous, unpleasant, hazardous work. Two of the nurses, Mary Francis and Mary George, contracted cholera and died.[14] In spite of all the sacrifices and organized efforts, the disease swept through Baltimore as it had other port cities. The death toll reached 853, or 1 in 96 of the city's residents.[15] Although this was a substantially lower death rate than was experienced by many other urban areas, the city was devastated.

Not so the countryside. Baltimore was the only place in the state that was profoundly affected. Numerous cases were noted outside the city, but they seemed to pose no great threat to others who were well. Only the state's hub of transportation and port of entry for immigrants was vitally affected by the epidemic. As a result, many who could afford to leave temporarily fled the city for safer terrain.

In Frederick, however, the citizens were not convinced that they would be spared. Their sense of alarm was exacerbated in June 1832 by the appearance of Halley's comet. Prayer was offered, and in August more worldly steps were taken. At a public meeting, concerned Frederick citizens organized a new Board of Health; as they noted, "whereas it has pleased Divine Providence to visit the most populous cities and towns throughout our land with a most direful disease termed cholera . . . and not knowing that our city may remain exempt from the dreadful malady . . . we conceive it not only prudent but proper that such means should be used as are within our power to preserve the health of our citizens and to be prepared to assist in the amelioration of any unfortunate who may become the victims."[16] Frederick appointed three people to oversee the efforts in each of the town's seven wards.

These preparations were not premature. In August, several people died of cholera at an almshouse just two miles from town. On September 1, the first Frederick inhabitant—a man employed on the canal—died. In an attempt to subdue fear and maintain business as usual, the Board of Health insisted that the disease was not contagious, and the local newspapers supported this effort by largely ignoring the epidemic. Even when the editor of the *Frederick Examiner* finally acknowledged there was cholera in their midst, he blamed it on foreigners. His article assured residents that cholera did not prevail "to any extent among our citizens. Its subjects have been, with one or two exceptions, either Irish or German immigrants."[17] As the local Board of Health and the press signaled to Frederick's citizens, hardly anyone who mattered was affected by the disease.

For a time, their class-stratified message seemed to hold true. The death rates were substantially higher among poor immigrants and African Americans who lived and worked in poor conditions. Irish laborers on the canal dropped like flies and received little sympathy or prophylaxis. But then cholera spilled over the class barrier, just as it had over the Atlantic Ocean. By September 26, twenty-one people had died in Frederick; only six were immigrants, and nine were African Americans.[18] When cholera persisted in the town through the next year, native residents were struck down in significant numbers, but they continued to associate the disease with the "less desirable" members of society.

As Dr. Jameson noted in his report to Baltimore's Health Department, "We have to lament the loss of a few of our most respectable citizens, and cannot but sympathize in the afflictions of the lower orders of our citizens, and the vicious, who suffered more largely." Indeed, the "vicious," that is, those who lived in overcrowded, squalid conditions with contaminated water and food, fell prey in large numbers. Historian Charles Rosenberg noted that many middle-class Americans at that time believed that the "dishonorable" poor brought the disease upon themselves by their idle, dirty, and intemperate behavior. Those same middle-class persons and their physicians probably underreported outbreaks among the "better" elements because cholera was viewed as a "shameful disease."[19]

In 1832 and in subsequent epidemics, Marylanders and other Ameri-

The Maryland Hospital for the Insane stood on Loudenschlager's Hill. In 1872, Johns Hopkins paid $150 to buy the property for his proposed hospital and medical school. The hospital for the insane moved to Spring Grove in Catonsville. This picture is not dated. *Courtesy of the Alan Mason Chesney Archives, Johns Hopkins.*

One of the many Gettysburg field hospitals erected during the Civil War. This is a Union Second Corps facility. Such makeshift facilities later became models for permanent hospitals, along the pavilion design. *Photograph by Frederick Gutekunst. Courtesy of John S. Heiser, Gettysburg National Military Park.*

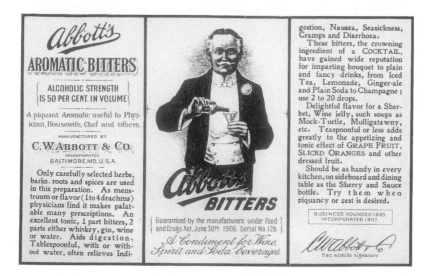

An early twentieth-century patent medicine advertisement from a Baltimore newspaper. *Courtesy of the Maryland Historical Society.*

An anatomy class at the University of Maryland in the late nineteenth century. Such classes could be conducted more openly by that time because cadavers were legally in more plentiful supply. *Courtesy of the University of Maryland Health Sciences and Human Services Library.*

THE NEW COLLEGE BUILDING,

OCCUPIED JUNE, 1881,

S. E. CORNER EUTAW AND FRANKLIN STREETS.

The Finest Building Devoted to Dental Education in the World.

The Baltimore College of Dental Surgery, which was the first dental school in the world, founded in 1840. *Courtesy of the University of Maryland Health Sciences and Human Services Library.*

A dental clinic at the University of Maryland's Dental Department (c. 1910). The building was constructed in 1903–4 and was used as a dental school until 1929. The building now houses the National Museum of Dentistry. In 1882, the University of Maryland had established its Dental Department, which merged with the Baltimore College of Dental Surgery in 1923 to form the Baltimore College of Dental Surgery, Dental School, University of Maryland, as it is still known today. *Courtesy of the National Museum of Dentistry, Baltimore, Maryland.*

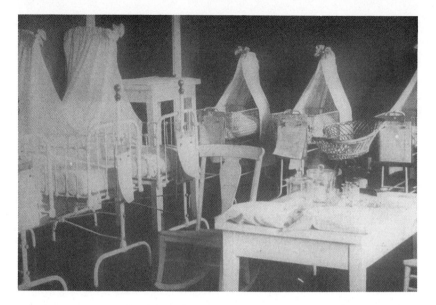

The nursery at the Hospital for Women in Baltimore (c. early twentieth century). *Courtesy of the University of Maryland Health Sciences and Human Services Library.*

A group of nurses from the early days of Provident Hospital (c. early twentieth century). *Courtesy of the University of Maryland Health Sciences and Human Services Library.*

Davidge Hall, the centerpiece of the University of Maryland, opened in 1812. *Courtesy of the University of Maryland Health Sciences and Human Services Library.*

The 1905 nursing class at the University of Maryland. *Courtesy of the University of Maryland Health Sciences and Human Services Library.*

Peninsula General Hospital (later Peninsula Regional) was opened in 1897 in a yellow-frame dwelling at Fitzwater and West Main Streets in Salisbury. This was the first hospital on the Eastern Shore, and it originally contained beds for six to nine patients. *Courtesy of Peninsula Regional Medical Center.*

Dr. George W. Todd, the founder of Peninsula General Hospital. *Courtesy of Peninsula Regional Medical Center.*

The west façade of the Johns Hopkins Hospital, facing onto Broadway (1890). *From the John Shaw Billings papers, courtesy of the Alan Mason Chesney Medical Archives, Johns Hopkins.*

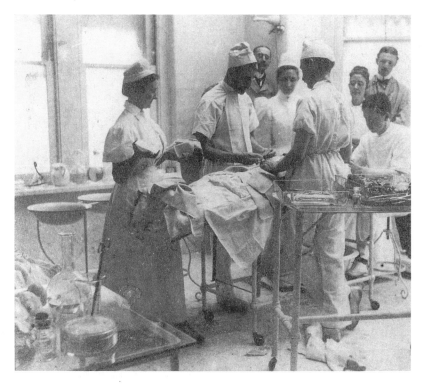

Dr. Howard Kelly performing gynecological surgery at the Johns Hopkins Hospital (1910). *Courtesy of the Alan Mason Chesney Medical Archives, Johns Hopkins.*

Nurses at Johns Hopkins Hospital taking care of indigent sick children on Christmas (1900), which was considered to be part of the mission of Hopkins Hospital. *Courtesy of the Alan Mason Chesney Medical Archives, Johns Hopkins.*

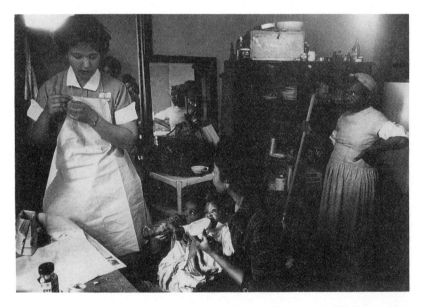

A student nurse from Johns Hopkins making a home visit to a mother and her babies (1964). *Courtesy of the Alan Mason Chesney Medical Archives, Johns Hopkins, and the Johns Hopkins Magazine.*

Dr. Elisha Stonestreet's office in Rockville, Maryland, was constructed during the post–Civil War era and served as a doctor's office for a half-century. *Courtesy of the Montgomery County Historical Society.*

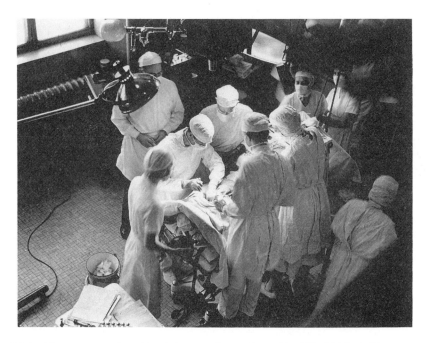

Vivien Thomas overseeing a blue-baby operation performed by Alfred Blalock. Thomas was an African-American technician who never received an M.D. degree but who worked at length on the blue-baby syndrome and provided a great deal of instruction to Blalock. Johns Hopkins Hospital eventually gave Thomas a position as instructor. *Courtesy of the Alan Mason Chesney Medical Archives, Johns Hopkins.*

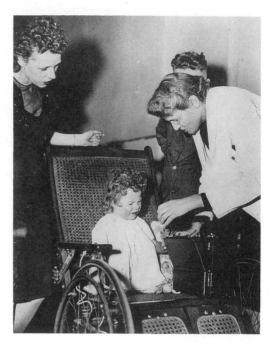

Dr. Helen Taussig with one of the "blue babies" she, Vivien Thomas, and Dr. Alfred Blalock were able to save (c. 1947). This baby girl has a hearing aid. *Courtesy of the Alan Mason Chesney Medical Archives, Johns Hopkins.*

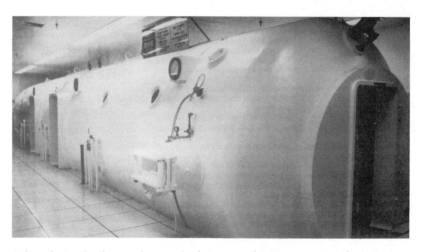

A hyperbaric chamber at the Maryland Institute for Emergency Medical Services (MIEMS) in 1978. Dr. R Adams Cowley organized the Shock Trauma Unit at the University of Maryland. Treatment in the chamber involves the administration of 100 percent oxygen under barometric pressure that is higher than normal and is used for patients who are suffering from such problems as carbon monoxide poisoning, gas gangrene, air embolism, and osteomyelitis. *From* Maryland Institute for Emergency Medical Services News, *June 1978. Courtesy of the University of Maryland Health Sciences and Human Services Library.*

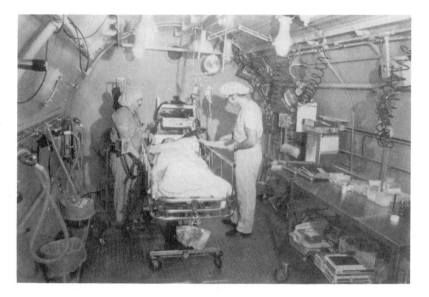

A physician (Ron Myers) and nurse (Tom Baker) prepare a patient inside the hyperbaric chamber at MIEMS. The treatments began in 1967, and the range of their application quickly increased. *From* Maryland Institute for Emergency Medical Services News, *June 1978. Courtesy of the University of Maryland Health Sciences and Human Services Library.*

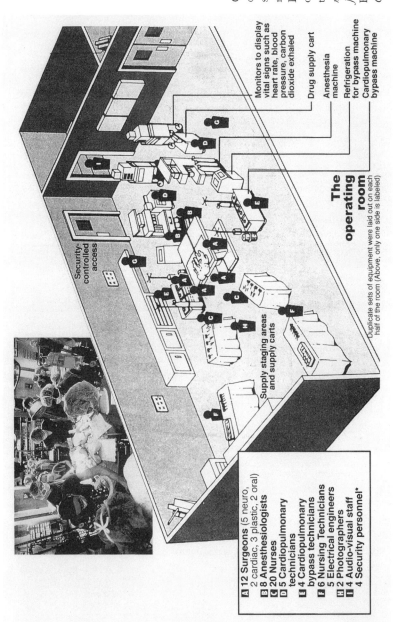

Composite picture of the operating room that was specially built for the separation of the Binder twins. Dr. Ben Carson was the head of this enormous surgical team. *Courtesy of the Department of Neurological Surgery, Johns Hopkins Hospital; the Baltimore Sun; and the Hearst Corporation.*

The operating room

Duplicate sets of equipment were laid out on each half of the room (Above, only one side is labeled)

Security-controlled access

Monitors to display vital signs such as heart rate, blood pressure, carbon dioxide exhaled

Drug supply cart

Anesthesia machine

Refrigeration for bypass machine

Cardiopulmonary bypass machine

Supply staging areas and supply carts

A 12 Surgeons (5 neuro, 2 cardiac, 3 plastic, 2 oral)
B 8 Anesthesiologists
C 20 Nurses
D 5 Cardiopulmonary technicians
E 4 Cardiopulmonary bypass technicians
F 6 Nursing Technicians
G 5 Electrical engineers
H 2 Photographers
I 4 Audio-visual staff
J 4 Security personnel*

cans were especially critical of the Irish. Thousands of desperately poor Irish were emigrating to the United States and were largely forced to settle in ghettos at their ports of entry. They were, then, doubly reviled, as poor and as immigrants. At a time when the Second Great Awakening was sweeping through much of the Midwest and Northeast, Roman Catholicism seemed to add another blot on the copybook of the Irish.[20] Although Maryland had a substantial Catholic population, many citizens found cause to blame recent Irish immigrants for the state's affliction.

From our late twentieth-century perspective, we can see that Maryland's immigrants actually made vital, positive contributions to a labor-poor country and state. Baltimore prospered during the antebellum years, when waves of Irish and Germans were entering Maryland.[21] Although there were many public health problems associated with that sudden bulge in the population, it was clear that the immigrants were substantially bolstering the economy. Many who had settled remained in the port city and supplied relatively inexpensive labor to the rapidly expanding sectors of small business and industry.

Medical professionals—many of whom prided themselves on long tenure in Maryland—did little to allay the hostile concerns expressed about immigrants. Sometimes, doctors added to the spirit of discrimination. Dr. Samuel B. Martin, Baltimore's Medical Officer during the 1832 epidemic, was deeply disturbed by the kinds of passengers he encountered in his inspections of vessels. Between April 30 and November 1, 1832, 11,946 people disembarked, of whom all but 400 were foreigners. Martin commented on what he had seen in that and previous years, reporting to the mayor and City Council, "I hope it will not be considered importunate if I once more beg the attention of our authorities to this growing evil, whereby a depraved population is, with so much facility, *poured* in upon us; the more able pass on to the interiors; but the *pauper part* are left on our hands."[22]

In the spirit of his time, Martin distinguished between the respectable and the unrespectable poor. He was concerned about crime, dirt, poverty, and disease. To him, crime was the simplest problem to solve. He suggested that all émigrés who had been convicted of a misdemeanor or crime before docking be sent home on the next sailing of the ship on which they had arrived. Dirt, too, he handled matter-of-factly, although not without complaining. He supervised the cleaning of quarantined vessels but frequently found it necessary "to cause the berths of passengers to be taken down, washed and stowed away" before he would permit them entrance to the harbor.

Although Martin's reports resonated with disgust, he pitied the emigrants in straitened circumstances. Indeed, he raised money to care for
the sick and the poor who were physically exhausted by their "tedious
passage across the Atlantic." Baltimore's mayor provisioned the poor,
and private citizens donated money to the most needy families.[23] While
that spirit of noblesse oblige seemed heightened under the threat of
cholera, it actually did little to abate fears of the "immigrant menace"
and their dreaded disease.

Those fears were exacerbated when an American ship, the *Brenda,*
docked in Baltimore's quarantine quarters on June 7, 1832, after a forty-
two-day trip from Liverpool. The vessel carried a large load of hardware,
dry goods, salt, and crates, as well as 123 passengers. During the voyage,
19 passengers had died, 5 from unknown diseases and 14 from cholera.
Martin first administered smallpox vaccinations to all whom he deemed
needed them and then detained all the passengers and their baggage at
the Lazaretto wharf. He later reflected that "the arrival of this ship caused
considerable excitement (though as has turned out, unnecessarily,) but
no means or attention was spared, which could possibly be afforded, to
protect the city from the introduction of *contagion* or *infection,* as well as
to render the situation of the emigrants as comfortable as the nature of
circumstances would permit."[24]

While Martin and some other members of the medical profession
used the terms *contagion* and *infection,* they actually did not know the cause
of cholera.[25] Nor was it just cholera that was a puzzle. The nature of all
infectious diseases had been debated for centuries. Two main theories
held sway, with a third acting as an intermediary. Miasmatic theorists believed that infectious diseases were atmospherically induced by miasma
(or vapors) arising from dirt. Contagionists, on the other hand, thought
that infectious diseases were caused by specific contagious elements or
organisms. The third, compromise theory maintained that diseases were
caused by specific contagia but only when atmospheric or social conditions facilitated them, analogous to the suitable soil that allowed the seed
to germinate.[26] Notions of contagion and *contagion animatum* had circulated for several centuries, and these ideas guided Baltimore's response
to the crisis.

In the first half of the nineteenth century, the anticontagionists — or
sanitarians, as many considered themselves — frequently dominated, and
they focused attention on environmental improvements to prevent the
development of miasma. Strengthening their cause were the commercial
interests who recognized that quarantine restrictions militated against

the free movement of their trade.[27] Within Maryland's medical community, the contagionists and the anticontagionists mounted a tense debate. This was reflected in the contrasting approaches taken by Drs. Martin and Jameson in their honorary consulting positions with the Baltimore Health Board. Martin, a contagionist, made every effort to maintain quarantines and repeatedly stressed their necessity. Consulting Physician Jameson, an anticontagionist, countered, "The information which I had early collected from Europe of the nature, &c. of Cholera, by direct and immediate correspondence with personal friends, enabled me to determine positively at an early period of the present year, that this disease is not contagious." He exhorted city officials to adopt "measures calculated to purify our atmosphere." The city should, he said, stop wasting "our time and money in providing prohibitory measures against contagion."[28] Baltimore authorities, however, played it safe. Confronted by conflicting expert opinion and lacking any basis for a choice, they applied both contagionist and anticontagionist measures. They maintained street cleaning and quarantine efforts for the duration of the epidemic.

The medical community was also uncertain about treating the disease. The "regular" medical profession agreed that treatment was essential but remained divided about the specific nature of the therapy. The range of potential therapies, as we noted in an earlier chapter, was small. Doctors tried the staples: bleeding, purging, stimulants, opium, calomel, and various other drugs and saline solutions. But none did much good, and physicians were left in dismay.

Given the extremely high mortality rate, the afflicted desperately looked for treatment elsewhere. Some turned to the numerous unorthodox sects that had leapt into the breach. The Thomsonians, who were among the most popular of the irregular groups at the time, promoted their botanic system.[29] In all probability, their gentler, less depleting regimen yielded better results — or at least a less tormented road to death. But their popularity during this period angered Maryland's regulars, prompting the Medical and Chirurgical Faculty to launch aggressive legislative action to curtail botanic practice.[30]

Neither political nor medical measures improved either the therapeutics or the prophylaxis in the 1830s or, for that matter, by the time Americans experienced the next cholera epidemic in 1849. Nor was there any indication that states, Maryland included, were better organized to cope with cholera. In this and other states, health boards had largely stagnated and street cleaning efforts that had received so much attention during the previous epidemic had not been sustained.[31] Maryland responded in the familiar ad hoc fashion. Members and consultants on Baltimore's Board of Health seemed astonishingly nonchalant as late as 1848, despite the imminent threat of another invasion from Europe. Francis Donaldson, physician to the Marine Hospital, and D. H. Lawrence, health officer of the Port of Baltimore, made no mention of any precautions. In fact, that year the board cut expenditures on street cleaning and farmed out the work to contractors. The health commissioner was persuaded "to look with an eye of indulgence on the operations of the present board of contractors," whose work was admittedly below par, because of the savings.[32]

The Medical and Chirurgical Faculty, however, was not so shortsighted. Its members, who maintained professional and personal ties with European doctors, were considerably less blasé. In 1832 they had abdicated responsibility to the Board of Health, but this time they were much more active. In the fall of 1848, the Faculty's Executive Committee had already convened a meeting to plan sanitary measures for Maryland. The Committee on Cholera, comprising Drs. Theobald, Baer, and Readel, read to the gathering a report that offers insights into the state of knowledge at the time and also shows how little had changed since 1832:

> Humidity and impurity of atmosphere are considered powerful predisposing factors. Cleanliness counteracts these agencies and should be insisted on. There should be a fortnightly inspection of premises, etc., and during epidemics additional dispensary physicians should be appointed. The committee recommends the use of chloride of lime freely, warm baths, attention to clothing, avoidance of exposure and especially temperance in eating and drinking. If the bowels are constipated rhubarb should be preferred, if the least lax, lead and opium, or calomel and opium, with rest in bed. It is also recommended that an apothecary be selected in each ward where the poor may procure the above remedies free of cost.[33]

The Faculty ordered the report dispatched to every town and village in Maryland, urging all of its members to be prepared.

Ultimately, the Board of Health was forced to act. By December 2, 1848, cholera had arrived in New York, and by January it had returned to Maryland.[34] The Board of Health quarantined the *Silas Richards,* a ship from Rotterdam, after three aboard had died from the disease. On this occasion, Marylanders were spared. The cholera epidemic reached Philadelphia and then moved back north, leaving Baltimore and the rest of the state unaffected.[35] No credit, however, redounded to the Board of

Health, which had been found sorely lacking as a public health institution.

The only notable exception to the board's lackadaisical performance was its handling of smallpox. When this disease struck in Maryland, city and state officials, as well as the medical profession, maintained active and ongoing prevention programs. In England, smallpox had been identified as a common epidemic disease since Elizabethan times and as an endemic disease since the early eighteenth century. It had traveled to the Americas in the seventeenth century. Although less prevalent than in Europe, it was still greatly feared in the United States.[36]

Efforts to protect against smallpox by inoculation had been popular in Maryland for much of the eighteenth century. Lady Wortley Montagu had introduced the variolation technique to Europe in 1717. By administering a small amount of smallpox matter (from scabs or pustules of an infected person) either through a small incision or through inhalation, physicians attempted to induce a mild case of smallpox and thus immunity. Inoculation was, however, a dangerous technique that proved to be a steady source of infection.

By the early 1800s, inoculation was giving way to the much safer vaccination technique (using cowpox matter) that Edward Jenner had developed in England.[37] Smallpox vaccination was available in Maryland as early as 1798, and physicians were vaccinating Baltimoreans in 1800. Gradually, the Jennerian technique took hold throughout the state, and by 1850 Maryland had pronounced inoculation illegal.[38] The medical community produced and administered vaccine through formalized channels on a planned, ongoing basis. The profession almost unanimously welcomed the arrangement, as did much of the lay population. But opposition to vaccination persisted, despite the overwhelming evidence that it was successful. For a variety of reasons, ranging from religion and concern for personal freedom to fear of any medical procedures, some did not want this form of prophylaxis.[39] One result of this resistance was government intervention and, as a result, a fierce debate that surfaced with each new epidemic.

Smallpox vaccination was compulsory for some in Maryland in the early nineteenth century. As noted above, unvaccinated immigrants who were detained at the Lazaretto wharf had no choice. In theory, neither did susceptible citizens of neighborhoods where the disease existed. In 1832, the Baltimore City Council ordained that the Board of Health's consulting physician undertake the task of tracking down and vaccinating all such persons. That year alone, Dr. Jameson vaccinated 673 people.[40] Of course, some escaped, creating a problem that public health workers have continued to face to the present day. In the nineteenth century, registration and compliance were especially problematic in this and some other public health functions.

In another effort to combat that problem, the city passed an ordinance on April 25, 1834, requiring physicians to report all cases of smallpox that came to their notice. Baltimore then instigated immediate vaccination procedures in affected neighborhoods. This measure proved highly effective, and by the next year Deputy Consulting Physician Samuel Annan reported that all outbreaks had been contained. Lay suspicion was apparently being abated; Annan's superior, Jameson, noted that the public was gradually becoming more confident in the vaccinators and their program.[41]

Despite this success, the city's leaders were still left pondering what to do with indigent smallpox patients. Landlords frequently evicted tenants suffering from the dangerous disease. Homeless smallpox victims were found sleeping in marketplaces and in the streets, causing "annoyance and alarm" to other citizens. The commissioners of health recognized the need for a special hospital that would care for the poor and maintain the quarantine. In 1936 Baltimore began work on a smallpox hospital, a facility all the more needed after fire destroyed the Lazaretto wharf near the quarantine station.[42] Until the hospital was finished, there was no facility to house immigrants with smallpox.

By early 1837, the new smallpox hospital was ready, but the city had no capability to run such an institution. As was often the case in early America, the city leased it to the Washington Medical College for the first five years because the school had an interest in the project and the staff to run the operation. The city was able to provide a special vehicle as an ambulance exclusively for the transportation of smallpox patients. Within the first nine months, forty-four patients entered the hospital on the city's account. By the end of the year, twenty-six had been discharged as cured, fourteen had died, and the remaining four were still under care. By 1837, too, Baltimore was reconstructing the Lazaretto facilities.[43]

Soon, however, Baltimore began to experience one of the common paradoxes of public health—effective prevention seemed to be making a cure unnecessary. During 1843, 2,254 free vaccinations were administered. This was in addition to the vaccinations that private doctors gave to those of greater financial means.[44] The city's vaccination program was so successful, in fact, that it virtually put the smallpox hospital out of business. For more than twelve months, the institution had only one patient and that due to the arrival in port of the barque *Leda*. Treatment seemed unnecessary when prevention was proving to be so effective.

It soon became apparent that, in the foreseeable future, both prevention and cure would continue to be necessary. Waves of immigrants continued to arrive in the city, and smallpox continued periodically to wash through Baltimore. The annual morbidity and mortality rates varied significantly. In 1846 there was only one death attributed to smallpox, but the following year 115 succumbed. The city found it absolutely essential to continue supporting the smallpox hospital as well as the vaccination campaign.[45]

The city's ongoing, well-organized campaign drew energy from numerous sources. The relationship between the Washington Medical College and the city was mutually satisfactory and beneficial. Individual physicians cooperated by reporting cases of the disease and supporting the vaccination efforts. The Medical and Chirurgical Faculty also appropriated funds to support Baltimore native Dr. Lucius O'Brien, who ran a vaccine institute in the city.[46] Through the antebellum years, the Faculty continued to promote vaccination in Baltimore and in the counties.

Maryland's response to smallpox was its most sustained and successful public health policy during those years. Even the programs that did not elicit a well-organized and effective bureaucracy—the cholera efforts, for instance—were nevertheless important. They taught significant lessons, giving public health an additional impetus in a country with a relatively weak tradition of public action. These were programs that the voting public could understand and appreciate.

Many of the public programs also fostered a desire for improved sources of knowledge in a "scientific" vein, and this in turn gave rise to a "statistical movement" in public health and medicine. In this and other regards, British influence was strong. Edwin Chadwick's 1842 monograph on "the sanitary conditions of the laboring classes" was influential, and during this era, statistical thinking in relation to medicine began to catch on in America.[47] Baconian methods of observation and induction that had long been applied in scientific circles were gradually adopted by the medical profession.[48] Americans began to pay more attention to census data and vital statistics. Between 1857 and 1860, there were four National Quarantine and Sanitary Conventions in Philadelphia, Baltimore, New York, and Boston, respectively.[49]

As this movement gathered momentum, many city authorities and sanitarians concluded that one of their major priorities had to be clean

water. The municipalization of water supplies had begun in Europe and
by this time had proven highly effective. Gradually, towns and cities in
the United States had begun to follow suit. By 1860, 136 communities
in America had pipe systems, over 40 percent of which were publicly
owned and operated. New York, Boston, and Philadelphia already had
extensive municipal systems.[50] Although Baltimore had apparently been
the first community in the United States to form a water company to
fight fires (1792), the city initially eschewed municipalization and explored other means of providing improved sources of drinking water.[51]
In 1804 the city turned to a private, joint-stock company, which developed a system for piping water from the Jones Falls through hollowed
logs.[52] That same year, the city government granted permission for similar pipes to be laid to carry water from a spring near Harford Road to
the docks and surrounding neighborhood. There was particularly heavy
demand for water at Fell's Point when large ships docked and needed to
be replenished for long voyages.[53]

As urban growth continued, additional water was needed, and the
city finally selected the Jones Falls as the most convenient source. Still
depending on the private sector, the city allowed the Baltimore Water
Company to dig a reservoir on high ground at what is now the corner of Cathedral and Franklin Streets, then well outside the city limits.
The firm constructed pumping stations and water wheels at this site. By
1838, the company needed another reservoir and built a new one with a
three-million-gallon capacity at the intersection of the present Chase and
Charles Streets. Six years later, it completed a third, the old Mount Ver-
non Reservoir. All of the firm's water mains were made from bored hemlock with wrought-iron bands and cast-iron valves. The company hewed
service pipes from cedar logs with about one-inch-diameter bores and
brass ferrules. While the firm's water was often not the most desirable
(there was contamination from privies and farmland run-off), it accommodated the city's domestic, business, and fire needs for many years.[54]

By the early 1850s, however, it was evident that a private corporation
did not have the resources needed to keep up with Baltimore's expansion. In 1854, the city took over the Baltimore Water Company and began
to build an entirely new system. The municipal organization built Lake
Roland, an impounding reservoir with a 400-million-gallon capacity at
a 220-foot elevation and began to dig a four-mile-long tunnel to carry
water from the lake into two new reservoirs in Hampden and what is
now Mount Royal. This massive feat of planning and engineering was

not completed until 1862, but once in operation, it could deliver twenty million gallons of relatively clean water a day.[55]

Similar developments took place outside Baltimore, although in smaller urban areas, spring water sufficed much longer. Frederick, one of the most progressive towns in this regard, used a private organization to construct a waterworks in 1825. Several prominent townsmen organized a company that used wooden pipes to bring water from a spring northwest of the town. This was a popular enterprise, but by 1839 increased demand persuaded the town government to step in, take over the operation, and fund its expansion. After raising the necessary capital with a lottery, the public organization was able to develop an adequate, if somewhat tenuous, water supply that satisfied the city's needs for some years to come.[56]

As should be evident, public health in Maryland developed in an uneven, sporadic manner during these years. The society was growing rapidly but was still far from wealthy, and public institutions were rudimentary, at best. Rapid growth in Baltimore constantly strained the resources and capabilities of the public sector. The state's citizens had, nevertheless, continued through trial and error to attempt to improve conditions. In the process they had laid an intellectual and institutional foundation for what would become in the decades ahead a strong and successful state public health movement.

The Civil War and Its Aftermath, 1861–1875

The Civil War was a distinct watershed for public health in Maryland, as it was throughout America. Although therapeutics and medical technology changed very little, the war forever altered public health practices and organizations. Activists who were distressed by events during the early phases of the war successfully organized the United States Sanitary Commission and the Ambulance Corps and developed significant innovations in military hospitals.

Initially, however, the Civil War yielded no benefits for Maryland; instead, it tore the state apart. The state was geographically, economically, and emotionally on the border between North and South, and its citizens differed sharply and sometimes savagely over their allegiances. The most northerly of the slave states, Maryland had relied upon human bondage labor for two centuries. During the several decades before 1860, however, the state's economy had changed in decisive ways. Planters and farmers diversified their crops, and as early as 1815 wheat and other grains had replaced tobacco as the chief agricultural product. Since wheat, corn, livestock, fruit, and vegetables were all less labor-intensive than tobacco, they diminished the need for year-round fieldhands and made slavery economically less viable. These changes took place unevenly, however, leaving certain parts of the state affiliated with the South both economically and emotionally. On the plantation-dominated Eastern Shore, southern sympathies ran deep, as they did in parts of western Maryland. Proximity to Pennsylvania and communication links with New York and with England shepherded northern and urban Marylanders toward the Union fold.[57]

As secession became imminent, most Marylanders felt compelled to pick a side. Citizens held meetings across the state. On December 17, 1860, for example, a gathering in Frederick County attempted to lead the state into the southern cause. This effort failed, but the question could not be avoided after news arrived of the secession of South Carolina and the federal attack on Fort Sumter (April 12, 1861).[58] Seven days later, there was a riot in Baltimore. Secessionists attacked Union soldiers of the Massachusetts Sixth Regiment, and many in the North began to identify the city as a "mobtown."[59]

In the months that followed, most of the fighting occurred south of Washington, but by the summer of 1862 the struggle had spread into Maryland.[60] The Battle of South Mountain (September 14, 1862) was the first major encounter, followed three days later by a terrible fight along Antietam Creek. In that confrontation, Union and Confederate losses totaled more than 23,000. During the Maryland campaign, including Harpers Ferry, the Union lost 26,023 killed, wounded, or missing; Confederate losses were 13,385.[61]

In addition to the loss of lives, there was severe economic hardship. This was especially true after Confederate forces crossed the Potomac and in June 1863 launched the Gettysburg campaign. They captured the main line of the Baltimore and Ohio Railroad, ending service from Sykesville to Rawlings Station, 160 miles to the west. They also disrupted road transportation by destroying every important bridge between Cumberland and Harpers Ferry. Water traffic, too, suffered.[62] The naval forces on both sides seized schooners, and passengers had good cause to be fearful of an attack. Both merchants and their customers were hard-pressed for vital supplies.

With less food, fewer jobs, and a struggling economy, Maryland's ad hoc public health system was under considerable pressure. Poverty-related illnesses increased, and public health workers lacked the resources to provide help. Many of the programs were staffed by volunteers, and women frequently found it necessary to adopt new roles, filling the places left open when men joined the conflict. Although women were not permitted to join regiments, there were plenty of openings for them in caring for the sick and injured. At Antietam, Clara Barton, the founder of the American Red Cross, had her hands full with the "mischief and misery" of war. She had already survived trial by fire at Cedar Mountain and at the Second Battle of Bull Run and was discouraged by how little effort was made to supplement the work of the Sanitary Commission, the Christian Commission, and the Army Nurses. She applauded the efforts of those groups but thought that they failed to provide sufficient help where it was most urgently required—at the fighting front. She attempted to remedy that situation.[63]

On September 13, 1862, Barton hurried to Harpers Ferry in anticipation of General Lee's invasion. The government provided her with a wagon, eight mules, and a driver, and after loading nursing supplies, food, and blankets, she joined the Union convoy. Although loyal to Lincoln, Barton also provided food to some starving, stranded Confederate troops, helping to establish the Red Cross's principle of nonpartisan benevolence. At the battle of Antietam, Barton set up her nursing headquarters just north of Sharpsburg, with her field hospital behind General Joseph Hooker's line.[64] In that forward position, she provided the help she could, under horrible conditions. During the battles of western Maryland, Barton gave to the troops what Florence Nightingale had given to those fighting in the Crimea.

Her efforts were badly needed because, at the onset of the war, the Army Medical Department had been dreadfully unprepared. There were not enough nurses or doctors, and many of the appointed physicians were both underqualified and ill-equipped. In combat, soldiers frequently had to serve as an ambulance crew, dragging their wounded comrades off the battlefields. Other unskilled soldiers and convalescents provided much of the care for the injured once they reached the field or general hospitals. All of these institutions were poorly organized and staffed.

The war aroused among physicians and philanthropists, men and women, an intense interest in public health questions. A group of concerned New York women organized the United States Sanitary Commission, and after President Lincoln made this an official, federal organization, the commission appointed officers to investigate the public health status of the Union troops.[65] There was much to explore; of the approximately 300,000 Union troops who died, two-thirds were killed by disease and only one-third by the enemy. Camp conditions, sanitation especially, seem to have been chiefly responsible for such illness. Rations were often short, and the normal diet consisted of beans and fried foods. Not surprisingly, nearly 30 percent of the men became ill during the first months of the war. Dysentery, typhoid fever, smallpox, and malaria decimated the Union forces.[66]

The experience of coping with these complex problems gave impetus to certain public health reforms. That was especially true in the case of hospital design. In Frederick alone, there were twenty hospitals for the care of Union and Confederate soldiers wounded at South Mountain and Antietam. Chief Surgeon Dr. R. F. Weir and Assistant Surgeon Dr. John S. Goldsborough supervised the largest of these, the U.S. General Hospital, which accommodated nearly a thousand patients. Like most such military organizations, it was a hodgepodge of permanent and temporary structures. The central, two-story, stone building was used as both the army's hospital and General Braddock's quarters. After patients overflowed the main building and the seven surrounding frame structures, the staff began to place them in tents and other buildings in Frederick.[67]

In this case and others, army doctors found that their makeshift pavilion design proved very healthful for patients. In Maryland, several facilities, including the hospital at Point Lookout in southern Saint Mary's County, were constructed with a mind to keeping the wounded and the sick in small, separate units with an adequate circulation of air.[68] These experiences prompted calls for new public health policies and programs, calls that became more forceful after the new discipline of bacteriology began to gain adherents, first in Europe and then in the United States.

The Public Health Profession and Bacteriology,
1875–1900

In the aftermath of the war, Maryland continued to suffer. The defeat of the South and the dismantling of slavery left many African Americans and poor whites in dire economic straits. Insofar as the state's problems bred policy responses, those activities were conducted by public health personnel and institutions that were themselves experiencing substantial changes in the postwar era. Public health was beginning to undergo an extended process of professionalization. Frederick County and Frederick township led the way in founding boards of health under the new state law of March 18, 1886, that ordered each county to establish such an organization. The law mandated boards to arrange preventive measures when any epidemic disease threatened and to levy fines of up to fifty dollars for violating health regulations. This measure also mandated county boards to appoint a "well-educated physician" as health officer, to keep systematic records, and to hold regular meetings.[69]

In Frederick, the new board replaced the ad hoc organization that the county had maintained since the 1832 cholera epidemic. The need for a permanent, ongoing organization was clearly demonstrated in the eighties by the large number of deaths in the town, especially of children, from diphtheria. During the nineteenth century, diphtheria had become endemic throughout the United States, and it was particularly familiar to urban residents.[70] Epidemic and endemic diseases that strike children have been and continue to be especially heart-wrenching, and they have often provoked strong demands for public action. In Frederick, the disease was killing about fifty children annually.

The Frederick board and Dr. F. B. Smith, the town's first health officer, responded to complaints from fellow citizens by launching an investigation of the diphtheria crisis. On October 28, 1886, Smith reported on sanitary conditions in the county. He found that "the disease has been limited to no particular locality of the city, appearing at different times during the last four years in all parts of the town, exempting no class or condition from its baneful influence." Between August 1881 and February 1882, there had been 125 deaths. As for causes, Smith was less certain. Frederick, he said, possessed an "unquestionably pure water supply," so he had looked elsewhere. "Believing that filth in the form of decomposing vegetable and animal matter, under certain favorable conditions of the atmosphere, [is] chiefly responsible for the maintenance, if not the origin, of the disease, my attention has been almost entirely directed to bringing to light the greatest agencies which exist in our city for its formation."[71]

Looking for miasmatic sources, Smith found much to criticize in the town's cannery, hog pens, stables, compost heaps, slaughter shops, privies and cesspools, tanneries, Carroll Creek, streets, alleys, gutters, and sewers. At the corn canning establishment, he said there was "much to commend and much to condemn." The corn was handled in a clean, healthy manner. Yet Smith discovered "inadequate and filthy privies" on the premises. He also found rotting in the sun "an area of at least 100 feet square covered to the depth of from three to ten feet with green corn cobs, tomato offal, and the manure of from 80 to 150 horses and mules." Equally disconcerting were the town's cesspools and privies: "Frederick has no uniform system for construction of these unfortunately neces- sary conveniences . . . . Many, situated above ground, in wet weather spread their filth over surrounding premises. Many consist of merely a pit, allowing all liquid to soak into the surrounding earth, and after satu- rating the earth give forth in their evaporation noxious vapors." More attention to miasmatic sources was needed, Smith said, just as it was on Frederick's thoroughfares, which were poorly drained and filthy.[72]

These suggestions fell on receptive ears. Local residents, the business community, aldermen, and the state and local boards of health worked together in an effort to solve Frederick's problems. Concerned about diphtheria, the townsfolk supported vigorous public health action. The Mercantile Association of Frederick helped the Board of Aldermen deal with some of the worst sanitary problems. Police officers examined prem- ises in their districts, especially those identified as nuisances.

The Mercantile Association perceived a beneficial blend of profit and health in a public system for garbage removal and street cleaning. As their committee noted:

> A few years ago our beautiful mountain city enjoyed the reputation
> of being the healthiest city in the State. Now the impression is wide-
> spread that we have a city full of disease and death, and leaving out of
> the account all the horrors and fears of ourselves and [our] wives for
> the safety of our children; and coming down to the sordid matter of
> dollars, we say that something must be done to improve the health of
> our city or we, as merchants, will be seriously affected by the decrease
> in our trade, caused by our customers being afraid to visit our city.[73]

Concerns for commerce coalesced with the fear of disease to unite the community. The aldermen, mercantile association, and Board of Health supplied disinfectants gratis to those prepared to scrub their dwellings, streets, and places of employment. Stirred into action, this combine served a clean-up notice on the corn cannery proprietor and placed new restrictions on hog pens and slaughterhouses. They appointed two in- spectors to assist in uncovering public health hazards and established comprehensive regulations for handling garbage. The merchants were elated, and they optimistically commented that "the condition of the city as to cleanliness is vastly superior to what it has been in any time in the past; that the health of the city has greatly improved, and we have recently been free from diseases as far as any community could expect."[74]

Helpful as these improvements were, neither Frederick nor the rest of the state was, of course, protected from diphtheria. Without an understanding of the cause of the disease, physicians could neither prevent nor cure.[75] Ironically, medical researchers in Europe were developing the knowledge that was needed in the same decade that Frederick was mounting its clean-up campaign. The resulting breakthroughs in medical understanding would have dramatic implications for Maryland's medical institutions, including those in public health. In 1882, Robert Koch identified the TB bacillus, and the following year Edwin Klebs publicized his discovery of the bacillus now known as *Corynebacterium diphtheriae*. The following year, Friedrich Loeffler proved its pathogenic role, and within a few years that information had percolated into scientific, medical, and public health circles in the United States. Maryland's William Welch, who maintained close connections with continental Europe's scientific community, was one among several eminent Americans who published on the subject.[76]

In New York City, the Health Department opened a modest diagnostic laboratory in the early 1890s, and Dr. William Hallock Park, who was in charge of diphtheria studies, soon became one of the leading human conduits carrying European concepts of bacteriology to the United States. Park assisted physicians in the diagnosis of culture material taken from patients suspected of having diphtheria. That enabled practitioners and public health workers to authorize the sequestration of patients until their cultures repeatedly came back as negative.[77] Though quarantining was an important step in reducing the morbidity and mortality rates, it was a relatively old-fashioned, passive step.

Despite these advances in understanding, children were still dying from diphtheria at an alarming rate.[78] Intubation could prevent asphyxiation in many cases, but that technique dealt only with the symptoms, not the source of disease.[79] The first effective therapy came from Europe, where Louis Pasteur, among others, was applying the new bacteriological principles to the prevention and treatment of disease.[80] In 1880, he had announced that he was able to prevent chicken cholera by giving hens an attenuated form of the bacillus. Following similar methods, in 1886 he had induced immunity to anthrax and rabies in experimental animals.[81] These innovations held out a promise for the human population as a new science, immunology, began to take shape.

Out of this setting came a revolutionary treatment for diphtheria. In

1888, Roux and Yersin isolated diphtheria toxin, and three years later von Behring and Kitasato produced an antidiphtheria serum.[82] They had been studying the toxin-destroying capacity of blood serum removed from animals that had been immunized and labeled the active element "antitoxin."[83] These developments and Koch's evidence supporting the germ theory of disease opened a completely new era for therapeutics, medical science, and public health.

In the years after 1895, the new serum treatment for diphtheria sharply reduced mortality rates for the disease in Maryland, as it did in other parts of the United States where residents could afford it. Now public health authorities and Med Chi's physicians at last had available both a science-based analysis of the cause of the disease and a relatively effective cure. They could also conduct extensive epidemiological studies of the disease "to elucidate the question of contagion in families and other important questions in connection with diphtheria control."[84]

During these same years near the end of the century, economic growth in the state and especially in Baltimore was generating additional economic resources, some of which were directed into public health programs against diphtheria and other infectious diseases. By the 1890s, Baltimore was the third largest port in the United States, and the city's commerce was pumping new revenue into both the private and public sectors of the city and state.[85] Wealthy individuals and companies were making donations and establishing foundations to support public health ventures ranging from local vaccination plans to such ambitious projects as the professional development of public health. Out of that economic, intellectual, and social context emerged a new institution that would transform public health in Maryland, the United States, and many countries around the world during the following century.

SEVEN

Public Health

Professional Responses to the
Rise of Scientific Medicine,

1900–1940

I n the realm of public health, the new medical sciences had an effect opposite to that they had on the institutions of medical education in Maryland. Instead of centralizing the institutional base, the new theories of disease causation and transmission inspired a significant new phase of institutional experimentation and expansion in state and local public health. Ideas were not the only source of growth. But in this case they were clearly significant in shaping a coherent pattern of development.

The political context in late nineteenth- and early twentieth-century Maryland was favorable to pragmatic experiments with new public health programs. Throughout America, local and state governments were becoming more involved in many aspects of American society, particularly those involving economic and urban affairs. Progressive reform movements had momentum in Maryland, just as they did in Washington, D.C. In Baltimore, the demands for change produced a new city charter in 1898. Like most such progressive reforms, this substituted centralized, functional organization for the ward-level politics that middle-class reformers found so unpalatable. Carefully planned undertakings coordinated by engineers, inspectors, and commissions began to replace many of the ad hoc projects funded by ward systems.[1]

One important product of that movement was the effort to pass pure food and drug laws, a movement that accelerated sharply in the 1890s, especially after the Spanish-American War. In that brief conflict, lasting only a year (1898–99), 968 Americans died of battle injuries or accidents, but six times as many succumbed to disease. Magnified and publicized by the new "yellow press," these casualty figures prompted renewed efforts to eliminate problems such as those stemming from contaminated foods. A team of investigators headed by Dr. Walter Reed also focused attention on the typhoid fever that resulted from the poor water and sewage systems in the U.S. Army's camps.[2]

Those experiences and a widespread movement for regulation produced a new federal law, the Pure Food and Drug Act of 1906.[3] That act became the prototype for subsequent legislation at the state level and had a strong influence on politics in Maryland. There was a long tradition of laws against adulteration, but enforcement had normally been lax, and corporate enterprise, which was national and even international in scope, had in most localities outgrown the state regulatory process.[4] Even after late nineteenth-century developments in scientific technology permitted more extensive and accurate analysis of contents, most states had been incapable of regulating food or drugs effectively. In this, as in other aspects of American government, new administrative capabilities were needed in the public sector.

By 1909, thirty-nine states had taken new "steps to protect their citizens from the cupidity of unscrupulous manufacturers," and Maryland shortly joined this movement. The federal government's provisions applied to interstate transportation; as a result, goods that were shipped into the state were stamped with labels accurately describing their contents. Once those goods arrived in Baltimore or on the Eastern Shore, however, wholesalers and retailers could, legally, repackage them and sell them under fraudulent labels. The press, especially the *Baltimore News,* turned this issue into a cause célèbre. Muck-raking articles drew widespread public attention to the resulting adulteration of food and drugs.[5]

Just as Maryland's legislators were prepared to take action, however, a political spat threatened to undermine the passage of a new law. The state Board of Health and the Maryland Agricultural College each claimed the right to become the new regulatory agency. Since the opponents were unable to resolve their differences, the governor stepped in and established a commission to settle the disagreement, appointing Dr. G. Milton Linthicum, president of the Medical and Chirurgical Faculty, to chair the group. The Faculty had long expressed a strong interest in improving the purity of drugs. Its member physicians were disturbed about the reliability of the medicines that they prescribed and those that their patients purchased over the counter or by mail order. Independently, the Faculty had formed its own committee to promote the bill and was supporting the Maryland Pharmaceutical Association, which had already drafted a bill that seemed satisfactory to the food-producing businesses, grocers, canneries, confectioners, and drug associations.

As to the question at hand—that is, which organization should have authority over the regulatory process—the Faculty saw "no good reason whatsoever for considering the Agricultural College in this connection." [6] The Board of Health had, after all, been the de facto enforcer of food and milk standards for two decades. The Pharmaceutical Association and some other groups opted for a compromise, but meanwhile the bill languished for months. [7]

In the midst of these debates, Dr. Harvey W. Wiley addressed Med Chi's members at a special meeting on December 16, 1909. Wiley, chief of the Bureau of Chemistry at the U.S. Department of Agriculture, had been involved in food and drug regulatory matters for twenty-five years. He was well aware of the problems of state-level control, and he emphasized his point with a story drawn from Maryland. It involved a man who, when discovered and brought to court in Washington, D.C., had admitted "that he made two kinds of goods, one a pure article properly branded, to be shipped outside the state; the other an adulterated and misbranded article, to [be] used by the citizens of Maryland." Wiley, who was tough and a little condescending, told the Faculty that the most important issue was to pass some version of the state bill, although his own preference was for one modeled after the national statute (much of which he had written). [8]

Dr. Lyman F. Kebler, chief of the Drug Division of the Bureau of Chemistry at the U.S. Department of Agriculture, seconded Wiley's call for quick passage of a state law. At the customs house in Baltimore, he said, he had seen powdered olive stones imported for human consumption as a food additive. He suggested, too, that the regulations on medical devices and standard dosages needed to be tightened; laudanum, for example, could still legally contain a wide range of strengths of opium. Kebler warned that the numerous soft drinks containing stimulants were "a forerunner of the cocaine habit." [9]

Med Chi doctors ultimately followed Wiley's advice and backed the pure food bill written by the governor's commission. Compromising, they helped end the political bickering and managed to achieve one of their major objectives. Under the new statute, the state Board of Health exercised authority over the regulatory process. As the editor of Med

Chi's *Bulletin* noted, there was a "moral" in this "story." "It is a splendid exemplification of the immense influence which a united profession can wield."[10] Indeed, there was much for the Faculty to celebrate when Governor Crothers signed Maryland's Food and Drugs Act into law on April 5, 1910.[11]

The revolution in the medical sciences also focused fresh attention on the quality of milk supplies in Maryland. Bacteriologists could now provide scientific data that would help public health workers identify milk hazards. A broad range of the state's citizens — bacteriologists, chemists, doctors, veterinarians, dairy farmers, transporters, distributors, and retailers — had all become involved in a clean milk movement that resulted in the passage of a new regulatory measure in 1908. Milk production and distribution was an economically important enterprise. In these years, Baltimore alone was receiving 29,000 gallons of milk daily: 23,000 by rail from 1,900 distant farms and 6,000 by wagon from 160 city and suburban dairies. Three hundred and twenty-five distributors handled milk from the railroads, and twenty-five from the local producers. More than 1,000 wagons were delivering milk to customers' doorsteps, and about 3,700 shops retailed it.

In this complex system, inspection was a nightmare. At first, the state and city health departments rejoiced to have the 1908 milk law and commented on "a very noticeable improvement in the commercial value of the milk and a wonderful improvement in the condition of the local producing dairies." But the bacteriological count indicated virtually no improvement, and Baltimore's eight milk inspectors were not armed with a bacteriological standard to use in the prosecution of offenders. During August 1911, when the inspectors took fifty-eight counts, the results ranged from 100,000 to 21,000,000 bacteria per cc; only eleven counts were under 1,000,000 at a time when 500,000 was the standard for a warning.[12] The inspectors concluded that

> the entire problem of milk production in the country sifts itself down to the labor that is employed. These men are too often independent, lazy, careless and disobedient, and at best are apt to perform their work in a purely disinterested manner, and not giving a "whoop" for the milk that is produced. They fail to keep the cows clean, they fail to keep the stables clean daily, they fail in personal cleanliness, and fail in milk handling. They know nothing about bacteria and cared less.[13]

Education, the inspectors concluded, was the key. They applauded the efforts in many of Maryland's rural public schools to teach agriculture and urged every such school to ensure that "the young generation may learn and appreciate the proper methods of caring for and milking cattle."[14]

Convincing people of the dangers of dirty milk turned out to be a long, difficult struggle. In 1911, 568 babies in Baltimore died as a result of bad milk, but the public remained apathetic.[15] Normally, children's diseases provoked strong public reactions, but in this case there was very little concern expressed about these deaths. The Medical and Chirurgical Faculty and the Women's Civic League joined forces in annual attempts to reshape lay attitudes toward clean milk. In 1912, Med Chi's annual conference had three evening meetings and an exhibit on milk, but the movement's leaders concluded that the message did "not reach the people most in need of enlightenment."[16] Tradition seemed to outweigh medical science in the popular culture.

Despite this apathy, the state and city gradually broadened and tightened the system of controls. In 1917, Baltimore passed an ordinance ensuring that virtually all of the city's milk would be pasteurized. By the mid-1920s, an enlarged crew of inspectors was making daily tests "to detect adulteration by addition of water and skimming off of butter-fat, and to make bacterial counts for evidence as to conditions of production." When they found a high bacteriological count, they visited the milk producer; if a second visit failed to yield results, the inspectors barred the farmer from selling milk in Baltimore. At that point, the producer had to convince the commissioner of health that he should not revoke the farmer's permit to produce milk for sale.[17] The iron rod of regulation worked in this case. By the mid-1930s, milk-borne typhoid fever and septic sore throat had at last become things of the past.[18]

The same combination of middle-class professionals (many of them physicians) and middle- and upper-class women activists who had joined forces to achieve milk regulation was effective in promoting other public health reforms. Improvements in sanitation were particularly appealing to many women activists because they involved domestic issues on a grand scale or, as it has been termed, "municipal housekeeping."[19] It was during these years and as a result of these reform movements that, as Elizabeth Fee has explained, the term *hygiene* was becoming inextricably linked with public health.[20]

The Sewerage Commission was typical of the new approach to urban problems.[21] In Baltimore Dr. Hampson Jones pointed out the incalculable harm being done in terms of death and illness due to the filth, flies, and mosquitoes associated with the city's thousands of privy wells and surface drains. Nor was he alone in calling for change. In 1906, the Sewerage Commission's report outlined plans for new sanitary sewers

and an entire storm-water system. Although these innovations were bud-
geted at $14 million and $4.5 million, respectively, Baltimore launched the
massive venture and by late 1911 was beginning to use parts of the new
system. In this case, engineers joined hands with physicians and women
advocates of reform to eliminate a major hazard to public health.[22]

In Maryland's small towns and rural areas, similar sanitation problems
were arising, as we noted earlier in our discussion of Frederick County.
In fact, studies at that time indicated that typhoid fever had become
more prevalent in the country and small towns, where it was associated
with the use of surface privies, than it was in the city. Concerned about
hookworm as well as intestinal diseases, public health activists launched a
campaign urging farmers to adopt improved means of sewage disposal.[23]

Education and regulation were both needed in urban Maryland as
well, where on balance the worst public health problems still existed.
Two industries in particular, ready-to-wear clothing and the iron and
steel works at Sparrows Point, had a decisive influence on public health
in Baltimore.[24] At the turn of the century, Baltimore was the nation's
leading clothing producer. While the so-called rag trade provided jobs
for many domestic and foreign migrants, the city's sweatshops were frequently death traps. In overcrowded, ill-ventilated workrooms, poor,
undernourished workers labored for long periods, readily communicat-
ing the agents of infectious diseases, including tuberculosis.

Since Koch's identification of the tubercle bacillus, public as well as
medical and scientific perspectives on the disease had been changing.
The romanticized image of the frail and fading consumptive gradually
gave way to a harsher picture that placed the tuberculous patient in poor
living conditions.[25] This negative image was sharpened by a growing recognition that society, as well as individuals, paid a high price for TB. In
1909, one investigator placed the annual cost to the nation at $330 mil-
lion, a large sum at that time. People who could have been in their most
productive working years were dying at a rate of 150,000 per year.[26] Economic and humanitarian considerations stirred public health officials and
philanthropists to action.

Both groups largely saw education as the most promising means of
reducing the incidence of tuberculosis and of improving the life expectancy of those who contracted the disease. Through 1910, the Maryland
Association for the Prevention and Relief of Tuberculosis and Med Chi's
Committee on Public Instruction led this effort. That year, Med Chi concluded that additional efforts at physician education were needed. The
Faculty formed a committee, headed by Dr. John Girdwood, who orga-

nized a meeting, with papers on "Sources of Infection" and "The Doctor's Duty in Tuberculosis." However, "apathy and indifference" kept all but sixty physicians away from the session. Girdwood was rightly concerned

> that the average doctor does not make the diagnosis of tuberculosis until the disease is moderately and often far advanced, that a great many do not tell the patient the truth after they have made a diagnosis, that less than 50 per cent of practicing physicians in this city avail themselves of the opportunity for free examinations of sputum provided by the Health Department, that not more than 37 per cent of the physicians of the State of Maryland are reporting their cases to the State Board of Health, and that not more than one-third are willing to give instructions to the patient and his family, as provided by law, and for which the State pays a fee.[27]

Despite this discouraging picture, Girdwood's committee decided to press on, instructing Maryland's physicians in diagnostic methods and marshalling a network of organizations to further their cause. The committee worked with the various antituberculosis agencies throughout the city and the state to enforce existing laws, to make physicians report cases, and to establish hygiene and prevention courses for grammar school children.[28]

Many doctors, Med Chi's committee concluded, did not believe they could arrest or cure the illness and were poorly informed about Maryland's treatment facilities. For so-called incipient cases, Maryland had three private and two public sanitaria. The State Sanitarium and the Eudowood Sanitarium could handle up to 300 incipient cases, and both institutions took nonpaying patients. The major problem involved those classified as "far advanced." Accommodations for such cases were insufficient, especially for those outside Baltimore. The Baltimore Municipal Tuberculosis Hospital maintained 160 beds for these far advanced patients, Eudowood had 30 beds, and the Jewish Home for Consumptives, 36. Although the last two facilities accepted patients from any part of Maryland, they primarily served the city.[29] Small town and rural residents dying of the disease were left to their own devices; the extremely difficult task of caring for them usually fell on family, friends, neighbors, and charity workers. Meanwhile, those caregivers and their contacts were all exposed to tuberculosis and could unwittingly spread the disease.

In an effort to cope with this problem, Maryland's doctors supported a visiting nurse program. Trained nurses treated tuberculosis patients in their homes and provided education for the patients' families. The nurses advised any family member they suspected of having the disease to consult a doctor. This assisted in identifying patients in the incipient stage, while something could be done and while there was time to limit communication. Symptoms in the initial stages were often not severe enough to drive people to a doctor, and many sought medical care very late.[30]

The available therapies were of limited efficacy. Eight years after Koch had proven the specific etiology of tuberculosis, he announced his discovery of tuberculin, an antitoxin serum prepared from a culture of living human tubercle bacilli. Unlike the serum treatment for diphtheria, however, tuberculin proved to be substantially short of a miracle cure. Although popular around the world, it frequently caused fevers, revived old tuberculous patches, and had mixed results as a curative agent. Not until later was its value as a diagnostic tool identified.[31]

The primary treatment involved rest, fresh air, and a wholesome diet, all provided in a sanitorium.[32] In 1906, the Maryland legislature created its first such facility, the State Tuberculosis Sanitorium near Sabillasville. The General Assembly allocated $10,250 to purchase 198 acres in the heart of the Blue Ridge Mountains and spent $200,000 constructing and equipping the facility. The state selected this site partly because of its proximity to the Western Maryland railroad, which erected a special stop named Sanitorium Station. When the institution's first superintendent, Victor Cullen, arrived on New Year's Day in 1908, there were still no roads and his buggy had to plow through mud "up to its hubs." He was the only person there that day, and he said it "looked like the most discouraging problem he had ever faced." But the facility—an administration building, infirmary, eight pavilions for patients (each with twenty beds), a powerhouse, living quarters for the staff, and a dining hall—was completed the following year, and Cullen made it his life's work. He spent the next forty years treating tuberculosis patients at what became known as the Victor Cullen Center.[33]

Part of an effort to heal the treatable lower class, the sanitorium was open to all white citizens of Maryland who had been residents of the state for at least a year. In addition to the racial bar, the institution would admit only patients deemed curable, and those with any financial resources (about 20 percent) were required to pay between $3.50 and $7.00 per week. Concerned that their patients were barred from the state facility, physicians from the African-American community followed the lead of the state's Jewish population and garnered support for a separate sanatorium. By 1923, these efforts had finally succeeded, and the

Maryland Tuberculosis Sanatorium was operating a "colored branch" at Henryton.[34]

The Henryton facility initially experienced difficulties. It was unpopular with patients, and despite the dire need for treatment in the African-American community, only about two-thirds of the beds were occupied during the first year. As Baltimore's African-American doctors discovered, potential patients were discouraged by the sanitorium's inaccessible location, which meant that patients rarely received visits from friends and family. Isolated and surrounded by far advanced patients (who were dying or too ill to be good company), patients were unhappy at Henryton and discouraged others from using the sanatorium. The director, Dr. Sloan, formerly the superintendent of the Eudowood Sanatorium at Towson, succeeded, however, in rallying his fellow physicians to support the Henryton establishment, and gradually the branch overcame its initial reputation and problems.[35]

During these years, the new understanding of bacteriology helped public health officials treat tuberculosis and prevent some other diseases, but they were still largely helpless in the face of viral infections. This became obvious when the influenza pandemic of 1918–19 swept through the state. Those Americans serving during the Great War had already experienced the usual gamut of wartime contagious disease—typhus, typhoid, tuberculosis, and cholera. But none proved as deadly as influenza. More American servicemen succumbed to influenza and its secondary bacterial pneumonias than to enemy fire. Civilian populations suffered just as badly, and while no one really knows how many people died worldwide, the best estimates exceed twenty million. Of those deaths, approximately 549,000 occurred in the United States.[36]

Although influenza seems to have made regular appearances in northern Europe in the nineteenth century, none of those waves of infection had been as deadly as the 1918–19 pandemic.[37] This virulent strain of the virus first struck troops in England and France, and by August 1918, returning soldiers had carried the disease to the United States. Like cholera, it first spread through the port cities. Soon America's entire population was at risk.[38]

During the autumn of 1918, Dr. William Welch visited some of America's troops and was reportedly more depressed by what he encountered than ever before in his career. At Camp Devens, near Boston, he was met by a steady stream of men carrying their blankets as they left for the hospital. There were too few attendants, and the patients were largely left to care for themselves. Welch saw young men who were blue from lack of oxygen and observed the same evidence of oxygen deprivation in lungs opened in the autopsy room. If the experience shocked Welch, one can well imagine how the so-called Spanish flu affected the public health workers, doctors, nurses, and lay volunteers who saw men digging mass graves.[39] In the United States, 2,899 soldiers and civilians died in August 1918, 10,481 in September, and 195,876 in the following month.[40]

Earlier that year, the Medical and Chirurgical Faculty of Maryland had heard an optimistic report on the triumphs of military medicine. Colonel Victor Vaughn, serving in the Army Medical Corps, wrote to his colleagues:

> The importance of medicine in war has been amply demonstrated during the past years. Without modern sanitation, infection would have long since supplanted warfare in its destructive effects; but preventive medicine has demonstrated its effectiveness in all the great armies of Europe, both those of our allies and our enemies. The only signal victories won so far have been those of medicine, both preventive and curative. Our old foes, the infections which in past wars have often proved more destructive than missiles and frequently decided the fate of nations, have been halted and forbidden admission to military camps.

But by fall, the Faculty was mustering its forces to deal with a deadly influenza pandemic that had gained admission to all civilian institutions as well as the military camps.[41] The Faculty's *Bulletin* editor rallied his profession to the cause. As he noted, during the summer of 1918, while members had been organizing the Volunteer Medical Service Corps in conjunction with the Office of the Surgeon General, they had had no idea "of any urgent demand for medical service outside of the military necessities. But early in the autumn the 'Spanish Flu' appeared in the United States and began its record of appalling disaster. From many neighborhoods came urgent appeals for medical aid, so that the Faculty was overwhelmed by requests to send doctors and nurses to stricken communities in various parts of Maryland and adjacent states."[42] Maryland's physicians and nurses responded to those pleas, whether civilian or military, but soon the epidemic raged so severely that their services were required at home. More than a few contracted the disease themselves and died.

Still, the source of the disease remained a mystery. Med Chi doctors, among others, observed that the survival of "so many older members of families where the young and middle aged have fallen victims forces us to believe that old people have in some way acquired immunity against it."[43] Certain pneumococcal entities, which were responsible for many of the deaths, had begun to be identified as early as 1884, but neither vaccine nor serum treatments had been particularly successful. They frequently produced severe reactions similar to symptoms of the disease.[44]

No one felt invulnerable, and the *Bulletin* commented, "Pale death was invading equally the homes of the rich and the homes of poverty."[45] In reality, the incidence of this disease (like many others) often followed class lines. Edgar Sydenstricker, one of America's and Maryland's leading public health authorities, conducted extensive studies of infectious diseases in Hagerstown in the immediate aftermath of the pandemic. He investigated morbidity in fifteen hundred to two thousand families.[46] Sydenstricker and his associates studied families from different economic groups in representative neighborhoods and found that morbidity figures varied by socioeconomic class. Wealthier residents were less susceptible than poorer families to a variety of infectious and other public health–related diseases. This matched Sydenstricker's findings during the 1918 pandemic, when, unlike many, he had concluded that even influenza attacked the poor in higher numbers than the rich.[47]

Since Marylanders were not inclined in these years to change the distribution of wealth and income in the state, they largely ignored Sydenstricker's conclusions. Although he was a respected figure in public health, his type of socioeconomic analysis pointed toward remedies that were out of the mainstream in Maryland politics and medicine at that time. Like most Americans, Marylanders were more interested in seemingly magic cures than in preventive medicine or uncomfortable epidemiological findings. The cutting edge was laboratory-based, bacteriological studies of specific diseases, and that was the type of science that shaped Maryland's and America's first professional school of public health.[48]

Maryland's New School for Professionals in Public Health

Maryland was the first state to open a school of public health, and the efforts to establish this institution were shaped decisively by the rise of the new laboratory-based medical sciences. During the early 1900s, the amateurs and volunteers who had dominated the field during the previous century had begun to give way to paid professionals. In the United States, however (unlike Great Britain), it was not clear initially just which professionals would gain authority. Lawyers, nurses, social workers, architects, statisticians, and a variety of other groups were all involved, but only the sanitary engineers had sufficient clout to give physicians a real challenge. As it turned out, even engineers had to yield to doctors armed with the tools of laboratory science and money from one of the country's leading philanthropic foundations.[49]

Ironically, the medical profession achieved control despite the fact that few contemporary doctors wanted to be public health officers. Compared with private-practice clinical medicine, public health was a poorly paid profession, and compared even with medical research, it was low-status work. The small minority of physicians who entered the preventive medicine arena were independently wealthy, had already established a secure clinical practice, or were so deeply committed to public health that income was a minor consideration. This paralleled the experience of America's first generation of twentieth-century medical scientists.

There were other differences and tensions between public health and medicine. Many private practitioners seem to have resented the emphasis that public health workers placed on the prevention of illness, rather than the cures that were the daily concerns of clinicians. Public health personnel perforce looked with more favor on government programs than did the average physician in private practice. From the perspective of physicians in Maryland and elsewhere in the United States, public health could never be more than a subordinate, quasi-profession.

During the 1890s and early 1900s, however, several forces converged to empower the public health movement and to support the notion of a fully developed, autonomous public health profession. Progressive reform highlighted the pleas of humanitarians to improve living and working conditions among working class Americans. Social efficiency, a popular idea at that time, seemed also to call for enhanced public health measures. Politically savvy public health promoters such as Hopkins's William Welch pointed out that these two goals were quite compatible. In a speech to the Sanitation Organization Society of Baltimore, Welch said that "from a mercenary and commercial point of view it is for the interest of the community to take care of the health of the poor. Philanthropy assumes a totally different aspect in the eyes of the world when it is able to demonstrate that it pays to keep people healthy."[50]

Impressive as Welch's arguments were, they would not have pushed public health over the threshold into full professional standing had not the medical sciences eased the transition. As bacteriology became an "ideological marker" of progress, the public health movement began to shift away from the intellectual orbit of the sanitarians and toward that of the medical scientists.[51] Like the new brand of epidemiology that developed in these years, laboratory research focused on specific diseases and did not raise awkward questions about social classes and the distribution of income in Maryland. These new and revamped disciplines greatly impressed foundation executives, and none more so than those at the Rockefeller Foundation. Having supported the Flexner Report's conclusions that medical education needed more extensive professionalization and more devotion to modern medical sciences, the Rockefeller organization began to look to a similar renovation for public health. The foundation's interests meshed neatly with those of a group of medical and scientific leaders who had become deeply involved in public health. Among the latter were William Welch, professor of pathology at Johns Hopkins Medical School; William Howell, professor of physiology at Hopkins; and Hermann M. Biggs, health commissioner for New York City.

Rather than cooperating to establish a national school of public health, the three competed in a style that was characteristic of U.S. political economy and would later become a familiar aspect of nonprofit development efforts. Each of these experts sought Rockefeller money for his own institutional vision. New York had a strong claim on support, as did the distinguished medical school at Harvard University. But Johns Hopkins had the inside track. Abraham Flexner had been impressed by the medical school and, after submitting his 1910 report to the Carnegie Foundation, had sustained a friendship with Welch. In 1914, Flexner, as secretary of Rockefeller's General Education Board, turned his investigative eye on establishments that were schooling public health officers. They were, he found, too few and too poorly organized to meet the needs of the time. Against that background, the board arranged a meeting on October 16, 1914, in New York City to discuss various proposals for upgrading professional training in this field. Welch was one of the eleven public health representatives who made their pitch to the Rockefeller Foundation.[52]

Two years of study, debate, and site visits followed, and in 1916 the foundation announced that Hopkins had won first prize. Boston, Chicago, New York, Philadelphia, Saint Louis, and Washington, D.C., had lost to Baltimore in the competition for Rockefeller support. To the chagrin of Harvard University, Abraham Flexner had strongly supported Hopkins, where a new school of public health could be organized in close cooperation with the existing scientific laboratories.[53] In June 1916, the foundation's Executive Committee allocated $267,000 to launch the School of Hygiene and Public Health at the Johns Hopkins University.[54]

As the school's name indicated, the professional struggle over the identity and authority of public health was still not settled. Welch, who was profoundly influenced by the German model of modern science, envisioned an institute of hygiene oriented almost exclusively to research. Rockefeller's kingpins, however, sought more emphasis on applied public health and public health administration. By and large, though, Welch got what he wanted—first-class resources that attracted top-ranking researchers and teachers—and, not surprisingly, he compromised with the foundation along the way. Research ranked first in the new institution, but applied work and administration had important secondary roles.[55]

The faculty at the new school undertook a remarkable range of work in the 1920s and 1930s. Internationally as well as nationally, the School of Hygiene and Public Health defined and frequently dominated the work that was generally acknowledged to be at the front edge of the field. Elmer McCollum, the head of chemistry, conducted groundbreaking nutritional studies; he discovered vitamins A and D and demonstrated their roles in health and illness.[56] Robert Hegner and his team of investigators carried out pioneering studies in the United States and the tropics in the discipline of medical zoology. Hegner, who was a prolific author and inspiring teacher, created a large program that attracted students from around the world. Charles Simon, who had been professor of clinical pathology and experimental medicine at the University of Maryland, joined the School of Hygiene's Department of Medical Zoology in 1919. His voluble pro-German sentiments had led to ostracism at Maryland. At Hopkins, however, where science came first and politics barely seemed to matter, he was able to help establish a new field of research on filterable viruses. Under Welch's mantle, immunology and bacteriology flourished, and the school trained the next generation of students how to isolate and treat specific diseases and how to establish and manage public health laboratories.[57] Welch had become a towering figure in the discipline and in national health circles. He was enormously active in Washington, D.C., and abroad, and in 1931 he served as one of the chief experts for the National Advisory Health Council.[58]

Maryland's Public Health Network

The School of Hygiene and Public Health at Hopkins often overshadowed the rest of the state's elaborate network of public health institutions and individuals. Yet what was most impressive by the early 1930s was not any single organization but the broad range of the institutions involved in improving the health of the public in this state. Med Chi played an important role in encouraging and coordinating outreach to the lay population across the state. So, too, did two of the state's leading newspapers, the *Sun* and, especially, the *American,* both of which ran health bulletins. Maryland physicians had for some years used the papers to communicate with a broad public audience.[59]

There were also clinics that addressed health problems directly. In addition to those run by the Babies' Milk Fund Association, there were Baby Welfare and Pre-School Clinics, which the Bureau of Child Welfare had established. By 1925, there were six in Baltimore, operating in the eastern, western, and northwestern sections of the city. The Robert Garrett Clinic, headed by Dr. Gustav Woltereck, was open six days a week, and the others, run by pediatricians Drs. John S. Fenby and William K. Skilling, were held in public schools. Like the schools, they were racially segregated, as were virtually all such Maryland institutions before World War II.

The object of the clinics was to keep well children well, a distinctively twentieth-century theme stemming from the hygiene side of public health. Such clinics served children from early infancy to school age, and when home nurses made their initial visit after the birth of a child, they encouraged mothers to take all of their preschool children to the clinics (unless they were already under the supervision of a private physician). At each facility, doctors and nurses weighed and examined children and gave advice about feeding. Nurses frequently monitored cases by means of home visits. In addition, clinics served as vaccination centers, where the staff emphasized the importance of vaccinating all children before the age of one year. Some parents were not persuaded, but wherever parental consent was forthcoming, the clinics administered smallpox and diphtheria vaccinations.[60]

Effective as these measures were and elaborate as the network of institutions and like-minded practitioners had become, public health in Maryland, and especially in Baltimore, was severely challenged by the Great Depression of the 1930s. This was especially true for the African-American population of the city. Since the end of Reconstruction, the gap between African Americans and Caucasians in the state had narrowed in some regards, although there was still a significant difference reflected in the mortality figures. Neither death nor life was color-blind.[61] For a time Maryland had the highest recorded African-American mortality rate of any state in the country.[62]

The racial contours of Maryland's medical and public health systems would not be changed decisively until the state and nation had escaped the hold of the depression. It would, in fact, be some years after World War II before this state and others would take the first major steps to eliminate the deep gulf that separated African Americans from the rest of the state's population in medicine, as in so many other aspects of life.

By the time that happened, Maryland's elaborate network of public health organizations and activities—an amalgam of private, nonprofit, and public institutions—had already made a significant difference to African Americans and to all other residents of Maryland. The difference was captured, in part, in the average figures for life expectancy. Between 1900 and 1940, the entire nation, Maryland included, had experienced a stunning change that could not be explained by reference merely to new therapies. The sources of this transformation were, instead, largely in more humble places, like sewers and drinking water. Americans in 1900 could look forward to an average life of approximately forty-seven years. When these figures are broken down by race, there were substantial differences. African-American life expectation was only thirty-three years. By 1940 the same figures were almost sixty-three years and fifty-three years, respectively; the gap between African Americans and the rest of the state's population had begun to close long before the civil rights movement began to transform race relations in the state. This was a remarkable change in a generation and a half, and public health was primarily responsible for the improvement.

Driven by reform ideologies, by new concepts of scientific medicine, and by the medical profession, Maryland had created an elaborate framework of new public health organizations. For the first three decades of the twentieth century, this diverse set of institutions had been sustained by the economic expansion of Maryland's commercial and industrial sectors. The Great Depression had sorely tested this array of interlocking organizations. But public health in the state had emerged at the end of the 1930s as an extremely innovative set of institutions, with strong professional leadership and a viable consensus about the best means of protecting the health of the state's population. In this case, decentralization and diversity served the long-term interests of medicine in Maryland very well.

EIGHT

Modern Medicine

Strains and Successes in
Maryland Health Care,
1940–1999

On January 27, 1940, Baltimoreans heard a fifteen-minute radio drama on the evils of quackery.[1] Med Chi and the Baltimore City Health Department jointly sponsored this program as part of a series called *Keeping Well*. The dialogue on WFBR featured a nefarious Quack Doctor and his victim, a gullible young man.

"Notice the lights on the panel young man," says the Quack. "The red light and the amber light are both burning. The purple light flickers. Yours is not a hopeless case but it will be stubborn."

Frightened, the young man, who suspects he has syphilis, replies. "Gee, Doctor—three lights. Are you sure everything will be all right? I'm going to be married in six months."

Quack Doctor, soothingly: "It's a good thing you came to me—for only by this method of automatic electric diagnosis would it have been possible to have accurately charted your symptoms and plotted the indicated cure. And let me tell you—not a single hospital in the city has one of those machines."

"I'm glad I read your advertisement," the young man says. "My buddy wanted me to go to one of those clinics over at Monumental . . ."

"Antiquated methods my dear boy. They use you like one of their guinea pigs and it would have been months, maybe years, before they could have cured you. This machine removes the ever present margin of human error in making its diagnosis. I know now exactly what to prescribe for you—why, the fight is half won!"

The young man, immensely relieved, exclaims, "Golly, Doc, science is a wonderful thing!"[2]

This attempt at drama tells us much about medicine in Maryland as America was on the brink of entering World War II and was, as well, just entering one of the great transitions in the history of the profession. The reverence for science, even a false science, was evident, and the fascination of Marylanders and other Americans with science, including scientific medicine, would grow much stronger during the 1940s and 1950s. That reverence would have a solid basis in experience as Marylanders logged impressive advances in clinical medicine and research during America's therapeutic revolution. Despite these revolutionary changes, however, and despite the efforts over the previous century of the Medical and Chirurgical Faculty to drive out irregular practitioners, quackery was obviously still a problem.[3] It would continue to be a problem to the present day.

While science was triumphant in the teaching hospitals, many of the state's citizens would continue to use home cures, much as they had through the previous century. Even housecalls carried over into the post–World War II years, although more and more of Maryland's health care was provided within a hospital or a doctor's office. Many of the state's more senior doctors still have fond memories of their visits to patients' homes, and some are ready to point out that such visits often helped the doctor to achieve a better understanding of the patient's situation and to provide care that was tailored to individual needs.[4]

Those visits could also be eye-opening reminders that modern scientific knowledge had not by any means eradicated traditional beliefs. In the mid-1940s, for example, Dr. Charles O'Donnell was asked to attend a two-year-old boy with measles who lived on a farm in Baltimore County. When O'Donnell arrived, the child was nowhere in sight, but the doctor was assured that the boy could be found in the "mud room." Entering the room, O'Donnell still could not find his patient. But after scraping around in a corner, he uncovered the little boy, whose family had placed him under a pile of manure "to bring out the measles."[5] Confronted by deep-set folk wisdom, the leaders of scientific medicine had to be satisfied with partial victories and a slow, uneven advance.

War Again

The progress of the regular medical profession accelerated after the United States entered World War II in December 1941. Initially, it was not evident to practitioners in Maryland that mobilization would have any positive aspects. The state sent more than its quota of doctors into military service: 718 physicians, of whom 577 were from Baltimore and 141 were from the counties.[6] Nurses, too, were leaving for the battle-front in large numbers, a situation that Dr. Merrill L. Stout, director of the Hospital for Women of Maryland, called "critical."[7] This placed the remaining medical personnel and the state's medical institutions under substantial strain.[8] Short-handed, they were confronted by a large in-flux of new workers and medical problems as war production increased throughout the state.

Industrial activity, which had already picked up speed before the war, increased sharply as the United States mobilized for a two-front struggle in Asia and Europe. Bethlehem Steel and the Glenn L. Martin Com-pany received major orders from the federal government, which placed $185 million in contracts with defense plants in Maryland. Factories in Baltimore, Cumberland, and Frederick were hard-pressed to produce the steel and rubber products, ships, and airplanes that were needed in the war effort.[9] Unemployment became a thing of the past, and depres-sion fears were put aside. African-American laborers left their homes to the south of Maryland in large numbers and flocked to the high-paying jobs opening in the state's steel mills and shipyards. Maryland Drydock alone needed twelve thousand new employees to handle its war work.[10] By 1943, the aircraft plants in Baltimore and Hagerstown employed fifty thousand people, many of whom were women because of the shortage of male labor.[11]

As Baltimore's population swelled, hospitals became crowded. The city's civilian population increased by 134,000 people between April 1940 and November 1943.[12] At Johns Hopkins, the staff of the Diagnostic Clinic saw a 50 percent increase in the number of admissions (from 1,879 in 1940 to 2,708 in 1945).[13] While this was happening, the major hospitals were becoming severely understaffed as large numbers of medical stu-dents, nurses, and physicians left to serve with the Allied forces. Mary-land sent 242,023 women and men into the military.[14] Johns Hopkins organized two hospital units, as did the University of Maryland; all four saw service in the Pacific theater of war.[15]

Personnel from the medical schools at Johns Hopkins and the University of Maryland also made important contributions to the war effort through research. During these years, they and their colleagues made significant advances in medical science — in surgery, in blood transfusions, in the field of tropical diseases, and in vaccines and antibiotics.[16] On the battlefronts, it became clear that tremendous improvements in medical treatment had been accomplished since the previous world war. The mortality rate from wounds, for example, was reduced by 50 percent. In the 1940s, blood and blood products were much more readily available; sulfonamides and then penicillin enabled physicians to cope with battlefield infections; field hospital and triage organization was greatly improved, as were the facilities for transporting the wounded.[17]

By the end of the war in 1945, Marylanders had good reason to believe that government-supported, large-scale programs in science and technology had been key ingredients in the Allied victory. They were ready to believe, too, that similar efforts would enable the United States to solve many of its peacetime problems, including those involving disease, in new ways. These convictions and elite support for new approaches to medical science led to the creation of a large, federally subsidized system for promoting research. During the postwar era, this new system had a decisive influence on medicine in Maryland.

A New Era of Expansion

A long era of prosperity followed the Allied victory in World War II, and Maryland benefited from two decades of economic expansion. After a brief phase of adjustment to peacetime conditions, employment in the state steadily increased as the commercial, governmental, construction, and financial sectors of the economy generated new jobs and income. The birth rate in Maryland and across the United States shot up in what became known as the "baby boom" years. Maryland's population increased by 11.6 percent during the 1940s, by 32.3 percent during the 1950s, and by another 26.5 percent in the 1960s. This kind of increase over three decades resulted in a greatly increased demand for consumer goods.[18] The growth, however, was unevenly distributed; rural areas were losing population to towns, cities, and suburbs; meanwhile, Baltimore City had begun to lose out to the Baltimore and Washington suburbs. This demographic shift was partly mirrored by a medical profession that had, since the prewar years, been moving away from the rural and into the urban areas.[19] While developments such as this caused problems for those who remained in the country, for the state economy as a whole, these were favorable years of low inflation and steady economic expansion.[20]

The population increases put pressure on the medical system while the prosperity enabled Americans to finance an impressive expansion of a new framework of public and nonprofit institutions dedicated to research in the medical sciences. As a result, the United States became a world leader in this and other areas of scientific inquiry for the first time in the nation's history. New developments in virology, cell tissue culture, biochemistry, and enzymology were followed by astonishing breakthroughs in molecular genetics and recombinant DNA technology. The results included a new understanding of disease at the molecular level, as well as new diagnostic capabilities. Meanwhile, surgery was being transformed by a combination of technological developments and the experience gained first under wartime conditions and then in such leading centers as Johns Hopkins and the University of Maryland.[21]

At the forefront of the developments in medical science was the National Institutes of Health (NIH) in Bethesda, Maryland.[22] NIH became the core of a vast, loosely linked research system that included hospitals, universities, medical schools, public health facilities, industry, and individual practitioners. The scientists and physicians working in this system were able to produce groundbreaking results across a variety of biomedical fronts, making the NIH one of the world's leading research institutions. NIH was a flexible organization that attracted large numbers of outstanding researchers, many of whom spent a few years in Bethesda and then carried their research forward in other settings. Whether working at NIH or in other establishments, they continued to communicate through an elaborate network of personal contacts, professional associations, and journals.[23]

The flow of information in this expanding system was overwhelming, but fortunately Maryland had a related national institution dedicated to preserving and organizing medical information. The National Library of Medicine (NLM) grew out of the Surgeon General's library, which John Shaw Billings had meticulously built up in the post–Civil War years. By the 1940s, the library already included a very extensive collection, but the additions in the years following 1945 were staggering. Finally, in 1962, the government moved the library to specially constructed facilities in Bethesda. The NLM gives Maryland doctors and medical scientists access to an enormous body of worldwide data.[24] It also contains one of the world's largest medical history collections and, as such, is of great value to scholars throughout the United States and abroad.[25]

At Johns Hopkins, the increased federal support for biomedical research had a significant effect on the medical school, gradually shifting the balance away from clinical services and toward research personnel and programs. In addition to providing grants for specific projects, the federal government began to extend funding to training programs. By 1968, the Medical School was receiving almost $28 million from research grants, an increase of over $25 million since 1947.[26] Hopkins researchers during these years produced work of fundamental importance in (among others) the neurological sciences, immunology, studies of renal function, enzymology, the biochemistry of the cell, pediatric surgery, transplantation, reproductive endocrinology, and biomedical engineering. The number of full-time faculty members and postdoctoral fellows increased, and major building programs followed as Hopkins took full advantage of the nation's newfound willingness to support innovation in the medical sciences.[27]

Each scientist and postdoctoral fellow had a particular story to tell us, as did each of the programs, departments, and divisions of Johns Hopkins. None of these individual histories would be truly representative of the changes that took place during this era of growth, but seen individually, they can be considered as illustrative of what was happening at the research powerhouse that was being created in East Baltimore. It is in that spirit that I offer a brief description of one such clinical researcher and his work.

Dr. John Eager Howard, the great-great-grandson of a hero of the American Revolutionary War, was a graduate of the Johns Hopkins Medical School. After a few years of experience at the Massachusetts General Hospital, he returned to Hopkins, was appointed to a faculty position in 1934, and launched his clinical studies of hypertension and renal disease. His work led to improvements in the diagnosis of unilateral renal disease, to extensive studies of tumors that possess endocrine-like activity, to an improved understanding of calcium metabolism and kidney stones, and to new approaches to therapy for diabetic acidosis. In 1964 he received a Modern Medicine Award, and four years later the Passano Foundation named Howard as the twenty-eighth scientist to become a foundation laureate.[28]

John Eager Howard's career marked a significant crossroad at Hopkins. His research was solidly grounded in the clinical tradition, but his explorations, in their later stages, crossed the border into fundamental biochemical research on, for instance, steroids. That latter style of research was already under way in the laboratories of scientists like Albert Lester Lehninger and would, in the years that followed, take the leading role in the School of Medicine at Hopkins. Lehninger, who directed the Department of Physiological Chemistry, discovered the role that mitochondria play in respiratory metabolism; he also conducted fundamental studies of energy-coupling mechanisms involving oxidative phosphorylation in the cell. His work opened a new research pathway in the analysis of cell metabolism.[29]

The university's School of Hygiene and Public Health experienced a similar expansion in the postwar era. New departments and divisions were added, along with a substantial number of additional senior faculty members. Here, too, research—often with an epidemiological thrust—and the grants that sustained it became central to the school's mission.[30]

While Hopkins was gaining national and international recognition for its research, the University of Maryland Medical School was steadily developing its own areas of scientific expertise. During this postwar era, it became evident to anyone concerned enough to study the case that Abraham Flexner had been wrong when he had advocated concentrating all of Maryland's medical education in one institution. Dr. Theodore E. Woodward, who had graduated from the University of Maryland program and went on to chair the Division of Medicine at that institution for twenty-five years, was one of those who led his school into the new era of research. Typical of the programs that were evolving in the postwar years was one that focused on scrub typhus fever (with Woodward directing the clinical studies). A three-sided alliance involving the University of Maryland, the U.S. Army Medical Service Graduate School, and the Institute of Medical Research in Kuala Lumpur conducted this study, which established the first cure for this infectious disease. The discovery was significant enough to win nomination for a Nobel prize.[31]

Equally notable was the research conducted by Dr. R Adams Cowley.[32] Cowley was too young to participate directly in World War II medical action, but this young heart surgeon learned a great deal from its immediate aftermath and from subsequent American military engagements. While practicing his profession in France in 1946, he was demoralized by the seemingly callous manner in which field hospital triage functioned. Although it was obviously better than the systems it had replaced, the triage of that day still set aside to die some of the most severely injured patients. They were sacrificed to devote attention to those whose chances of survival were better.

Cowley thought they could do better than that, and he also decided that experience in the distant past pointed to a solution. A century earlier most surgeons had profoundly grooved in their minds the fact that speed was of the essence. The availability of anesthesia had dulled that sense, but Cowley decided that it needed to be restored. He became convinced that excellent surgical techniques should be performed with rapidity to prevent shock and raise the odds of survival.[33]

Back in Maryland, Cowley pushed his explorations in surgery and in animal studies.[34] Why, he asked, did so many patients survive heart surgery only to succumb to shock, infection, coma, and death within hours or days? "What we've discovered," he concluded, "is that if you stay in shock for very long, you're dead. Maybe you'll die in ten minutes or maybe you'll die next week, but you're dead. So if you're in shock we have to work fast. You've got, at most, sixty minutes. If I can get to you, and stop your bleeding, and restore your blood pressure, within an hour of your accident . . . then I can probably save you. I call that the golden hour."[35]

In 1961, Cowley organized a high-tech, two-room laboratory in the hospital where patients who were dying were closely monitored. In the Clinical Shock Trauma Unit, as it was known, the basic aim was to study death. As patients fell further and further into shock, every possible vital sign and metabolic action was measured and recorded by the doctors and nurses. While many died as expected, about half—surprisingly—survived. By monitoring their status closely, the medical attendants were able to change the patients' blood oxygen levels and buffers regularly, keeping them alive. By 1963, his results were so impressive that the Department of Health, Education and Welfare provided Cowley with $800,000 toward building the trauma unit he envisaged.[36]

In subsequent years, Cowley's Shock Trauma Unit became a model for hospitals across the country and in numerous other nations. It was a tribute to the dogged determination of one medical innovator and his supporters. It was a product more of powerful medical convictions than of professional diplomacy. It developed, not by coincidence, in a state system of hospitals that was decentralized, loosely coordinated, and thus open to the influence of a medical entrepreneur.[37]

Maryland's hospitals, which had grown with the state's population and economy, continued to thrive in the postwar years. By 1954, there were seventeen hospitals in Baltimore alone (including City Hospitals); their bed capacity ranged from 903 at Johns Hopkins to only 86 at Doctors' Hospital, and together this complex array of institutions logged over 1.25 million patient days that year. The occupancy rate varied from a high of 86.5 percent at Mercy to a low of 53.8 percent at Baltimore City Hospitals. The rates at Johns Hopkins and University, the city's two largest institutions, were 82 percent and 79 percent, respectively.[38]

Baltimore City maintained its hospitals, and the state government sustained University Hospital; the remaining fifteen were privately owned and operated on a nonprofit basis. Religious denominations owned and operated eight of the private organizations. One, Provident Hospital and Free Dispensary, continued to function exclusively for African-American patients, and ten others "admitted Negroes as in-patients in 1953." State-aided care had become important by this time, and Johns Hopkins, Mercy, and Provident were the leading providers of welfare-financed medical care in the state.[39] Meanwhile, more and more Marylanders were covered by Blue Cross plans, which in 1947 charged only two dollars for a family membership that included maternity care.[40] Federal funding had also promoted the expansion of the system, providing over $5 million to support additions and improvements to hospitals in Baltimore and the rest of the state between 1948 and 1952. The institutions receiving cost-sharing grants ranged from a new Garrett County Memorial Hospital, to new health centers in Harford, Saint Mary's, and Anne Arundel Counties, to the Associated Jewish Charities' new tuberculosis hospital in Baltimore.[41]

At Provident, the staff had created an intricate network of informal relationships with other medical personnel and institutions in the state. Provident residents were able to attend postgraduate courses at the University of Maryland School of Medicine, as well as some departmental staff conferences at the Johns Hopkins Hospital. These links were maintained by the chiefs of the medical and surgical services at the African-American hospital, both of whom were members of the faculty at Hopkins, and by the chiefs of obstetrical and pediatric service, who were professors at the University of Maryland. Provident aligned with Morgan State College and the Henryton TB Sanatorium to provide training to its nursing students.[42] While these informal ties could not make up for the segregation that existed in medicine, as it did in most other aspects of Maryland society in the 1950s, they do suggest that important physicians were attempting to change conditions some years before the civil rights movement blossomed in the state and nation.

Throughout the rest of the state, there were twenty-five general hospitals. Few communities were building new institutions during these years of expansion, but substantial efforts were made to construct additions to the existing facilities. All of these hospitals were regulated by the state under a licensing program that was introduced in 1945.[43] Although Maryland's population growth was taking place largely in the Baltimore-Washington suburbs, the hospital facilities on the Eastern Shore and in western Maryland were able during these years to upgrade and expand their facilities. Peninsula General (one of the hospitals we considered in a previous chapter) was able to benefit from the new sources of government funding, as did one of its much larger counterparts in Baltimore, the University of Maryland Hospital.[44]

One of the reasons more beds were needed throughout the state was the relatively long period that patients stayed in the hospital. In the 1950s, the average length of stay was between eight and nine days, and for patients unable to pay for their care, the average was over fourteen days. Patients and sometimes their families resisted discharge, often for financial reasons; at times, bureaucratic impediments kept patients in the hospitals longer than they needed to be there. Whatever the reason, the long stays put economic pressure on the entire hospital system, pressure that was beginning to be studied but was not yet a critical problem during this long era of expansion and prosperity.[45]

During these years, many of the state's hospitals extended their involvement in the burgeoning field of mental health, a discipline that had been popularized by the recognition of psychological trauma incurred during the war.[46] There was an "explosion"—to use Gerald Grob's word—in studies of the mentally ill. It was no coincidence that, in 1946, the U.S. government passed the National Mental Health Act and shortly thereafter established the National Institute of Mental Health.[47] In the immediate aftermath of the war, the state Board of Mental Health developed a construction program that would substantially increase the number of state hospital beds devoted to patients with psychiatric problems. By the early 1950s, there were seventeen special hospitals with over ten thousand beds devoted exclusively to mental health.[48]

These were, as well, years of expansion and progress in public health. In Baltimore, where many of the state's most serious problems existed, the city Health Department was able virtually to eradicate diphtheria. In 1920, the department had examined 60,000 specimens for diphtheria organisms, and the annual rate per 100,000 was almost 185. With the development of an effective toxin-antitoxin and the implementation of an efficient public program for distribution of the preventive medicine through private physicians and clinics, the city cut the average number of cases to 17 by 1950–54 and 1 (in a transient family) by 1956.[49]

Baltimore's organization was part of what had become by this time a fairly elaborate set of public health institutions. The State Department of Health coordinated its work with county-level advisory committees, county health departments, private physicians, and other government agencies. In 1951 and again in 1966, the state reviewed and revised the organization of this system to improve public health operations in an era in which federal involvement was steadily increasing. "Public health agencies are doing more and spending more," the 1966 report said, "yet opportunities and demands for services continue to multiply." The state was confronting the "paradox of progress"; each advance seemed to foster new demands for service.[50]

The "progress" was impressive. The state had taken part in the mass immunization programs against poliomyelitis in the early 1960s and was continuing to push for 100 percent vaccination among preschool-age children.[51] While 97 percent of the school-age children had been vaccinated against smallpox, many parents were still waiting until school enrollment to get their children immunized. The same was true for diphtheria, pertussis, and tetanus, as well as measles, for which a vaccine had recently been developed. In an effort to cope with this latter deficiency, the state department, Med Chi, the local health organizations, and the Jaycees had launched a joint campaign ("End Measles Menace") that had already vaccinated sixty-five thousand children.[52] To many, it seemed that the combination of new preventive medicines, vigorous public health action, progress in medical research, expansion of the hospital system, and advances in medical education were lifting the state over a significant threshold. Maryland seemed to be realizing the full benefits of the Therapeutic Revolution.

An Era of Tensions and Trials

Rather unexpectedly, the long period of growth and optimism came to an end for Maryland and the rest of the nation in the 1970s. Oil shocks and inflation created new hardships for consumers and businesses alike. American firms encountered competition from foreign companies that were often more efficient and innovative. Leading industries such as automobiles and steel lost market shares to their overseas competitors, and unemployment increased in the eastern cities, Baltimore included. The economic setting for medicine in Maryland was transformed from one of optimism and growth to one in which new concerns for economy and efficiency threatened traditional institutions and practices.

In the 1970s, Maryland and the entire country began to go through a period of restructuring and reorientation that is still going on in the late 1990s. For the first time since the Great Depression of the 1930s, large numbers of middle-class Marylanders found their lives disrupted by political and economic changes that they could barely understand, let alone control. White-collar and blue-collar workers had much in common as prosperity faded in the 1970s. In government, in the private sector, in education, and in what came to be identified as the health-care industry change became the norm. The pressures to adapt to new conditions in new ways reshaped all of the institutions and affected most of the individuals involved in providing and receiving medical care in Maryland.

Centripetal Forces

One of the basic responses to this new situation was organizational change. At the forefront of that transition were the health maintenance organizations (HMOs). They were, in part, a response to the need to spread risks and cut costs in the provision of health care. They were not new. In fact, such organizations had a relatively long history. What was new was the manner in which they mounted a challenge to the traditional individual practices that had long characterized health care in the state.[53] HMOs disrupted the relationships with clients that medical practitioners had long maintained and that many (if not most) thought were an essential aspect of protecting the health of Marylanders.

What was driving the change? To some, the answer was the system of third-party payments that had steadily pushed up medical costs faster than the rate of inflation and certainly faster than the increase in the incomes of most Marylanders. To others, the answer was the overexpansion of a system of medical provision and research that could simply no longer be sustained in an era of fierce competition and resistance to further expansion of governmental expenditures. To yet others, the answer rested in the inevitable necessity to bring to health care some of the efficiencies that had long been realized through economies of scale and scope in other parts of the American political economy. Technical and scientific change in modes of treatment also pressed for new institutional arrangements.

Whatever the factors driving this transformation, the transition to managed health care took place very quickly and more completely than most had anticipated would be the case. Seen in the historical perspective of Maryland's medicine over the past two centuries, this was the fastest and most dramatic transition health care in the state had ever experienced. It took place much faster, for instance, than the turn-of-the-century transition to scientific medicine grounded in the germ theory of disease. As one might expect, rapid change created a great deal of tension within the medical profession and the institutions we have been describing in this history.[54]

Nor did the changes stop there. Pharmaceutical benefit organizations (PBOs) began to transform another element of health care. These organizations handled pharmaceutical purchases for more and more citizens in this state, as in others. These businesses developed formularies that were used to determine which drugs were most economical. The companies signed up large numbers through employer health plans and used their bargaining power to lower prices, much as the chain stores had many years ago in the grocery business.

Both HMOs and PBOs cut into the close, personal relationships that existed between many physicians and their patients. Of course, those personal ties had already been impinged upon by specialization and by the tendency of many urban Marylanders to turn to hospital emergency wards for their medical attention.[55] But the new health-care organizations took those changes to another level, leaving many doctors concerned that they were being forced to abandon an essential personal element that had long characterized the profession.[56]

The new drive to increase efficiency at the cost of personal relationships had a dramatic effect on hospitals. They were already being affected by successful efforts to reduce hospital stays. In Maryland, as elsewhere, these efforts left the state with many surplus hospital beds, as did the use of drugs instead of hospital treatments for mental problems.[57] At the Liberty Health System (descendent of the Provident Hospital and Free Dispensary and the Lutheran Hospital), the pressures were felt particularly acutely because the institution had a very high percentage of indigent patients.[58] In fact, however, this new health-care environment affected every hospital in the state, including Johns Hopkins and the University of Maryland.

The transition to new styles of organization had a significant influence, too, on medical education. As more and more Marylanders used managed health-care organizations, these institutions put more and more pressure on the teaching hospitals to reduce costs. Why, the HMOs asked, should they pay for the higher costs of a teaching hospital? Their profits were at stake, and they were likely now to turn to the lowest-cost provider.

As this happened, medical education came under another type of pressure. As education had become increasingly centralized and specialized in the second half of the twentieth century, doctors had become ever more concentrated in urban areas. Rural areas of this state and others suffered. Throughout the country, programs were established to offer financial encouragement to medical students who were willing to set up their practices in rural America upon graduation. These efforts, however, had very limited success. Most doctors who had trained in large urban hospitals had become accustomed to extensive, up-to-date facilities and to the specialties that often commanded more professional respect and almost always provided higher incomes than did general practice in a small town. This, however, left many patients without the service they needed, and some medical school administrations in Maryland and elsewhere continued to look for solutions to this persistent problem.[59] The University of Maryland, in particular, has attempted in recent years to develop new approaches to this aspect of medical care.[60]

Paradoxically, these changes were accompanied by a series of dramatic breakthroughs in medical science. Although leading institutions such as NIH were feeling the effect of budget cuts, biochemistry, enzymology, and molecular genetics were during these years producing a profoundly new understanding of human disease and its treatment.[61] At Hopkins, Victor McKusick was one of the founders of medical and clinical genetics, a field that has become central to medical science and that was carried forward in the school by Nobel laureates Daniel Nathans and Hamilton O. Smith. Their research and that of other distinguished Hopkins men and women researchers helped open a broad new front for scientific exploration.[62] Recombinant DNA technology is already being used to produce new vaccines and pharmaceuticals, as well as a new understanding of disease.[63] This process of discovery continues today and seems likely to produce changes in medicine comparable to those that took place at the beginning of the twentieth century.[64] At both Hopkins and the University of Maryland, these developments in medical science and the political economy of medicine reverberated through the systems of medical education, bringing changes in everything from curricula to personnel and building programs.[65]

Centrifugal Forces and Diversity

While these powerful changes were making for greater centralization in medicine, there was in Maryland a countercurrent that actually made for greater diversity in medical practice and personnel. The civil rights movement of the 1950s and 1960s began, for instance, to transform the role of African Americans in medical education and practice. At the Johns Hopkins Hospital, the number of African-American house officers increased steadily from seven in 1973–74 to twenty-nine by 1989–90. In nursing, the number increased from one in 1984–85 to eighteen (8 percent of the class) by 1993–94. By 1986, 10 percent of the medical students and 5 percent of the house staff were African Americans.[66] The figures were even higher at the University of Maryland, which had moved faster to accommodate African-American students in the 1970s.[67]

For a change, young African Americans in the state did not lack role models in medicine. A few persons in particular stand out. Roland T. Smoot was a graduate of the Howard University Medical School and a member of the Provident Hospital medical staff. He also served as an assistant professor of medicine at both Johns Hopkins and the University of Maryland School of Medicine. An active member of Med Chi for many years, Smoot became in 1983 the first African-American president of the Faculty.[68] The change at Med Chi was rather startling. In 1947, Dr. W. Houston Toulson had written to the American Medical Association (AMA) to inquire about "the admission of negro physicians." Toulson said, "It seems fitting that the negro not be denied educational advantages and post-graduate advancement, but in the South it is difficult to find a way to arrange this without causing a certain social embarrassment, particularly, inasmuch as in many counties the meetings are held in the physicians' homes and many of the other meetings are dinner gatherings." In the years that followed, Med Chi, indeed, found a way to avoid "social embarrassment" and in 1983 to elect an African American to its highest position of leadership.[69]

By the 1970s, this significant shift in race relations was already taking place, but as Dr. Levi Watkins discovered, it had yet to work its way very far down in Maryland society. Watkins, who was born in Montgomery,

Alabama, was no stranger to segregation. In 1970, after graduating from Vanderbilt Medical School (having been the first African American to matriculate at that institution), he came to Johns Hopkins as an intern. At Hopkins, he discovered that "most of the blacks were in the basement. They were custodians or they worked in the cafeteria, not on the staff or faculty."[70] As Watkins knew, he was an unusual faculty member at Hopkins and across the nation. By his early thirties, he had become one of America's few African-American cardiac surgeons and one of the very few working in academe. In that position he was conscious of his ability to serve as a role model, and as a member of the medical school's admission board, he traveled the country encouraging minority students to apply to Hopkins.[71]

By the 1980s, the situation in Maryland and in medicine had changed even more. Thus, Dr. Benjamin S. Carson could in 1984 become the director of pediatric neurosurgery at the Johns Hopkins Medical Institutions. He was the youngest person to have reached that position in the United States, and three years later he became internationally renowned for an astonishing accomplishment in surgery. He and his team separated the conjoint Binder twins, two seven-month-old boys who were fused at the back of their heads. The infants had been flown from Germany for this procedure, after their mother had been unable to find another surgeon who thought both of her babies could survive independently. Carson did, but his procedure required a specially constructed operating room and a seventy-member surgical team. The head of that team was a young African-American man who had grown up in a poor, single-parent household, had chosen one of the most challenging fields in medicine, and had become a hero to his patients and their parents, to medical students, and to young people of all races.[72]

The gender as well as the racial balance in Maryland medicine had by that time also shifted markedly. Slightly over one-quarter of the state's 21,781 physicians were women, with most of them practicing in either Montgomery County or Baltimore City (like their male peers).[73] They, too, had many role models to emulate, both in research and in the practice of medicine. One of the most prominent was Helen B. Taussig, who at Hopkins had been a partner with Alfred Blalock in developing a revolutionary procedure for dealing with congenital heart disease in newborns, the "blue baby" operation.[74]

Diversity extended as well to the basic approaches Maryland physicians were using as they practiced medicine. It is easy to see the development of our modern systems of health care as a steady line of success with, perhaps, an occasional delay in discovery. But anyone who studies medicine over the long run knows that the process of change is not linear. While scientific medicine has made great strides in recent decades, old methods have often still proven to be useful. Not all new methods have been clear improvements from the patient's perspective, so alternative medicines have continued to thrive, even though they had been rejected by the majority of the state's physicians and medical researchers. In the 1950s and 1960s, for example, most doctors in Maryland dismissed alternative therapies and the use of vitamin supplements. Today, however, we see a marked revival of alternative medicines and a strong interest in everything from herbs, to vitamins, to more unusual products such as shark cartilage. The Saint John's Wort that was used in ancient Greece and employed by herbalists when Med Chi was founded has recently been "rediscovered" as an effective cure in many instances of mild to moderate depression. Evidently, it raises serotonin levels in the brain. The use of leeches has also enjoyed something of a revival in some reputable medical circles.

Complementary medicine seems to be on the rise over the last few decades across the state, perhaps indicating that the old anxieties about medical boundaries have at last gone away. Acupuncture has become extremely popular as one form of alternative therapy, and the University of Maryland has established a new Complementary Medicine Program. Instead of attempting to drive alternative medicine out of Maryland, practitioners involved in this innovative scheme have embraced other ways of treating their patients. They have attempted to integrate the best that orthodox western medicine has to offer with the best that unorthodox and nonwestern medical systems can bring to therapeutics.

Like Maryland's Shock Trauma Unit, the Complementary Medicine Program was the first of its kind in the United States and, like the Shock Trauma Unit, it was initially developed largely as the brainchild of one determined leader. Like Cowley, Dr. Brian Berman was unwilling to accept the status quo; he, too, went beyond the current boundaries of medical practice and education; he also had spent time abroad and imported ideas he had gathered in Europe. Berman, who was born in 1950 in Freeport, New York, had received his medical degree from the Royal College of Surgeons in Dublin, Ireland. He then served his residency in family medicine at the University of Maryland from 1979 to 1981. While this was an excellent residency program, Berman became frustrated with some of the limitations of modern orthodox therapeutics, especially in the treatment of patients suffering from chronic pain.

Seeking new approaches, Berman went outside the regular medical profession. He worked from 1984 through 1987 in London, where certain branches of alternative medicine were well established and he could receive sound training. In England, he studied acupuncture and homeopathy, while also conducting clinical work in a private practice. Returning to Baltimore, he established in 1991 a program in which he and others could continue to explore what had now come to be known as complementary (not alternative) medicine. As the program's report indicates, its initial diagnostic areas of interest were "dysfunction or illness due to chronic pain and stress. The initial therapies of interest to CMP [the Complementary Medicine Program] are traditional systems of medicine such as Traditional Chinese Medicine, homeopathy, manipulation, electromagnetic and mind/body therapies."[75]

There was still tension between those dedicated to scientific and to complementary medicine, but the battles of the 1990s are muted in comparison with those that raged in the state during the nineteenth century. The University of Maryland program had the support of both the state government and the School of Medicine. Berman launched CMP with a million dollar grant from the Laing Foundation, which was matched by the university, and by 1997 he had collected a staff of twenty-eight persons. In 1995, the NIH's Office of Alternative Medicine provided additional funding and made CMP one of the nation's ten Centers for Alternative Medicine Pain Research and Evaluation.[76] In its new official capacity, alternative medicine had clearly arrived by the 1990s.

A Crisis in Public Health

Neither alternative nor scientific medicine had any answer for the new public health crisis that Maryland encountered in the 1980s and 1990s. Reorganized by the state and revitalized by the new preventive medicines of the 1960s and 1970s, the State Department of Health and Mental Hygiene and its supporting organizations in the counties and cities seemed capable of dealing with most of the situations it encountered. Like other states, Maryland had attacked the problem of "overreliance on major institutions" and confronted the pressing issues of environmental health. Dr. Neil Solomon, secretary of the Maryland State Department of Health and Mental Hygiene, had confidently guided all of the state's public health programs toward an "holistic approach."[77]

The state department thus pressed forward with its multiphased effort to improve vaccination levels. In Maryland in 1977, despite the availability of vaccines, a mere 58 percent of two-year-old children had received all of the protection provided against such preventable infectious diseases as measles, mumps, rubella, polio, diphtheria, whooping cough, and tetanus. The problem in this state and others was so serious that President Jimmy Carter and U.S. Secretary of Health, Education and Welfare Joseph Califano launched a national campaign. In Maryland, State Senator Rosalie Silber Abrams, chair of the Maryland Immunization Action Committee, and Dr. Solomon started a similar effort.[78] Plenty of vaccine was available, both for those who could afford it and for those who could not; the problem was that parents frequently did not bother to have their children vaccinated until it was required for them to enter school.[79] With the right kind of directed effort, however, it seemed likely that the state's public health organizations could deal with that problem. It was well within the state's capabilities. But the new crisis of the 1980s was not.

When the AIDS pandemic reached Maryland, at around the same time that it struck much of the rest of the United States, it was baffling to everyone. Americans, like the inhabitants of other modern, Western countries, were suddenly hit with a very hard lesson. The majority of people in those countries had largely come to assume that, with the great resources available and the great expertise in their health-care systems, nothing like the cholera pandemic of the nineteenth century could happen in the late twentieth century. They gradually came to see that this was not the case and that they were not as secure as they thought they were.

To the community of health-care providers and scholars, another important lesson would be learned from AIDS. While some advocated centralizing medical and scientific resources and others favored decentralization, attempts to understand and cope with the disease, as well as to develop prophylaxes, treatments, and cures, soon made it apparent that society needed a variety of highly concentrated efforts spread across a very broad front. In effect, both centralization and decentralization were needed to deal with this crisis. Too little was known to concentrate all of the resources and personnel on one approach. But each of the most promising approaches needed substantial support if it was going to succeed. Fortunately, in this instance, there was very little competition between the two approaches because it quickly became obvious that everyone needed all the help they could get.

The U.S. government's centralized facilities and personnel in the Public Health Service (PHS), the NIH, and the Centers for Disease Control

(CDC) made crucial contributions to the response to AIDS. The government reporting system indicated during the summer of 1981 to designated Surgeon General Dr. C. Everett Koop that it had recently received reports of twenty-six gay men who had an extremely rare form of cancer known as Kaposi's sarcoma. By that August, the CDC provided the grim news that the organization had received reports of one hundred cases of the new immunodeficiency disease and that nearly half of the afflicted had died.[80] In the late twentieth century, a 50 percent mortality rate from what seemed to be a communicable disease was almost unimaginable. And worse news lay ahead. It soon became clear that over time hardly anyone survived.

In the ensuing effort to understand where and how this particular disease arose, centralized organizations again played a vital role. Their reporting and epidemiological analyses were essential. In the United States, by the end of 1986, over 27,000 cases of the disease had been reported.[81] By the close of the following year, there were 923 reported cases of AIDS in Maryland alone.[82] By the end of the decade, 43,339 cases had been recorded in the United States.[83] And this was in a society where there could be little doubt that AIDS was underreported because this particular malady carried an even greater social stigma than other sexually transmitted diseases; for a time it was associated primarily with the gay population and with drug users. Indeed, it was initially termed GRID, gay-related immunodeficiency.[84] That was an extremely unfortunate association because it contributed to the lack of public interest in the infection. As the disease's epidemiology was unraveled, some of the stigma dissipated, but sadly, some of that apathy turned to antipathy as individuals who were evidently not gay became ill.[85]

Gradually, the nation's complex information networks were able to convince much of the American population that groups other than gay men were being infected with HIV. Gradually, the epidemiology of the disease and the different routes of its transmission were elucidated: sexual contacts, needle usage, exposure to blood and blood products. Infected mothers, it became apparent, were passing the infection to their babies. By this time, the acronym GRID had been discarded and, after some discussion, replaced by AIDS (acquired immune deficiency syndrome). Government agencies could never act quickly enough for those who are affected by a disease, but in historical terms, the government acted swiftly this time. In addition to the PHS, NIH, and CDC, the National Cancer Institute and the National Institute of Allergy and Infectious

Diseases became deeply involved in the effort to bring this new plague under control.[86]

In December 1985, Maryland Governor Harry Hughes assembled the Governor's Task Force on AIDS, consisting of representatives from the medical, public health, and scientific communities, lawyers, state agency personnel, and lay persons. The group met weekly with the goal of determining the best policies to cope with HIV/AIDS around the state. One of the early recommendations of the task force was that AIDS was such a sensitive illness that confidentiality was an unusually important issue and, as a result, its members recommended against mandatory public reporting. This was accepted by the Maryland General Assembly, which made reports of AIDS cases available only under seal to courts.[87]

Information was, of course, needed to find appropriate methods to treat and perhaps prevent this terrifying pandemic. The earlier the virus could be detected the better, at least from the perspective of government agencies, scientists, public health workers, and blood bank staffs.[88] There was still no treatment available, and while the NIH and some of the large pharmaceutical companies were scrambling to try to develop a vaccine, a cure, or a palliative, identification was clearly needed by all of these parties. By March 1985, that problem was partly solved by the Food and Drug Administration's introduction of the ELISA test, which could be used to indicate the presence of HIV antibodies in the blood.[89]

In the years of work that followed, one could see the virtues of both centralization and decentralization. Long-term government support for basic research played a crucial role in this country and abroad. In a surprisingly short period, investigators accumulated a massive data bank as well as breakthrough discoveries that have been crucial in the attack upon this unusual retrovirus. In France in 1983, Louis Montagnier and his team of researchers isolated the retrovirus responsible for AIDS. Within months thereafter, Robert Gallo at the NIH also reported his laboratory's discovery of the virus.[90]

Private, nonprofit, and public agencies then attempted to develop the vaccines or antiviral compounds that would enable physicians to cope with the infection. Sometimes cooperating and frequently competing, pharmaceutical companies in the United States and abroad experimented with vaccines and various types of enzyme inhibitors that might destroy or control the virus. A diverse array of facilities in Maryland continues to address the problems HIV has created. The NIH has become one of the leading centers for analyzing how HIV works and how to block its

deadly activity. Dr. Anthony Fauci (NIH) and Dr. Robert Gallo (now at
the University of Maryland) have played leading roles in the research on
HIV. By the time effective antiviral agents had been developed by pharmaceutical companies, Dr. John Bartlett at Johns Hopkins had become
one of the international leaders in supervising treatment and conducting clinical studies of the disease. Less visible are all the state and local
agencies that have been helping AIDS patients and their loved ones day
by day.[91] Organizations such as HERO in Baltimore provide counseling, as well as practical assistance. Diverse, often locally based groups
frequently lack substantial resources, but they are still able to cope with
the immediate needs of those with AIDS. Many Maryland organizations
have been active counseling patients who have contracted the disease and
organizing prevention instruction.[92] Privately organized groups, such as
the Sabin Foundation and the Ryan White Fund, have also made essential contributions in the widespread efforts to cope with this disease.

The struggle against HIV/AIDS provides an appropriate place to end
this narrative of medicine in Maryland over the past two hundred years.
The current efforts to deal with this frightening infection have been
shaped by many of the developments discussed in the previous pages.
For one thing, the HIV/AIDS struggle illustrates very clearly how much
progress has been made in the scientific understanding of disease. In
a relatively short period, by historical standards, society has acquired a
substantial understanding of the etiology of the disease and the viral
entity that causes it. Maryland scientific leaders and institutions have
played leading roles in that intricate process of discovery, a process characterized by both cooperation and the type of rivalry that characterizes
all modern research systems. All of these institutions and researchers are
deeply embedded in the national and international systems of medical
science, systems that have become significantly more important since
World War II. Virtually every advance in Maryland medicine since that
time has taken place with support from outside the state. Although there
is no doubt that this support has improved the research done in Maryland, it has left the state's scientists hostage to developments that are
frequently beyond their control.

The problems this can create became particularly evident during the
recent phase of contraction and reorganization in Maryland medicine.
As a result, the progress made in understanding HIV/AIDS was not
matched by an increased ability to provide assistance to those suffering
from the infection or to develop and maintain successful prevention pro-

grams. The epidemiology of the disease also indicates that there is still much to do before racial and class lines in medicine are obliterated. In that sense, the HIV/AIDS crisis is an appropriate symbol of both the progress achieved and the problems remaining to be solved, in this state and others, as we near the end of the twentieth century.

Epilogue

M edicine in Maryland over the past two hundred years has been a
history of remarkable experimentation and change. As we have
seen in the previous chapters, there have been substantial changes in
ideas, institutions, and practices, many of which have involved the Medical and Chirurgical Faculty of Maryland and its members. They have
played leading roles in shaping many of these developments. As the
state's economy and population expanded, Maryland's capacity to sustain
innovations in medicine, as well as the need for change, both increased.
For several decades, the capacity lagged the need significantly, and this
gap gave rise to numerous experiments in public health, in education,
in hospital development, and in medical, dental, and pharmacological
practices. The authority of the state government provided a small measure of central control over these experiments in the first half of the
nineteenth century, but on balance, very little control was exercised and
the process of change continued to be ad hoc, even haphazard.

Throughout, medicine remained largely a local enterprise. Much of it
continued to be domestic, practiced by nonprofessionals, and grounded
in a variety of different therapeutic concepts. The regular medical profession held a relatively tenuous position in most settings, largely because it
had very little to offer in terms of treatment.

During the second half of the nineteenth century, this situation began to change, gradually at first and then more rapidly in the 1880s and 1890s. The primary factors reshaping medicine in Maryland were the rise of new medical sciences, which substantially expanded therapeutic and institutional capabilities. This inspired increasing confidence in the regular profession and exerted mounting pressure on the alternative medical sects and their institutions.

The pressure to conform to a modern scientific model became even greater in the early twentieth century, as symbolized by the Flexner Report of 1910. By following the dictates of Flexner without deviation, Maryland would have had a much narrower medical history. But the state and its professions opted for greater diversity than Flexner proposed, much to the advantage of its medical practitioners, their institutions, and its citizens. The diversity that seemed problematic to the medical elite proved favorable to the majority of the residents of this state over the long run. Marylanders, it would seem, have done a tolerably good job of balancing their desire for expertise and efficiency in medicine with their interest in preserving a democratic tradition and a diverse, innovative society. Certainly, the state has ranked among the leaders in the United States in fostering institutions that have created new medical knowledge over the past two hundred years.

Of course, the benefits of improved medical knowledge and therapeutics were never distributed evenly. Racial, class, regional, and gender differences remained decisive. Not until the post–World War II era did significant changes in these relationships take place, and even then — as we saw in the previous chapter — they continued to hold powerful sway.

In the recent past, the pace of change seems to have accelerated, making the tasks of Med Chi ever more difficult to perform at the same time that they were becoming more important to the profession. The explosion of new medical knowledge has transformed the health-care professions, their educational institutions, and their therapeutics. Much of that knowledge was generated by research institutions like Johns Hopkins and the University of Maryland; some of it now came from alternative sources that had once been denied legitimacy. The dual processes of centralization and decentralization were taking place simultaneously. While this furthered innovation, the reorganization of the profession's institutional and economic bases raised serious questions for practitioners, politicians, and patients.

Both processes seem likely to continue through the foreseeable future. On the one hand, the outlook for the development of new treatments is extremely favorable. On the other hand, however, pressures to economize on individual care and public health efforts make the future seem less attractive. Still, most of us can be very glad that, when we become ill or are injured at the end of the twentieth century, we have a much greater panoply of treatments available to us than we would have at the end of the eighteenth century. Certainly, we live much longer. Few Americans die from contaminants in their water supply. Few die from gangrene. Surgery is relatively safe and relatively pain-free. Many cancers are curable. Scarcely any women die in childbirth. Few children below the age of five die from once-common killers.

Hence, we head toward the millennium with a Janus-faced ego—looking back to the tremendous accomplishments that have given the average citizen a substantially longer life expectancy and looking with less certainty toward the future, wondering how our health-care system will cope with what is around the corner. HIV/AIDS, the Ebola scare, and resistant germs and viruses give us serious pause, as do the economic problems our society is facing.

The past fortunately provides some guideposts for coping. History suggests that we should not try to hold on to past ideas and institutions with too much dedication if we are going to remain creative. Janus was, after all, the Roman god of doorways, passages, and bridges. Medical professionals will have to find many new doors to open, new passages to explore, and new bridges to cross if the state's future is to be as productive as its past.

Notes

ONE: Conflicts and Compromises: Domestic Medicine, Orthodoxy,
Sectarianism, and Quackery, 1799–1899

1. William Faris Diary, 1792–1804, MS 2160, Maryland Historical Society.

2. This was also the case in the more rural areas of Great Britain, where a multitude of different practitioners was rarely at hand and professional boundaries were often acknowledged only in the breach.

3. See also the education and career of Dr. James Smith of Baltimore, as described in Whitfield J. Bell Jr., *The Colonial Physician and Other Essays* (New York: Science History Publications, 1975), 131–32.

4. Eugene Fauntleroy Cordell, *The Medical Annals of Maryland, 1799–1899* (Baltimore: Williams and Wilkens, 1903), 18.

5. Norman Gevitz, "Andrew Taylor Still and the Social Origins of Osteopathy," in Roger Cooter, ed., *Studies in the History of Alternative Medicine* (New York: St. Martin's Press, 1988), 155.

6. William G. Rothstein, "The Botanical Movement and Orthodox Medicine," in Norman Gevitz, ed., *Other Healers: Unorthodox Medicine in America* (Baltimore: Johns Hopkins University Press, 1988), 29–51.

7. The Shiplap House was built about 1715 and is one of the oldest surviving houses in Maryland. It was a waterfront tavern and is now a museum.

8. George B. Scriven, "Doctors, Drugs, and Apothecaries of Seventeenth Century Maryland," *Bulletin of the History of Medicine* 37, no. 6 (1963): 516–22.

9. Cordell, *Annals*, 13, 305.

10. Ibid., 652.

11. *Maryland Journal and Baltimore Advertiser,* Nov. 30, 1779, 1, notice dated: Baltimore, Nov. 28, 1779, from Ch. Wiesenthal, M. Haslett, John Boyd, Th. Andrews, S. S. Coale, F. Ridgeley, H. Beard, and John Labesius.

12. The term *quackery* often had a rather vague application during the nineteenth century. Physicians commonly used it to mean all attempts at medicine or healing or claims of special medical knowledge by persons who were not medically licensed. This, usually deliberately, missed the distinction between nonallopathic practitioners who received training in their particular sects and those who possessed no training. For the duration of this book, except in quotations, members of nonallopathic groups will be identified either by the sect name or by the terms *nonallopathic, unorthodox,* or *irregular,* despite the fact that to many in the nineteenth century nonallopathic medicine was their regular practice. The terms *quack* and *quackery* will be reserved for persons who were completely unqualified and untrained but who claimed to possess medical knowledge in their practice. In the latter instance, fraud was involved.

For a discussion of the application of the term *quackery,* see Roy Porter, "Before the Fringe: 'Quackery' and the Eighteenth-Century Medical Market," in Cooter, *History of Alternative Medicine,* 1–27.

13. *Maryland Journal and Baltimore Advertiser,* Nov. 25, 1785, 2.

14. *Maryland Journal and Baltimore Advertiser,* Dec. 13, 1785, 3.

15. *Maryland Journal and Baltimore Advertiser,* Dec. 23, 1785, 2.

16. Letter from Charles Frederick Wiesenthal in Behalf of the Faculty of Baltimore, Baltimore, Dec. 4, 1788, in *Maryland Journal and Baltimore Advertiser,* Dec. 5, 1788, 3; Cordell, *Annals,* 13–17.

17. Laws of Maryland, passed Jan. 20, 1799, Lib. JG, no. 3, fol. 224.

18. Ibid., sec. 4.

19. For an excellent discussion of jurisdiction in various professional settings, see Andrew Abbott, *The System of Professions: An Essay on the Division of Expert Labor* (Chicago: University of Chicago Press, 1988).

20. "An Act to Establish and Incorporate a Medical and Chirurgical Faculty," 1799, sec. 3; Cordell, *Annals,* 43. Persons incorporated at the time the act was passed into law on Jan. 20, 1799, were as follows:

Gustavus Brown, William Lanidale, Barton Tabbs, Elijah Jackson and William A. Roach of St. Mary's County; James M. Anderson, junior, Morgan Browne, junior, Edward Scott, Robert Geddes and Edward Warrell of Kent County; Charles Alexander Warfield, Richard Hopkins, Wilson Waters, Thomas Noble Stockett and William Murray of Anne-Arundel County; Thomas Bourne, Thomas Parran, Joseph Ireland, Daniel Rawlings and James Gray of Calvert County; John Parnham, Gustavus Richard Brown, Daniel Jenifer, John M. Daniel and Gerard Wood of

Charles County; Thomas Cradock, Thomas Love, John Cromwell, Philip Trapnell and Christopher Todd of Baltimore County; Perry E. Noel, Stephen Theodore Johnson, Tristram Thomas, and Ennalls Martin of Talbot County; Levin Irvin, Arnold Elzey, Ezekiel Haynie, John Woolford and Matthias Jones of Somerset County; Edward White, James Sulivane, Dorsey Wyvill, William Hays and Howes Goldsborough of Dorchester County; Abraham Mitchell, William Miller, Elisha Harrison, John Grome and John King of Cecil County; Richard J. Duckett, William Beanes, junior, William Marshall, William Baker and Robert Pottinger of Prince-George's County; Upton Scott, James Murray, John Thomas Shaaff and Reverdy Gheselin of the City of Annapolis; James Davidson, John Wells, Samuel Thompson, Robert Goldsborough and John Thomas of Queen-Anne's County; John Neille, Thomas Fassett, George Washington Purnell, John Purnell and John Huston of Worcester County; Philip Thomas, Francis Brown Sappington, William Hilleary, John Tyler and Joseph Sim Smith of Frederick County; John Archer, Thomas A. Birkhead, Elijah Davis and Thomas Archer of Harford County; Jesse Downes, John Young, junior, Benjamin Keene, Joseph Price and Henry Helm of Caroline County; George Brown, John Coulter, Miles Little John, George Buchanan, Lyde Goodwin, Ashton Alexander, Arthur Pue, Daniel Moores and Henry Stevenson of the City of Baltimore; Richard Pindell, Samuel Young, Peter Waltz, Jacob Schnievley and Zachariah Clagett of Washington County; Edward Gantt, Charles Worthington, Joseph Hall, Zadok Magruder, junior, James Anderson and Charles A. Beatty of Montgomery County; Benjamin Murrow, James Forbes and George Lynn of Allegany County.

21. "An Act to Establish a Medical and Chirurgical Faculty," sec. 3, p. 43; J. Thomas Scharf, *History of Baltimore City and County,* with a new introduction by Edward G. Howard (Baltimore: Regional Publishing, 1971), 741.

22. Richard Harrison Shryock, *Medical Licensing in America, 1650–1965* (Baltimore: Johns Hopkins Press, 1967), vii–19; "An Act to Establish a Medical and Chirurgical Faculty," sec. 6.

23. Shryock, *Medical Licensing in America,* 23–29. One of the responses was to organize on the national level by establishing the American Medical Association (1847). James G. Burrow, *A.M.A.: Voice of American Medicine* (Baltimore: Johns Hopkins Press, 1963); Paul Starr, *The Social Transformation of American Medicine: The Rise of a Sovereign Profession and the Making of a Vast Industry* (New York: Basic Books, 1982).

24. Scharf, *History of Baltimore City and County,* 742.

25. Christian E. Jensen, *Lives of Caroline County, Maryland, Physicians, 1774–1974* (Denton, Md.: Baker Printing, 1986), 147–48.

26. Theodore E. Woodward, *Carroll County Physicians of the Nineteenth and Early Twentieth Centuries* (Westminster, Md.: Historical Society of Carroll County, 1990), 49–50.

27. Laws of Maryland, 1838, chap. 281; Cordell, *Annals,* 102.

28. This was generally true throughout the United States; see Lamar Riley Murphy, *Enter the Physician: The Transformation of Domestic Medicine, 1760–1860* (Tuscaloosa: University of Alabama Press, 1991), 70–71.

29. James H. Cassedy, "Why Self-Help? Americans Alone with Their Diseases, 1800–1850," in Guenter B. Risse, Ronald L. Numbers, and Judith Walzer Leavitt, *Medicine without Doctors: Home Health Care in American History* (New York: Science History Publications/USA, 1977), 31–48.

30. John S. Haller Jr., *Kindly Medicine: Physio-medicalism in America, 1836–1911* (Kent, Ohio: Kent State University Press, 1997), 13–14.

31. Haller, *Kindly Medicine,* 15–16.

32. Murphy, *Enter the Physician,* 70–100; Gevitz, "Andrew Taylor Still," 157.

33. Haller, *Kindly Medicine,* 17; Dr. James H. Miller, "Thompsonalgia," report to the Trustees of the Baltimore County Alms House and address to the Friendly Botanic Society of Maryland, Jan. 16, 1836, Library of the Medical and Chirurgical Faculty of Maryland.

34. Shryock, *Medical Licensing in America,* 32; Walter I. Wardwell, *Chiropractic: History and Evolution of a New Profession* (St. Louis: Mosby Year Book, 1992), 25.

35. Constitution and Minutes of the Third Branch of the Thomsonian Friendly Botanical Society, March 3, 1835, Peter Perine Papers, MS 654, Maryland Historical Society. Peter Perine was a businessman engaged in the manufacture and sale of pottery.

36. James Stabler to Friends, Jan. 26, 1836, MS 147, box 18, Maryland Historical Society. It is unclear whether this letter was addressed to personal friends or to Stabler's Quaker Friends.

37. Maryland House of Delegates, Dr. Williams' Remarks on the Bill to Incorporate the Thomsonian National Infirmary, March 1835, in "Address of the Friends of the Thomsonian Botanic System of Medicine, to the People of Maryland, April 1835," 5, 12, 6–7, Library of the Medical and Chirurgical Faculty of Maryland. In May 1835, Dr. James H. Miller, physician to the Alms House of Baltimore County, used his annual report to castigate the Thomsonians and to establish the superiority of the "regulars." Miller was attempting to explain the higher mortality rates in the almshouse:

> The most prolific source is the too prevalent vulgar practice of over stimulation, by the steam and scalding portions of a now popular impyricism. The bare mention of this latter cause may to some seem invidious, but I trust I shall be shielded from all such imputations by you [the almshouse trustees], and those who know me, and are acquainted with the *sphere of private practice in which I move, a society far elevated above the influence of vulgar in-*

fatuation, both by intelligence and moral worth; yet in addressing you, the guardians of the class which requires protection from the arts of designing or misguided imposters, acting upon their native or acquired imbecility, I feel officially bound to render the outlines of the reasoning and *facts* upon which my declaration is founded.

Miller, "Thomsonalgia," 4 (Miller's emphasis).

38. Maryland House of Delegates, Williams' Remarks, 4.

39. For other experiences with Thomsonian treatment, see the letter from Isaac Briggs Jr. to his mother, Hannah Briggs, Forks of Patapsco, March 12, 1831, and the letter from Elizabeth Stabler to Isaac Briggs, Sharon, Md., Oct. 20, 1843; both in MS 147, Maryland Historical Society. Isaac Briggs Jr. said that he had suffered from "Rheumatism in my head . . . . In the evening I stopped at the boarding house of an acquaintance John Parry, a respectable pedagogue in Baltimore. He gave me some of the Rheumatic drops and which I applied both *ex* and *in*ternally and in 5 minutes and 3 and a half seconds the said pains which had hurted me were completely chased out and I aint hearn of 'em sence." It seems likely that Thomsonian treatments continued to be used long after the coherent sect had disappeared.

40. Isaac Briggs to Francis O. Stabler, Oct. 12, 1873, vertical files, Maryland Historical Society.

41. Roger Cooter, *The Cultural Meaning of Popular Science: Phrenology and the Organization of Consent in Nineteenth Century Britain* (Cambridge: Cambridge University Press, 1984).

42. Roger Cooter, *Phrenology in the British Isles: An Annotated, Historical Bibliography and Index* (Metuchen, N.J.: Scarecrow Press, 1989), vii–ix; Stephen Jay Gould, *The Mismeasure of Man* (New York: W. W. Norton, 1981), 92, 93, 97; David de Giustino, *Conquest of Mind: Phrenology and Victorian Social Thought* (London: Croom Helm, 1975); John D. Davies, *Phrenology. Fad and Science: A Nineteenth-Century American Crusade* (New Haven: Yale University Press, 1955).

43. Report of the first meeting of the Baltimore Phrenological Society, Feb. 17, 1827, MS 1102, Maryland Historical Society.

44. For an example see "The Mental Faculties, and the Relative Size of Their Organs in the Case of T. L. Stansbury," MS 2830, Maryland Historical Society.

45. "Report of a Case of Amativeness" [n.d., c. 1828], Maryland Historical Society.

46. Throughout this book the spelling *homeopathy* will be used except where its more popular nineteenth-century and European spelling, *homoeopathy,* is directly quoted or is part of a name. On eclecticism see William G. Rothstein, *American Physicians in the Nineteenth Century: From Sect to Science* (Baltimore: Johns Hopkins University Press, 1972), 217–29.

47. Lester S. King, *The Medical World of the Eighteenth Century* (Chicago: University of Chicago Press, 1958), 159–62; Samuel Hahnemann, *Organon of Medicine,*

trans. Jost Kunzli, Alain Naude, and Peter Pendleton (Los Angeles: J. P. Tarcher, 1982).

48. Hahnemann, *Organon of Medicine,* 58.

49. Rothstein, *American Physicians in the Nineteenth Century,* 154–56. The amounts were so small that, when the substances were tested by the regular profession, they frequently were found to contain no detectable active ingredients.

50. Harris L. Coulter, *Divided Legacy: A History of the Schism in Medical Thought,* 3 vols. (Washington, D.C.: McGrath Publishing, 1973); John Duffy, *The Healers: A History of American Medicine* (Urbana, N.Y.: McGraw-Hill, 1976), 115–16; Anne M. Clover, *Homoeopathy Reconsidered: A New Look at Hahnemann's Organon* (London: Victor Gollancz, 1989). For a guide to the sources, see Francesco Cordasco, *Homoeopathy in the United States: A Bibliography of Homoeopathic Medical Imprints, 1825–1925* (Fairview, N.J.: Junius-Vaughn Press, 1991). Wardwell, *Chiropractic,* 26.

51. Martin Kaufman, *Homeopathy in America: The Rise and Fall of a Medical Heresy* (Baltimore: Johns Hopkins Press, 1971), 29.

52. Martin S. Pernick, "The Calculus of Suffering in Nineteenth-Century Surgery," in Judith Walzer Leavitt and Ronald L. Numbers, eds., *Sickness and Health in America: Readings in the History of Medicine and Public Health* (Madison: University of Wisconsin Press, 1985), 104; John Ellis, *Family Homoeopathy* (New York: Boericke and Tafel, 1879).

53. Rothstein, *American Physicians in the Nineteenth Century,* 159–60. The homeopathic dispensary was in Baltimore. See Henry Janes to Ch. John Lee, Baltimore, Oct. 1, 1880, vertical file, Henry Janes, Maryland Historical Society. Janes and Pratt were members of the Board of Managers that had incorporated the previously private Baltimore Homeopathic Free Dispensary in 1877. Nine other prominent citizens, five of whom had M.D. degrees, joined them in that capacity. Report for the Baltimore Homeopathic Free Dispensary, [c. 1880–81], vertical file, Henry Janes, Maryland Historical Society.

54. Harris L. Coulter, *Homoeopathic Influences in Nineteenth-Century Allopathic Therapeutics: A Historical and Philosophical Study* (Washington, D.C.: American Institute of Homeopathy, 1973).

55. Jensen, *Lives of Caroline County Physicians,* 65–66.

56. Ibid., 29–30. Another homeopathic physician who was well known on the Eastern Shore was Dr. G. W. Simmons (1844–c. 1925). Although Simmons was teased about his sugar pill remedies, he maintained that they did indeed make patients well; clearly, sufficient of his patients sustained him in that belief. See Jensen, *Lives of Caroline County Physicians,* 153.

57. Duffy, *The Healers,* 109.

58. On hydropathy (the use of water cures) in Maryland, see Harry B. Weiss and Howard R. Kemble, *The Great American Water-Cure Craze: A History of Hydropathy in the United States* (Trenton, N.J.: Past Times Press, 1967), 125–26. The two sites in Maryland were the Green Spring Hydropathic Institute in Baltimore County (1849) and C. C. Schieferdecker's establishment in Baltimore City (1856).

On the sect, see also Roy Porter, ed., *The Medical History of Waters and Spas* (London: Wellcome Institute for the History of Medicine, 1990).

On osteopathy (which initially emphasized manipulation of the vertebral bodies to improve blood and nerve flow), see Marcine J. Cohen, "Medical Social Movements in the United States (1820–1982): The Case of Osteopathy" (Ph.D. diss., University of California, San Diego, 1983), and Frank J. Helminski, "The Legal Creation of Osteopathic Medicine" (M.A. thesis, Wayne State University, 1981). Andrew Taylor Still (1828–1917), the founder of osteopathy, grew up when heroic medicine was in its prime in the United States. Andrew T. Still, *Autobiography of Andrew T. Still* (Kirksville, Mo.: Published by the author, 1897); Gevitz, "Andrew Taylor Still," 155–70.

On naturopathy (which emphasized natural healing) and chiropractic (which gave primary emphasis to spinal adjustments), see Wardwell, *Chiropractic,* esp. 1–50. See also J. Stuart Moore, *Chiropractic in America: The History of a Medical Alternative* (Baltimore: Johns Hopkins University Press, 1993); Pierre-Louis Gaucher-Peslherbe, *Chiropractic: Early Concepts in Their Historical Setting* (Lombard, Ill.: National College of Chiropractic, 1993); and Saul F. Rosenthal, *A Sociology of Chiropractic* (Lewiston, N.Y.: Edwin Mellen, 1986).

59. Erwin H. Ackerknecht, *Medicine at the Paris Hospital, 1794–1848* (Baltimore: Johns Hopkins Press, 1967); George Rosen, "The Philosophy of Ideology and the Emergence of Modern Medicine in France," *Bulletin of the History of Medicine* 20 (1946): 328–39; John Harley Warner, *The Therapeutic Perspective: Medical Practice, Knowledge, and Identity in America, 1820–1885* (Cambridge: Harvard University Press, 1986), 39–40.

60. Richard W. Wertz and Dorothy C. Wertz, *Lying-In: A History of Childbirth in America* (New Haven: Yale University Press, 1989), 1–2.

61. Jean Donnison, *Midwives and Medical Men: A History of Inter-professional Rivalries and Women's Rights* (New York: Schocken Books, 1977), 8.

62. Midwives had been using ergot for centuries before the regular profession began to recognize its value. Michael J. O'Dowd and Elliot E. Philipp, *The History of Obstetrics and Gynaecology* (New York: Parthenon Publishing Group, 1994), 26; Judith Walzer Leavitt, *Brought to Bed: Childbearing in America, 1750–1950* (New York: Oxford University Press, 1986), 98.

63. Laws of Maryland, 1867, chap. 185; James C. Mohr, *Abortion in America: The Origins and Evolution of National Policy* (New York: Oxford University Press, 1978); Carroll Smith-Rosenberg, "The Abortion Movement and the AMA, 1850–1880," in *Disorderly Conduct: Visions of Gender in Victorian America* (New York: Oxford University Press, 1985), 217–44.

64. Thomas Hersey, *The Midwife's Practical Directory; or, Woman's Confidential Friend: Comprising Extensive Remarks on the Various Casualties and Forms of Disease Preceding, Attending, and Following the Period of Gestation,* 2d ed. (Baltimore: n.p., 1836), 220–21.

65. Guenter B. Risse, Ronald L. Numbers, and Judith Walzer Leavitt, eds.,

Medicine without Doctors: Home Health Care in American History (New York: Science History Publications, 1977).

66. This theme is developed in Kathryn Kish Sklar, *Catherine Beecher: A Study in American Domesticity* (New York: W. W. Norton, 1973).

67. Hannah C. Williams' Recipe Book, c. 1819, MS 2211, Maryland Historical Society.

68. Griffith-Staats Cookbooks, c. 1860–90, MS 1765, Maryland Historical Society. See also J. Milner Fothergill, *A Manual of Dietetics* (New York: William Wood, 1886), which noted in its preface that "the value of feeding in disease is admitted to be as important as the administration of medicines."

69. Woodward, *Carroll County Physicians,* 13–15; Susan E. Cayleff, "Self-Help and the Patent Medicine Business," in Rima D. Apple, ed., *Women, Health, and Medicine in America: A Historical Handbook* (New Brunswick, N.J.: Rutgers University Press, 1992), 303–28. On advertising, see, e.g., Sarah Stage, *Female Complaints: Lydia Pinkham and the Business of Women's Medicine* (New York: W. W. Norton, 1979); James Harvey Young, *The Toadstool Millionaires: A Social History of Patent Medicines in America before Federal Regulation* (Princeton: Princeton University Press, 1961); James Harvey Young, *American Health Quackery* (Princeton: Princeton University Press, 1992); Stewart H. Holbrook, *The Golden Age of Quackery* (New York: Macmillan, 1959); Porter, "Before the Fringe," 10–11.

70. Millicent Gay and Jane North, "The Stonestreet Medical Museum: Rural Medicine in Montgomery County," *Maryland Medical Journal* 45, no. 10 (1996): 856–58; Cordell, *Annals,* 585. Dr. Stonestreet died in 1903 at the age of seventy-four, while going to visit a patient.

T W O: Medicine in the Hospital: The Mainstream Institutions, 1799–1940

1. Charles E. Rosenberg, *The Cholera Years: The United States in 1832, 1849, and 1866* (Chicago: University of Chicago Press, 1962); Morris Vogel, *The Invention of the Modern Hospital, Boston, 1870–1930* (Chicago: University of Chicago Press, 1980); Rosemary Stevens, *In Sickness and in Wealth: American Hospitals in the Twentieth Century* (New York: Basic Books, 1989).

2. Robert J. Brugger, *Maryland: A Middle Temperament* (Baltimore: Johns Hopkins University Press, 1988), 64.

3. Ackerknecht, *Medicine at the Paris Hospital* (see chap. 1, n. 59); Michel Foucault, *The Birth of the Clinic: An Archaeology of Medical Perception* (London: Tavistock Publications, 1973); Warner, *The Therapeutic Perspective* (see chap. 1, n. 59); Russell C. Maulitz, *Morbid Appearances: The Anatomy of Pathology in the Early Nineteenth Century* (Cambridge: Cambridge University Press, 1987).

4. Rosenberg, *Cholera Years,* 59, 63.

5. Brugger, *Maryland,* 100–102.

6. "History of Francis Scott Key Hospital" (unpublished manuscript, Department of Public Relations, Francis Scott Key Hospital).

7. Rosenberg, *Cholera Years,* 4–8.

8. Vogel, *Invention of the Modern Hospital;* Rosenberg, *Cholera Years.*

9. Hospital histories have tended to be either case studies of single institutions or broader, synthetic works exploring general trends. Examples of case studies include Lindsay Granshaw, *St. Mark's Hospital* (London: Kings Fund Historical Series/Oxford University Press, 1985); Dorothy Levenson, *Montefiore: The Hospital as Social Instrument, 1884–1984* (New York: Farrar, Straus and Giroux, 1984); and Joseph Hirsh and Beka Doherty, *The First Hundred Years of Mount Sinai Hospital of New York* (New York: Random House, 1952). Examples of general works include John Woodward, *To the Sick No Harm: A Study of the British Voluntary Hospital System to 1875* (London: Routledge and Kegan Paul, 1974); Rosenberg, *Cholera Years;* and Stevens, *In Sickness and in Wealth.*

Some local studies have examined city hospitals within their urban histories and in the context of widespread changes in hospitals: David Rosner, *A Once Charitable Enterprise: Hospitals and Health Care in Brooklyn and New York, 1885–1915* (Cambridge: Cambridge University Press, 1982); Vogel, *Invention of the Modern Hospital.*

And one has examined Baltimore City Hospitals: Jon M. Kingsdale, *The Growth of Hospitals, 1850–1939: An Economic History in Baltimore* (New York: Garland Publishing, 1989).

10. U.S. Census, 1890.

11. Charles E. Rosenberg, "Social Class and Medical Care in Nineteenth Century America: The Rise and Fall of the Dispensary," in Judith Walzer Leavitt and Ronald L. Numbers, eds., *Sickness and Health in America: Readings in the History of Medicine and Public Health* (Madison: University of Wisconsin Press, 1978), 157–71.

12. "The Oldest Charity in Baltimore: Baltimore General Dispensary," report for 1886, 3, Library of the Medical and Chirurgical Faculty of Maryland.

13. Ibid., 4–6.

14. Ibid., 7.

15. Ibid., 8.

16. Vogel, *Invention of the Modern Hospital,* 10–11.

17. Charles E. Rosenberg, *The Care of Strangers: The Rise of America's Hospital System* (New York: Basic Books, 1987), 317.

18. George H. Callcott, *A History of the University of Maryland* (Baltimore: Maryland Historical Society, 1966), 21–23; Cordell, *Annals,* 54–55 (see chap. 1, n. 4); Eugene Fauntleroy Cordell, *Historical Sketch of the University of Maryland School of Medicine, 1807–1890* (Baltimore: Press of Isaac Friedenwald, 1891), 1–14; Theodore E. Woodward, ed., *Two Hundred Years of Medicine in Baltimore: Outstanding Contributions of the University of Maryland Medical Alumni and Faculty* (Baltimore: University of Maryland at Baltimore School of Medicine, 1976), 2.

19. For insight into his controversies and accomplishments, see F. L. M. Pattison, *Granville Sharp Pattison: Anatomist and Antagonist, 1791–1851* (Tuscaloosa: University of Alabama Press, 1987).

20. Margaret Byrnside Ballard, *A University Is Born* (Union, W.V.: Old Hundred, 1965), 38–39.

21. Ibid., 42; Callcott, *History of the University of Maryland,* 42–43.

22. "The History of Medicine in Baltimore," *Baltimore* 24, no. 6 (1931): 51.

23. Cordell, *Historical Sketch,* 44–46; Ballard, *A University Is Born,* 42–43.

24. Ballard, *A University Is Born,* 72–74; Rosenberg, *The Care of Strangers;* Arthur L. Lomas, "As It Was in the Beginning: A History of the University Hospital," *Bulletin of the School of Medicine, University of Maryland* 23, no. 4 (1939): 200–202.

25. Lomas, "As It Was in the Beginning," 202.

26. Ibid., 204–5; Ballard, *A University Is Born,* 126.

27. Pattison, *Granville Sharp Pattison,* 128–30; Lomas, "As It Was in the Beginning," 191–93; Ballard, *A University Is Born,* 42–50.

28. Callcott, *History of the University of Maryland,* 244.

29. Lomas, "As It Was in the Beginning," 206–7.

30. Richard Harrison Shryock, "Nursing Emerges as a Profession: The American Experience," in Leavitt and Numbers, *Sickness and Health in America,* 203–5. For an alternate view of the professionalization of nursing, see Susan M. Reverby, *Ordered to Care: The Dilemma of American Nursing, 1850–1945* (New York: Cambridge University Press, 1987).

31. Callcott, *History of the University of Maryland,* 224–25.

32. Ibid. While in Egypt, Parsons contracted typhoid and was sent home. Harvey Cushing, "Louisa Parsons, First Superintendent of Nurses in the University of Maryland Hospital," *University Hospital Nurses Alumnae Bulletin* 3, no. 1 (1923).

33. Cushing, "Louisa Parsons"; Callcott, *History of the University of Maryland,* 225–26.

34. Lomas, "As It Was in the Beginning," 209; minutes of the Faculty of Physic, University of Maryland, University of Maryland Health Sciences Library, June 1896, 7–8; Callcott, *History of the University of Maryland,* 257; Randolph Winslow, "The University Hospital," *Therapeutica* 1 (1905): 21–22 (published by the nurses of the Training Schools, Maryland University Hospital, University of Maryland Health Sciences Library).

35. "Notables to Attend 'Preview' of New University Hospital," *Baltimore News Post,* Dec. 13, 1934.

36. Mrs. Charles R. Posey, President of the University Hospital Woman's Auxiliary Board, to Mr. George G. Buck, May 2, 1931, Maryland Room, Enoch Pratt Free Library, Baltimore.

37. H. L. Mencken, series of articles on the Johns Hopkins Hospital, *Baltimore Sun,* July 6–28, 1937.

38. Helen Hopkins Thom, *Johns Hopkins: A Silhouette* (Baltimore: Johns Hopkins Press, 1929); Alan M. Chesney, *The Johns Hopkins Hospital and the Johns Hopkins University School of Medicine: A Chronicle,* vol. 1, *Early Years, 1867–1893* (Baltimore: Johns Hopkins Press, 1943), 1.

39. This does not count almshouses or insane asylums. These calculations are based on several surveys and directories, but they are only estimates. Some small institutions may not have been recorded. Some closed within a few years of opening.

40. Suzanne Ellery Greene Chapelle et al., *Maryland: A History of Its People* (Baltimore: Johns Hopkins University Press, 1986), as cited in Brugger, *Maryland*, 1988, 771.

41. Rosenberg, *The Care of Strangers*, 118.

42. Ibid., 97–99; Harold Elk Straubing, *In Hospital and Camp: The Civil War through the Eyes of Its Doctors and Nurses* (Harrisburg, Pa.: Stackpole Books, 1993).

43. Gert H. Brieger, ed., *Medical America in the Nineteenth Century: Readings from the Literature* (Baltimore: Johns Hopkins University Press, 1972), 235; John D. Thompson and Grace Goldin, *The Hospital: A Social and Architectural History* (New Haven: Yale University Press, 1975).

44. Gert H. Brieger, "The Original Plans for the Johns Hopkins Hospital and Their Historical Significance," *Bulletin of the History of Medicine* 39 (1965): 518–28, 175–87; Chesney, *The Johns Hopkins Hospital*, 1:18–33.

45. Fielding H. Garrison, *John Shaw Billings: A Memoir* (New York: G. P. Putnam's Sons, 1915); John C. French, *A History of the University Founded by Johns Hopkins* (Baltimore: Johns Hopkins Press, 1946), 102–4.

46. Chesney, *The Johns Hopkins Hospital*, 1:10–12; Patrick A. McGuire, "Origins," in "Milestones in Medicine," *Baltimore Sun Magazine*, May 28, 1989, 7, 12. Hopkins permitted only the interest on his endowment to be used, and that had to accumulate before construction could be completed.

47. French, *A History of the University*, 115; Ethel Jones and Blanche Pfefferkorn, *The Johns Hopkins Hospital School of Nursing, 1889–1949* (Baltimore: Johns Hopkins Press, 1954), 27–51.

48. Hampton resigned in 1894 to marry a Hopkins doctor.

49. "The History of Medicine in Baltimore," *Baltimore* 245, no. 6 (1931): 52–53; *Johns Hopkins Bulletin* 1, no. 1 (1889), 15.

50. A. McGehee Harvey, *Science at the Bedside: Clinical Research in American Medicine, 1905–1945* (Baltimore: Johns Hopkins University Press, 1981), 38–59.

51. French, *A History of the University*, 104–6; Chesney, *The Johns Hopkins Hospital*, 1:74–97; A. McGehee Harvey, *Adventures in Medical Research: A Century of Discovery at Johns Hopkins* (London: Johns Hopkins University Press, 1974), 39–48.

52. The apparent hesitation in hiring Halsted may have been due to his noted cocaine addiction.

53. Chesney, *The Johns Hopkins Hospital*, 1:98–148.

54. Johns Hopkins to the Trustees of "the Johns Hopkins Hospital," Baltimore, March 10, 1873, as quoted in *Johns Hopkins Hospital Bulletin* 1 (1889): 4; Mencken, series of articles.

55. Mencken, series of articles.

56. *The Johns Hopkins Hospital, 1889–1939: A Brief Account of Its Founding and of Its Achievements during the First Fifty Years of Its Existence*, published in connection

with celebration of the fiftieth anniversary of the opening of the hospital (Baltimore: Press of Schneidercith and Sons, 1939), 35; Thomas B. Turner, *Heritage of Excellence: The Johns Hopkins Medical Institutions, 1914–1947* (Baltimore: Johns Hopkins University Press, 1974), 23–42.

57. Turner, *Heritage of Excellence,* 42–43.

58. Harvey, *Adventures in Medical Research,* 240, 333.

59. Turner, *Heritage of Excellence,* 134–45.

60. For more detailed descriptions of these and other innovations, see Harvey, *Adventures in Medical Research,* esp. 8–17, 39–46, 60–68, 114–23, 261–87, 302–5, 314–32.

61. Turner, *Heritage of Excellence,* 273–334.

62. James Y. Simpson, *Hospitalism: Its Effects on the Results of Surgical Operations* (Edinburgh: Oliver and Boyd, 1869); Leavitt, *Brought to Bed,* 13–35 (see chap. 1, n. 62).

THREE: Medicine on the Margins: A Complex Array of Institutions, 1799–1940

1. Rosenberg, *The Care of Strangers,* 4–5, 337, 341 (see chap. 2, n. 17); J. M. Toner, "Statistics of Regular Medical Associations and Hospitals in the United States," *Transactions of the American Medical Association* 24 (1873): 287–333. The hospitals Toner listed included only the "regular" establishments. He did not list homeopathic, osteopathic, or other "irregular" hospitals. Nor did he include dispensaries or institutions for the blind or the physically or mentally handicapped.

2. An authority on this subject, the nineteenth-century physician and public health reformer Stephen Smith, separated the nation's hospitals into three categories: military, quarantine, and civil. In this chapter, we concentrate on the civil institutions, leaving military and quarantine hospitals to be considered with other aspects of public health. Brieger, *Medical America,* 235 (see chap. 2, n. 43).

3. H. F. Hill to R. D. Coale, June 21, 1908, University of Maryland Health Sciences Library; Minutes of the Faculty of Physic of the University of Maryland, Sept. 15, 1908, 219.

4. See Rosenberg, *The Care of Strangers,* and Vogel, *Invention of the Modern Hospital* (see chap. 2, n. 1).

5. Address by Joshua J. Cohen at the Laying of the Corner-Stone of the Baltimore Asylum for the Israelites, Beth Machase Umisthor and the Addresses upon the occasion, Baltimore, June 25, 1866 (12th Tamus 5626), 6.

6. Ibid., 16.

7. The pewter plaque from the cornerstone of the Hebrew Hospital (1866) can be seen today at Baltimore's Sinai Hospital.

8. Records of Sinai Hospital, Baltimore, Md.

9. The outreach program was formalized in 1921. "Sinai Hospital, 125th Anniversary: Highlights of Events by Decade, 1863–1990" (prepared by Paul Uman-

sky, Sinai Hospital), 3, 4; Record Book of the Hebrew Hospital Asylum Association, 1922–25, vol. 13, June 19, 1922.

10. "Sinai Hospital, 125th Anniversary," 3.

11. Record Book of the Hebrew Hospital Asylum Association, Jan. 12, 1868, to Dec. 9, 1877, 1:17, 1:85, 1:226; Record Book of the Hebrew Hospital, 1922–25, vol. 13, June 19, 1922.

12. Samuel H. Long, "Report of 76 Cases of Typhoid Fever Treated in the Hebrew Hospital," *Hospital Bulletin* 6, no. 6 (1910): 105–9 (Medical Department of the University of Maryland).

13. Case history of Ezra W. Jones, Sinai Hospital Public Relations Department.

14. Rabbi William Rosenau to Mr. Leon Coblens, president of Hebrew Hospital, Baltimore, Jan. 8, 1926, Sinai Hospital; Record Book of the Hebrew Hospital, 1926–1927, vol. 14; State Tax Commission of Maryland to Hebrew Hospital, Baltimore, July 27, 1926.

15. Cordell, *Annals*, 336, 713–14 (see chap. 1, n. 4).

16. Harold J. Abrahams, *The Extinct Medical Schools of Baltimore, Maryland* (Baltimore: Maryland Historical Society, 1969), 71.

17. These themes are explored in Ornella Moscucci, *The Science of Woman: Gynecology and Gender in England, 1800–1929* (Cambridge: Cambridge University Press, 1990), and in Jane Eliot Sewell, "Bountiful Bodies: Spencer Wells, Lawson Tait, and the Birth of British Gynecology" (Ph.D. diss., Johns Hopkins University, 1991).

18. Regina Markell Morantz-Sanchez, *Sympathy and Science: Women Physicians in American Medicine* (New York: Oxford University Press, 1985); Virginia Drachman, *Hospitals with a Heart: Women Doctors and the Paradox of Separatism at the New England Hospital, 1862–1969* (Ithaca: Cornell University Press, 1984); Mary Roth Walsh, *Doctors Wanted, No Women Need Apply: Sexual Barriers in the Medical Profession, 1835–1975* (New Haven: Yale University Press, 1977).

19. Tenth Annual Report of the Hospital for Women of Maryland, of Baltimore City (hereafter cited as Hospital for Women), 1892, 9.

20. Ibid., 10–11.

21. The Second Annual Announcement and Catalogue of the Women's Medical College of Baltimore, for the session 1883–84.

22. See, e.g., the discussion in George Rosen, *The Specialization of Medicine with Particular Reference to Ophthalmology* (New York: Froben Press, 1944).

23. Tenth Annual Report of the Hospital for Women, 1892, 12; Twenty-second Annual Report of the Hospital for Women, 1904.

24. Twenty-second Annual Report of the Hospital for Women, 1904, 19.

25. Thirty-eighth Annual Report of the Hospital for Women, 1920, 59.

26. Twenty-ninth Annual Report of the Hospital for Women, 1911; Thirty-ninth Annual Report of the Hospital for Women, 1921, 17–18.

27. Fortieth Annual Report of the Hospital for Women, 1922, 19.

28. Fiftieth Annual Report of the Hospital for Women, 1932, 17.

29. Fifty-first Annual Report of the Hospital for Women, 1933, 16–17.

30. Forty-sixth Annual Report of the Hospital for Women, 1928, 18; Forty-seventh Annual Report of the Hospital for Women, 1929, 20; Fiftieth Annual Report of the Hospital for Women, 1932, 17.

31. Fifty-sixth Annual Report of the Hospital for Women, 1937, 14–15.

32. Fifty-ninth Annual Report of the Hospital for Women, 1940, 18.

33. Fifty-seventh Annual Report of the Hospital for Women, 1938, 20.

34. Fifty-eighth Annual Report of the Hospital for Women, 1939, 17.

35. Brugger, *Maryland,* 418–19 (see chap. 2, n. 2).

36. Vanessa N. Gamble, "The Negro Hospital Renaissance: The Black Hospital Movement, 1920–1940" (Ph.D. diss., University of Pennsylvania, 1987).

37. Leslie A. Falk, "Black Abolitionist Doctors and Healers, 1810–1885," *Bulletin of the History of Medicine* 54 (1980): 259–60.

38. "A Notable Baltimore First," *Baltimore Sun,* March 17, 1935.

39. Robert L. Jackson and Emerson C. Walden, "A History of Provident Hospital, Baltimore, Maryland," *Journal of the National Medical Association* 59, no. 3 (1967): 157; *Baltimore Sun,* July 19, 1931.

40. Helene Fuld School of Nursing of Provident Hospital, "History of the School of Nursing of Provident Hospital" (unpublished manuscript, Maryland Department, Enoch Pratt Free Library, Baltimore), 1.

41. *Baltimore Evening Sun,* Dec. 3, 1948, 33.

42. Jackson and Walden, "A History of Provident Hospital," 158.

43. Ibid.; *Baltimore Evening Sun,* Dec. 4, 1948; *Baltimore Sun,* March 17, 1935.

44. See "History of the School of Nursing of Provident Hospital," 3.

45. Jackson and Walden, "A History of Provident Hospital," 161.

46. Ninth Annual Report of Provident Hospital, Baltimore, 1937; Tenth Annual Report of Provident Hospital, Baltimore, 1938, 16, 27A; Richard B. Morris, ed., *Encyclopedia of American History* (New York: Harper and Brother, 1953), 363; Twelfth Annual Report of Provident Hospital, 1940.

47. Bliss Forbush, *The Sheppard and Enoch Pratt Hospital, 1853–1970* (Philadelphia: J. B. Lippincott, 1971), 16.

48. Philippe Pinel, *A Treatise on Insanity* (New York: Hafner Publishing, 1962), facsimile reprint of 1801 edition; Erwin H. Ackerknecht, *A Short History of Psychiatry* (New York: Hafner Publishing, 1968), 41–53; Andrew Scull, "Moral Treatment Reconsidered: Some Sociological Comments on an Episode in the History of British Psychiatry," in Andrew Scull, ed., *Madhouses, Mad-Doctors, and Madmen: The Social History of Psychiatry in the Victorian Era* (Philadelphia: University of Pennsylvania Press, 1981), 105–18.

49. Gerald Grob, *The State and the Mentally Ill: A History of the Worcester State Hospital in Massachusetts, 1830–1920* (Chapel Hill, N.C.: University of North Carolina Press, 1966); Michel Foucault, *Madness and Civilization: A History of Insanity in the Age of Reason* (London: Random House, 1965).

50. Nancy Tomes, *A Generous Confidence: Thomas Story Kirkbride and the Art of Asylum-Keeping, 1840–1883* (Cambridge: Cambridge University Press, 1984); Forbush, *Sheppard and Enoch Pratt Hospital.*

51. *Baltimore Sun,* Aug. 30, 1930.

52. Forbush, *Sheppard and Enoch Pratt Hospital,* 17–23.

53. Ibid., 27–76.

54. Ibid., 28–31.

55. "Sheppard Asylum," *Baltimore Sun,* Sept. 25, 1896; Forbush, *Sheppard and Enoch Pratt Hospital,* 38–39.

56. Forbush, *Sheppard and Enoch Pratt Hospital,* 51–58.

57. Ibid., 52–91.

58. Eldridge C. Price, "Medical Progress" (Philadelphia: Globe Printing House, 1881), 7 (reprinted from the *North American Journal of Homeopathy,* Feb. 1880); Jane Sewell, "Infinitesimals for the Insane: The Homeopathic Treatment of Mental Illness" (M.A. thesis, Johns Hopkins University, 1985).

59. Price, "Medical Progress," 7–8; Thomas Lindsley Bradford, *Homeopathic Bibliography of the United States* (Philadelphia: Boericke and Tafel, 1892), 393, 508. Cordell dates the establishment of the dispensary to 1874, but it was not incorporated until 1877. Cordell, *Annals,* 712.

60. AMA Directory, 1906, 1909, 1912, 1918, 1921; Maryland Manual, 1900, 1905, 1910, 1915; Abrahams, *The Extinct Medical Schools,* 264–65 (see chap. 1, n. 16)

61. Abrahams, *The Extinct Medical Schools,* 266.

62. Ibid., 266–67.

63. "From *Sun* 50 years ago," *Baltimore Sun,* July 15, 1962.

64. Alex Berman, "The Heroic Approach in Nineteenth-Century Therapeutics," in Leavitt and Numbers, *Sickness and Health in America,* 78–86 (see chap. 2, n. 11).

65. E. Richard Brown, *Rockefeller Medicine Men: Medicine and Capitalism in America* (Berkeley and Los Angeles: University of California Press, 1979); Coulter, *Divided Legacy,* vol. 3 (see chap. 1, n. 50); Kaufman, *Homeopathy in America* (see chap. 1, n. 51).

66. *Baltimore Evening Sun,* Jan. 24, 1954.

67. Starr, *Social Transformation of American Medicine,* 116–19 (see chap. 1, n. 23).

68. Abrahams, *The Extinct Medical Schools,* 266.

69. Brugger, *Maryland,* 321; U.S. Census, 1880 and 1940.

70. Peninsula General Hospital, Enlargement Campaign brochure, 1939. Various brochures were put together by the Peninsula Regional Hospital, as Peninsula General is now known.

71. First Annual Report of the Peninsula General Hospital of Salisbury, Maryland, 1898.

72. *Baltimore Sun,* July 27, 1939; Dec. 9, 1939; March 30, 1940; Dec. 29, 1940.

73. Brugger, *Maryland,* 434.

74. Material from Sacred Heart Hospital, Cumberland. In 1952, Allegany

Hospital changed its name to Sacred Heart so as better to indicate the institution's Catholic identity.

75. Sister M. Florence to Mother Superior, Mother House, July 29, 1911.

76. Ibid.

77. Material from Sacred Heart Hospital.

FOUR: Medical Education: Diversity, Expansion, and Decentralization, 1799–1876

1. Henry E. Sigerist, *The Great Doctors: A Biographical History of Medicine* (Garden City, N.Y.: Doubleday Anchor, 1958), 380.

2. Kenneth M. Ludmerer, *Learning to Heal: The Development of American Medical Education* (New York: Basic Books, 1985), 11.

3. Charles W. Turner, "Letters (1790–1800) of John Johnston, Rockbridge Medical Student and Doctor," *Journal of the History of Medicine and Allied Sciences* 14 (1959): 191–95.

4. Patricia Ann Watson, *The Angelical Conjunction: The Preacher-Physicians of Colonial New England* (Knoxville: University of Tennessee Press, 1991).

5. Cordell, *Annals,* 304–5 (see chap. 1, n. 4).

6. Martin Kaufman, *American Medical Education: The Formative Years, 1765–1910* (Westport, Conn.: Greenwood Press, 1976), 45–46; Ludmerer, *Learning to Heal,* 16.

7. Ludmerer, *Learning to Heal,* 16.

8. "Manuscript Lectures on Surgery Delivered by Philip Syng Physick, M.D., Professor of Surgery in the University of Pennsylvania," John Archer Jr., "Notes on Surgery," 1804, 87–88, MS 1650 in Dr. Randolph Winslow Papers, Maryland Historical Society.

9. Ibid., 13–14, 40–41.

10. Abraham Flexner, *Medical Education in the United States and Canada: A Report to the Carnegie Foundation for the Advancement of Teaching* (New York: Arno Press and *New York Times,* 1972), 3–6.

11. Abrahams, *The Extinct Medical Schools,* 1 (see chap. 3, n. 16); "Two Papers by John Shaw Billings on Medical Education," with a foreword by Alan M. Chesney, *Bulletin of the History of Medicine* 6, no. 4 (1938): 303.

12. A. E. Waller, "A Fictitious Medical Degree of the 1830's," *Bulletin of the History of Medicine* 20, no. 4 (1946): 505–12.

13. William Frederick Norwood, "American Medical Education from the Revolutionary War to the Civil War," *Journal of Medical Education* 32 (June 1957): 433–47.

14. Martin Kaufman, "American Medical Education," in Ronald L. Numbers, ed., *The Education of American Physicians: Historical Essays* (Berkeley and Los Angeles: University of California Press, 1980), 8.

15. Roy Porter, "William Hunter: A Surgeon and a Gentleman," in W. F.

Bynum and Roy Porter, eds., *William Hunter and the Eighteenth-Century Medical World* (Cambridge: Cambridge University Press, 1985), 7–34.

16. Ibid., 16.

17. Cordell, *Annals,* 15.

18. Ruth Richardson, *Death, Dissection, and the Destitute* (London: Penguin Books, 1988).

19. See, e.g., George E. Gifford Jr., ed., "Twelve Letters from Jeffries Wyman, M.D.: Hampton-Sydney Medical College, Richmond, Virginia, 1843–1848," *Journal of the History of Medicine and Allied Sciences* 20 (1965): 309–33.

20. Callcott, *History of the University of Maryland,* 18 (see chap. 2, n. 18).

21. William G. Rothstein, *American Medical Schools and the Practice of Medicine: A History* (New York: Oxford University Press, 1987), 25–27.

22. Cordell, *Annals,* 17–18, 337–38.

23. Callcott, *History of the University of Maryland,* 18–19.

24. Randolph Winslow, "A Brief Sketch of the Medical School of the University of Maryland, 1807–1920," *Bulletin of the School of Medicine* 21, no. 1 (1936): 76.

25. Cordell, *Annals,* 371.

26. Gifford, "Twelve Letters," 309–53.

27. As it turned out, however, two of the three previously uncredentialed petitioners resigned and were replaced before the school was in operation.

28. Winslow, "Brief Sketch," 76.

29. Callcott, *History of the University of Maryland,* 25–26, 76–77.

30. Gifford, "Twelve Letters," 319.

31. Cordell, *Historical Sketch,* 20–21 (see chap. 2, n. 18).

32. Richard W. Flint, "Notes on the History of the Four Oldest UMAB Buildings," August 20, 1993, 1, University of Maryland Health Sciences Library.

33. Pattison, *Granville Sharp Pattison,* 112 (see chap. 2, n. 19).

34. Cordell, *Historical Sketch,* 31.

35. Richard and David Gittings Papers, MS 1667, Maryland Historical Society.

36. Nevertheless, Gittings passed his days conversing with fellow passengers and reading Burns, Byron, and Shakespeare from the ship's large book collection. David Gittings to Charles Howard, London, Aug. 25, 1818, MS 1667, Maryland Historical Society; David Gittings to Richard Gittings, Chesapeake Bay, July 19; near Cape Henry, July 21, 1818, MS 1667, Maryland Historical Society.

37. David Gittings to Richard Gittings, Edinburgh, Oct. 2, 1818, MS 1667, Maryland Historical Society.

38. Ibid. Gittings quickly began to learn something about the tension that frequently developed between educational imperatives and the well-being of the patients. He reported that the students "teased the poor devils [patients] to death."

39. Cordell, *Annals,* 411.

40. Winslow, "Brief Sketch," 78.

41. Ibid.

42. Callcott, *History of the University of Maryland,* 66–69; Abrahams, *The Extinct Medical Schools,* 1–70.

43. Genevieve Miller, "A Nineteenth Century Medical School: Washington University of Baltimore," *Bulletin of the History of Medicine* 14, no. 1 (1943): 14–29.

44. Winslow, "Brief Sketch," 79.

45. Callcott, *History of the University of Maryland,* 80–81, 123–24.

46. Ibid., 157.

47. Hammond was responsible for organizing the Army Medical Library and the Army Medical Museum.

48. Winslow, "Brief Sketch," 80.

49. Several professors were recruited from southern ranks. Julian J. Chisolm became professor of diseases of the eye and ear, and Francis T. Miller became professor of anatomy and clinical professor of nervous diseases.

50. Cordell, *Historical Sketch,* 133–34.

51. Minutes of the Faculty of Physic, April 8, 1870, University of Maryland Health Sciences Library.

52. *The Baltimore College of Dental Surgery: Heritage and History,* 7, 8, University of Maryland Health Sciences Library Historical Collection (hereafter UMHSLHC).

53. Cordell, *Annals,* 432; Callcott, *History of the University of Maryland,* 83–85.

54. Cordell, *Annals,* 432; J. Ben Robinson, "Dr. Horace H. Hayden and His Influence on Dental Education," reprinted from *Dental Cosmos,* August 1932, 784–86.

55. Cordell, *Annals,* 686, 695; Robinson, "Hayden and His Influence," 786.

56. *Eighth Annual Circular and Catalogue of the Dental Department of the University of Maryland,* 1889–90, 3, UMHSLHC.

57. Callcott, *History of the University of Maryland,* 85. See also Cordell, *Annals,* 429.

58. Cordell, *Annals,* 105; Callcott, *History of the University of Maryland,* 86–87.

59. *Annual Announcement of the Board of Visitors of the College of Dental Surgery,* 1840, 2–4, UMHSLHC.

60. *Baltimore College of Dental Surgery,* 11.

61. *Annual Announcement of the Baltimore College of Dental Surgery,* 1840, 6, UMHSLHC.

62. Ibid., 6–7, 12.

63. Ibid., 7.

64. *Annual Announcement of the Baltimore College of Dental Surgery,* 1850, 11–12; *Annual Announcement of the Baltimore College of Dental Surgery,* 1874–75, 6–20.

65. *Baltimore College of Dental Surgery,* 14.

66. *Fourteenth Annual Announcement and Catalogue of the Baltimore College of Dental Surgery,* 1853–54, 7–8, UMHSLHC.

67. *Triennial Catalogue of the Baltimore College of Dental Surgery,* 1874–75, 1–5.

68. *Baltimore College of Dental Surgery,* 14.

69. *Annual Circular and Catalogue of the Maryland Dental College*, 1874, 6; *Triennial Catalogue of the Baltimore College of Dental Surgery*, 1874–75, 25.

70. *Forty-Sixth Annual Catalogue of the Baltimore College of Dental Surgery*, 1885–86, 1.

71. *Annual Circular of the Maryland College of Pharmacy*, 1873–73, 9.

72. Callcott, *History of the University of Maryland*, 92.

73. For an informative discussion of the problem of jurisdiction, see Abbott, *The System of Professions*, 1–113 (see chap. 1, n. 19).

74. Callcott, *History of the University of Maryland*, 93.

75. On the charter, see Cordell, *Annals*, 106. In regard to the college's location, the pharmacists were at least ahead of the physicians, who had initially been forced to teach in their homes. See Callcott, *History of the University of Maryland*, 93–94.

76. Cordell, *Annals*, 583–85.

77. Callcott, *History of the University of Maryland*, 94; Cordell, *Historical Sketch*, 113.

78. *Journal and Transactions of the Maryland College of Pharmacy* 1, no. 1 (1888): 19, UMHSLHC; Callcott, *History of the University of Maryland*, 94–95.

79. Callcott, *History of the University of Maryland*, 95; *Annual Circular of the Maryland College of Pharmacy*, 7–9; *Journal and Transactions of the Maryland College of Pharmacy* 1, no. 1 (1888): 1, 35.

80. Lewis H. Steiner, "Valedictory Address at the Annual Commencement of Maryland College of Pharmacy," *Journal and Transactions of the Maryland College of Pharmacy* 2, no. 2 (1861): 49–68.

81. *Annual Circular of the Maryland College of Pharmacy*, 3.

82. Ibid., 9–10.

FIVE: Medical Education: Science and Centralization, 1876–1940

1. See Richard H. Shryock, *The Unique Influence of Johns Hopkins University on American Medicine* (Copenhagen: Ejnar Munksgaard, 1953).

2. M. Carey Thomas had earned her bachelor's degree at Cornell University in 1877. She wanted to pursue a doctoral degree at Johns Hopkins but was refused admission because of her sex. She went to Europe for her Ph.D., and by 1893 she had become president of Bryn Mawr College.

3. Caroline Bedell Thomas, "How Women Medical Students First Came to Hopkins: A Chronicle," *JHU Staff Newsletter* 1, no. 4 (1975), Thomas Papers 1202, Alan Mason Chesney Archives, JHU School of Medicine (hereafter cited as AMCAJHU).

4. Kenneth M. Ludmerer, "Reform of Medical Education at Washington University," *Journal of the History of Medicine and Allied Sciences* 35, no. 2 (1980): 156–57.

5. A. McGehee Harvey, Gert H. Brieger, Susan L. Abrams, and Victor A.

198

Notes to Pages 89–92

McKusick, *A Model of Its Kind,* vol. 1, *A Centennial History of Medicine at Johns Hopkins* (Baltimore: Johns Hopkins University Press, 1989), 189–90.

6. Ludmerer, *Learning to Heal,* 214 (see chap. 4, n. 2). Another factor was, of course, the expense of supporting a full-time faculty.

7. Ibid., 129.

8. Shryock, *The Unique Influence,* 19. According to Shryock, a physician accepting one of Hopkins's full-time preclinical chairs when the medical school opened was exchanging an income of at least $10,000 per annum for a salary of $3,000 or $4,000.

9. Thomas Neville Bonner, *American Doctors and German Universities: A Chapter in International Intellectual Relations, 1870–1914* (Lincoln: University of Nebraska Press, 1963), 23.

10. "Two Papers by John Shaw Billings on Medical Education," with a foreword by Alan M. Chesney, *Bulletin of the History of Medicine* 6, no. 4 (1938): 285–310.

11. Gert H. Brieger, "The California Origins of the Johns Hopkins Medical School," *Bulletin of the History of Medicine* 51 (1977): 339–52. Gilman had been president of the University of California in the early 1870s, and the West Coast, unlike most of the West, was then making substantial strides in educational reform. These experiences shaped what Gilman did when he was planning the medical school.

12. John Field, "Medical Education in the United States: Late Nineteenth and Twentieth Centuries," in C. D. O'Malley, ed., *The History of Medical Education* (Berkeley and Los Angeles: University of California Press, 1970), 506.

13. Harvey et al., *A Model of Its Kind,* 190.

14. Bertram M. Bernheim, *The Story of Johns Hopkins: Four Great Doctors and the Medical School They Created* (Toronto: Whittlesey House; New York: McGraw-Hill, 1948), 35.

15. Flexner, *Medical Education,* 111 (see chap. 4, n. 10).

16. Chesney, *The Johns Hopkins Hospital,* 1:83–84 (see chap. 2, n. 38).

17. Harvey et al., *A Model of Its Kind,* 19–21.

18. Chesney, *The Johns Hopkins Hospital,* 1:108–13; Harvey et al., *A Model of Its Kind,* 22.

19. Bernheim, *The Story of Johns Hopkins,* 13; Chesney, *The Johns Hopkins Hospital,* 1:114–15.

20. It is not entirely clear why the trustees made this choice, but gynecology, as a rapidly growing field, promised to attract patients to the hospital, increasing the medical institution's revenues. The decision may also have been influenced by the unusual role women had played in founding the school and by the fact that it was obligated to train female physicians, many of whom could be expected to have a special interest in women's maladies.

21. Harvey et al., *A Model of Its Kind,* 16–19.

22. Chesney, *The Johns Hopkins Hospital,* 1:221; Harvey et al., *A Model of Its Kind,* 29.

23. Chesney, *The Johns Hopkins Hospital,* 2:2–3.

24. Chesney, *The Johns Hopkins Hospital,* 1:271–73; Ludmerer, *Learning to Heal,* 113.

25. Chesney, *The Johns Hopkins Hospital,* 2:9–10. Glover later married Professor Franklin Pierce Mall.

26. Ibid., 14–17.

27. T. Clifford Allbutt, "Medicine in the Nineteenth Century," *Bulletin of the Johns Hopkins Hospital* 9 (1898): 277–85. See also Chesney, *The Johns Hopkins Hospital,* 2:197–98, and Kenneth M. Ludmerer, "The Rise of the Teaching Hospital in America," *Journal of the History of Medicine and Allied Sciences* 38, no. 4 (1983): 389–414.

28. Harvey et al., *A Model of Its Kind,* 36; William Frederick Norwood, "Medical Education in the United States before 1900," in O'Malley, *The History of Medical Education,* 490.

29. Ludmerer, "The Rise of the Teaching Hospital," 403.

30. Shryock, *The Unique Influence;* Ludmerer, *Learning to Heal,* 104.

31. Ludmerer, *Learning to Heal,* 389.

32. Harvey et al., *A Model of Its Kind,* 37.

33. Ludmerer, *Learning to Heal,* 60–61. Following British custom, Halsted secured extensive experience for students by giving them positions as surgical dressers. Shryock, *The Unique Influence,* 23–24.

34. Ludmerer, "The Rise of the Teaching Hospital," 413–14.

35. Robert A. Harrell, "A History of the Pithotomy Club," 1980, 3–4, Pithotomy Society, AMCAJHU; Robert C. Sergott and Peter D. Olch, "The Society of Pithotomists, 1897–1980" (paper presented in part at the meeting of the American Osler Society, Kansas City, Mo., May 9, 1978).

36. Harrell, "A History of the Pithotomy Club," 5.

37. The other scene involved a spoof of a patient presentation by Dr. Bloodgood; the patient was an attractive young woman with a breast lesion. Ibid., 8, 14–15.

38. C. L. C. Horn to Dr. H. M. Hurd, April 26, 1907, Pithotomy Society, AMCAJHU.

39. Harrell, "A History of the Pithotomy Club," 5.

40. Ibid., 4; Sergott and Olch, "The Society of Pithotomists," 7. By opening up the membership, the club was able, among other things, to increase its financial resources.

41. Harrell, "A History of the Pithotomy Club," 9.

42. List of members and fellows of the Pithotomy Society, Pithotomy Society, AMCAJHU.

43. Morantz-Sanchez, *Sympathy and Science,* 114–17 (see chap. 3, n. 18).

44. Caroline Bedell Thomas, "American Medicine in the Twentieth Century: Some Personal Insights," Thirtieth Kate Hurd Mead Lecture in the History of Medicine, Philadelphia, 1, 13, Thomas Papers, AMCAJHU.

45. Letter from the special committee appointed by Dr. Remsen, May 20, 1909, AMCAJHU. Boarding House Inspection Committee members were Drs. Thomas B. Futcher (chair), Thomas McCrae, and Thomas R. Boggs.

46. "Student Life," AMCAJHU; Report of Committee to Investigate Conditions under Which Students Live and Work, folder 1, 1904, General Health, AMCAJHU.

47. By the 1930s, all first-year students received thorough physical examinations, and by 1938 Dean Chesney was overseeing plans to perform annual or semi-annual chest X-rays and tuberculin tests on all students (on a voluntary basis). This required extra financing. N. B. Herman estimated that it would cost the school $1,500 to test each of the three hundred students annually. N. B. Herman to Alan M. Chesney, Sept. 27, 1938; "Student Health," 1930s, AMCAJHU.

Surgeon Mark M. Ravitch has given us an informative portrait of student life during the Depression. When he entered Hopkins in 1930, there were seventy-five students in his year, and it was taken for granted, he said, that there would be six to ten women in each class. The women were mostly accommodated at the "Hen House" at 800 North Broadway. A few of the male students still lived at the Pithotomy Club or in other fraternity houses near the hospital. Most continued to live in boardinghouses around the hospital. These were run by women with a few spare rooms in their row houses who needed to supplement their incomes. In many cases, their children had grown and left home, and the medical students benefited from family-style meals. These consisted of "huge platters of fried chicken, pork chops, fried oysters, marvelous pies and other cheap foods of the day." These memories may romanticize landladies such as Mrs. Ningard and Mrs. Heanies; not all students may have fared so well. Nevertheless, as Ravitch pointed out, "during this Depression time, at least one of us was sustained by those dinners alone at a cost of perhaps $7 per week, eschewing breakfast and lunch." "Depression-Era Memories: Pittsburgh Surgeon Mark Ravitch Recalls Medical School in the '30s," *Hopkins Medical News* 9, no. 2 (1985): 11, box 87.05, AMCAJHU.

48. Harvey et al., *A Model of Its Kind,* 41–42.

49. No longer were the medical facilities relying on student fees for their income. In 1903, for instance, Halsted was paid $10,000 for an appendectomy and Kelly received $20,000 for some major operations.

50. See Brown, *Rockefeller Medicine Men,* 82 (see chap. 3, n. 65).

51. Flexner, *Medical Education,* 12, 133–34 (see chap. 4, n. 10).

52. Ibid., 234–35, 76.

53. "Depression-Era Memories," 11.

54. Sigerist, *The Great Doctors,* 385 (see chap. 4, n. 1); Harvey et al., *A Model of Its Kind,* 42–43.

55. Turner, *Heritage of Excellence,* 149–50 (see chap. 2, n. 56).

56. Chesney, *The Johns Hopkins Hospital,* 3:2–12, 262.

57. Curiously enough, Barker refused a full-time appointment. Despite all

of his efforts on the full-time front, he did not want to relinquish his extensive private practice. Harvey et al., *A Model of Its Kind*, 43–54.

58. Ibid., 57.

59. Donald Fleming, *William H. Welch and the Rise of Modern Medicine* (Boston: Little, Brown, 1954), 190.

60. Turner, *Heritage of Excellence*, 273–470; Harvey et al., *A Model of Its Kind*, 57–74.

61. Callcott, *History of the University of Maryland*, 204 (see chap. 2, n. 18).

62. Frederick C. Waite, "The First Medical Diploma Mill in the United States," *Bulletin of the History of Medicine* 20, no. 4 (1946): 495–504.

63. Callcott, *History of the University of Maryland*, 261.

64. Ibid., 264. The severe depression that began in 1893 might have had some influence on these figures. The elevated standards were even more troublesome for the proprietary schools, which relied on students' fees for survival.

65. Flexner, *Medical Education*, 5.

66. Ibid., 236.

67. Ibid., 39.

68. Ibid., 238–39.

69. Ibid., 238–39, 43.

70. Robert P. Hudson, "Abraham Flexner in Perspective: American Medical Education, 1865–1910," *Bulletin of the History of Medicine* 46, no. 6 (1972): 545–61.

71. Ludmerer, *Learning to Heal*, 197.

72. Winslow, "Brief Sketch," 84 (see chap 4, n. 24).

73. Callcott, *History of the University of Maryland*, 290–93.

74. *Bulletin of the School of Medicine* (University of Maryland), 24, no. 3 (1940): 139–41.

75. *Announcement of the Dental Department of the University of Maryland*, 1882–83, 2–3, UMHSLHC.

76. Ibid., 4.

77. *Annual Catalogue of the Dental Department of the University of Maryland*, 1883–84, 18–19, UMHSLHC.

78. Gardner P. H. Foley, "Milestones in the Development of the School of Dentistry" (paper presented at the University of Maryland, June 9, 1988), 11, UMHSLHC.

79. *Baltimore College of Dental Surgery*, 15 (see chap. 4, n. 52).

80. *Twenty-Third Annual Announcement and Catalogue of the Dental Department of the University of Maryland*, 1904–1905, 2–3.

81. *Baltimore College of Dental Surgery*, 15. At this time, the dental students and some of the staff transferred to the university's Dental Department.

82. Foley, "Milestones in the Development," 4–6.

83. Callcott, *History of the University of Maryland*, 331, 359; Foley, "Milestones in the Development," 6–7.

84. *Annual Catalogue of the Maryland College of Pharmacy,* 1891–92, 16–20, UMHSLHC.

85. *Sixty-Seventh Annual Announcement of the Maryland College of Pharmacy, University of Maryland, Department of Pharmacy,* 1910–11, 1–7.

86. *Catalogue and Ninety-sixth Announcement of the School of Pharmacy (Maryland College of Pharmacy),* 1939–40.

87. Minutes of the Faculty of Physic, University of Maryland, Sept. 17, 1872, UMHSLHC.

88. Abrahams, *The Extinct Medical Schools,* 71, 130 (see chap. 3, n. 16).

89. Alice Kessler-Harris, *Out to Work: A History of Wage-Earning Women in the United States* (Oxford: Oxford University Press, 1982), 3–72.

90. Sheila M. Rothman, *Woman's Proper Place: A History of Changing Ideals and Practices, 1870 to the Present* (New York: Basic Books, 1978).

91. Carroll Smith-Rosenberg, *Disorderly Conduct: Visions of Gender in Victorian America* (New York: Oxford University Press, 1985), 1; Sklar, *Catherine Beecher* (see chap. 1, n. 66).

92. Morantz-Sanchez, *Sympathy and Science,* 49, 64. Elizabeth Blackwell was the first to receive her medical degree on home shores, at Geneva Medical College in New York in 1849.

93. Ibid., 64–66; Catherine Clinton, *The Other Civil War: American Women in the Nineteenth Century* (New York: Hill and Wang, 1984), 83. Although Elizabeth Blackwell had gained her medical degree in America and had furthered her studies in Europe, upon returning to New York in 1851 she found herself entirely excluded from her profession's establishment. Male doctors would not admit her in their midst. Spurred on by this rejection, Blackwell, along with her physician sister, Emily, and Dr. Maria Zakrewska, organized the New York Infirmary for Women and Children in 1857. With a hospital in place, they then established the Woman's Medical College of the New York Infirmary. In addition to Blackwell's establishment, there was the New York Medical College and Hospital for Women (a homeopathic enterprise).

94. Abrahams, *The Extinct Medical Schools,* 71.

95. *Announcement of the Woman's Medical College of Baltimore,* for the session 1882–83, 3, Archives of the Medical and Chirurgical Faculty of Maryland (hereafter cited as Med Chi).

96. Morantz-Sanchez, *Sympathy and Science.*

97. *Third Annual Announcement and Catalogue of the Woman's Medical College of Baltimore,* 1884, 12–16. Students were furnished with a list of "desirable boardinghouses" that were available in the vicinity for $3 to $5 a week.

98. *Sixth Annual Announcement and Catalogue of the Woman's Medical College of Baltimore,* 1887–88, 3–4. This was in accordance with the membership requirements of the American Medical College Association.

99. *Eleventh Annual Announcement and Catalogue of the Woman's Medical College of Baltimore,* 1892–93, 3–4, 11–12.

100. Claribel Cone Manuscript Lecture Notes, Woman's Medical College of Baltimore, May 17, 1900, 3–4, Med Chi.

101. *Fifteenth Annual Announcement and Catalogue of the Woman's Medical College of Baltimore,* 1896–97.

102. Cordell, *Annals,* 359, 536 (see chap. 1, n. 4); Harvey et al., *A Model of Its Kind,* 138. By 1900, the Woman's Medical College had graduated 73 female physicians, whose geographic origins were as follows: Maryland, 25; New York, 7; Massachusetts, 6; Pennsylvania, 6; Ohio, 5; Virginia, 4; Illinois, 3; Nebraska, 2; New Jersey, 2; Tennessee, 2; Alabama, 1; Georgia, 1; Mississippi, 1; Missouri, 1; North Carolina, 1; South Carolina, 1; West Virginia, 1; Wisconsin, 1; New Brunswick, 1; Germany, 1; and Korea, 1. *Nineteenth Annual Announcement and Catalogue of the Woman's Medical College of Baltimore,* 1900–1901, 37–39.

103. Abrahams, *The Extinct Medical Schools,* 71–72. The school's associates took seriously the need to foster collegiality among female physicians and students. In 1885, they established the Medical Society of the Woman's Medical College. Members included faculty, students, and physicians throughout Baltimore. During the lecture seasons, they held monthly meetings at which papers were read and specimens exhibited. William Welch, William Thayer, William Osler, and Simon Flexner were among the "special lecturers," and their reputations helped draw attention to the society. In 1894, it boasted 104 members, and its officers launched a quarterly bulletin.

104. *Twenty-eighth Annual Announcement and Catalogue of the Woman's Medical College of Baltimore,* 1909–10. At the Good Samaritan Hospital, advanced students attended operations, and occasional clinics were held in the wards to discuss interesting cases. Fourth-year students obtained clinical clerkships. Other clinical facilities included the Dispensary of the Woman's Medical College (City Dispensary for the Northwestern District); the Presbyterian Eye, Ear and Throat Charity Hospital; and the Hospital for the Relief of Crippled and Deformed Children.

105. Flexner, *Medical Education,* 10–11, 237.

106. Graduates of Woman's Medical became respected and active members of their profession. The majority engaged in medical practice after graduation, working predominantly in the areas of gynecology, obstetrics, and general practice.

107. Abrahams, *The Extinct Medical Schools,* 73.

108. John Harley Warner, "Physiology," in Ronald L. Numbers, ed., *The Education of American Physicians: Historical Essays* (Berkeley and Los Angeles: University of California Press, 1980), 54. Some sects in the early nineteenth century, especially the eclectics, established their own societies and schools. By mid-century, the eclectics were doing well, so much so that, in the 1850s, the Eclectic Medical Institute of Cincinnati claimed to have the largest student body of any city besides Philadelphia and New York. Beginning in the 1820s and 1830s, however, homeopathy grew faster than eclecticism.

109. Kaufman, *American Medical Education,* 70–71 (see chap. 4, n. 6). New York and Pennsylvania were the initial strongholds of American homeopathy. In 1835, Constantine Hering had opened the Nordamerikanische Academie der Homoeopathischen Heilkunst in Allentown, Pa. By 1848, Hering and William Wesselhoeft had obtained a charter for a Homoeopathic Medical College in Philadelphia, which in 1869 became the Hahnemann Medical College. Francesco Cordasco, *Homoeopathy in the United States* (see chap. 1, n. 50). See also *The Bibliography of Homoeopathic Medical Imprints, 1825–1925* (Fairview, N.J., and London: Junius-Vaughn Press, 1991), xvii–xviii.

110. Martin Kaufman, *Homeopathy in America,* 29 (see chap. 1, n. 51). Homeopathy had established a sound reputation in New York during the 1832 cholera epidemic, and its standing was strengthened in the epidemics of 1848 and 1852. Throughout these crises, it was widely preferred over "orthodox" efforts. In 1844, the city's homeopaths had organized the American Institute of Homoeopathy as the first national association.

111. Price, "Medical Progress," 7 (see chap. 3, n. 58).

112. Abrahams, *The Extinct Medical Schools,* 264.

113. Ibid. The greatest number of students (thirty men and ten women) attended in the academic year 1898–99.

114. Ibid., 265.

115. Cordasco, *Homeopathy in the United States,* xviii.

116. Flexner, *Medical Education,* 238, 158–60.

117. Ibid., 236, 238.

118. Todd L. Savitt, "Lincoln University Medical Department—a Forgotten Nineteenth-Century Black Medical School," *Journal of the History of Medicine and Allied Sciences* 40, no. 1 (1985): 42–65.

119. Abrahams, *The Extinct Medical Schools,* 324–25.

120. James Nabwangu and Robert Gamble (1967) were Johns Hopkins's first African-American medical graduates. Black Graduates, JHU School of Medicine, AMCAJHU.

121. John B. Blake, "Anatomy," in Ronald L. Numbers, *The Education of American Physicians,* 38.

122. For some early observations on the counterflow, see George Dohrmann III, "Medical Education in the United States as Seen by a German Immigrant: The Letters of George Dohrmann, 1897–1901," *Journal of the History of Medicine and Allied Sciences* 33, no. 4 (1978): 477–506.

SIX: Public Health: A New Mission in an Urbanizing Sociey, 1832–1899

1. John Duffy, *The Sanitarians: A History of American Public Health* (Urbana: University of Illinois Press, 1990), 1.

2. Ibid., 2.

3. James H. Cassedy, *American Medicine and Statistical Thinking, 1800–1860* (Cambridge: Harvard University Press, 1984), 185.

4. Anthony S. Wohl, *Endangered Lives: Public Health in Victorian Britain* (London: Methuen, 1983), 118–19.

5. Rosenberg, *Cholera Years,* 14–15 (see chap. 2, n. 1).

6. Ibid., 14–16; Barbara Gutman Rosenkrantz, *Public Health and the State: Changing Views in Massachusetts, 1842–1936* (Cambridge: Harvard University Press, 1972), 4.

7. Theodore E. Woodward et al., "Marylanders Defeat Philadelphia: Yellow Fever Updated," *Transactions of the American Clinical and Climatological Association* 87 (1976): 71, 76.

8. Peter L. Beilenson and A. Soula Lambropoulos, "Baltimore City Health Department: Two Hundred Years of Progress and Partnership," *Maryland Medical Journal* 42, no. 8 (1993): 730.

9. Cordell, *Annals,* 94 (see chap. 1, n. 4).

10. Yellow fever was the first epidemic disease in Maryland that had led to political action on behalf of public health. In 1793, the governor appointed two quarantine physicians in Baltimore, one to deal with transportation on the water and one with transportation on the land. In 1794, he appointed a seven-member committee of health, and the following year the state organized the election of a board of health and a port health officer. In 1797, when Baltimore acquired a city charter, it was able to pass its own sanitary and quarantine ordinances. The following year, the city appointed a superintendent of street cleaning. Duffy, *The Sanitarians,* 46.

11. Report of the Commissioners of Health, Baltimore City Health Department, Dec. 31, 1832, Enoch Pratt Free Library, Maryland Room.

12. Rosenberg, *Cholera Years,* 20–23, 36.

13. Report of the Commissioners of Health, Baltimore City Health Department, Dec. 31, 1832.

14. Ibid.

15. Cordell, *Annals,* 94.

16. Quoted in T. J. C. Williams and Folger McKinsey, *History of Frederick County, Maryland* (Baltimore: Regional Publishing, 1967), 213.

17. Ibid., 214.

18. Ibid.

19. Consulting Physician's Report, Baltimore City Health Department, Dec. 31, 1832; Rosenberg, *Cholera Years,* 55–57. Many decades later, there would apparently be underreporting of HIV infections and AIDS-related deaths for somewhat the same reason.

20. Alan M. Kraut, *Silent Travelers: Germs, Genes, and the "Immigrant Menace"* (New York: Basic Books, 1994), 31–34.

21. William Travis Howard, *Public Health Administration and the Natural History of Disease in Baltimore, Maryland, 1797–1920* (Washington, D.C.: Carnegie Institute of Washington, 1924), 7.

22. Health Officer's Report, Baltimore City Health Department, 1832 (Martin's emphasis).

23. Ibid.

24. Ibid. (Martin's emphasis).

25. In 1883, it was discovered that cholera was caused by the bacterium *Vibrio cholerae,* which was ingested in food or water. The bacillus can survive for up to five days in meat and dairy products, up to fourteen days in water, and up to sixteen days in apples. It was most frequently transmitted by water contaminated with excreta from those already afflicted or by flies that hatched in or fed upon infected excrement and then contaminated food. Cholera patients are now treated with antibiotics and rehydration therapy.

26. George Rosen, *A History of Public Health* (New York: MD Publications, 1958), 287–89.

27. Erwin H. Ackerknecht, "Anticontagionism between 1821 and 1867," *Bulletin of the History of Medicine* 22 (1948): 562–93.

28. Consulting Physician's Report, Baltimore City Health Department, Dec. 31, 1832.

29. Cassedy, *American Medicine and Statistical Thinking,* 98, 185.

30. Cordell, *Annals,* 96.

31. Rosenberg, *Cholera Years,* 101–3.

32. Report from the Baltimore Marine Hospital, Baltimore City Health Department, Jan. 1, 1848; Report of the Health Officer of the Port of Baltimore, Baltimore City Health Department, Jan. 1, 1848; Report of the Board of Health, Baltimore City Health Department, Dec. 31, 1848.

33. Cordell, *Annals,* 120.

34. Rosenberg, *Cholera Years,* 104.

35. Report of the Health Officer of the Port of Baltimore, Baltimore City Health Department, Jan. 1, 1849; Report of the Board of Health, Baltimore City Health Department, Dec. 31, 1849.

36. Rosen, *A History of Public Health,* 99–100.

37. Derrick Baxby, *Jenner's Smallpox Vaccine: The Riddle of Vaccinia Virus and Its Origin* (London: Heinemann Educational Books, 1981); Paul Saunders, *Edward Jenner: The Cheltenham Years, Being a Chronicle of the Vaccination Campaign* (Hanover, N.H.: University Press of New England, 1982).

38. Howard, *Public Health Administration,* 99; Cordell, *Annals,* 46–47. Smallpox was, unfortunately, the only major nineteenth-century epidemic disease that yielded to this sort of preventive medicine. Wohl, *Endangered Lives,* 132.

39. Wohl, *Endangered Lives,* 132.

40. Consulting Physician's Report, Baltimore City Health Department, Dec. 31, 1832.

41. Report of the Commissioners of Health, Baltimore City Health Department, Dec. 31, 1834; Appendix, Consulting Physician's Report, Baltimore City Health Department, Dec. 31, 1835; Appendix, Consulting Physician's Report, Baltimore City Health Department, Dec. 31, 1834.

42. Appendix, Report of the Commissioners of Health, Baltimore City Health Department, Dec. 31, 1835; Appendix, Report of the Commissioners of Health, Baltimore City Health Department, Dec. 31, 1836; Appendix, Health Officer's Report, Baltimore City Health Department, Dec. 28, 1836.

43. Report of the Consulting Physician, Baltimore City Health Department, Jan. 28, 1843; Health Officer's Report, Baltimore City Health Department, Dec. 30, 1837; Health Officer's Report, Baltimore City Health Department, Dec. 26, 1837.

44. Report of the Consulting Physician, Baltimore City Health Department, Jan. 20, 1844.

45. Report of the Board of Health, Baltimore City Health Department, Dec. 31, 1847; Report of the Board of Health, Baltimore City Health Department, Dec. 31, 1848.

46. Cordell, *Annals,* 94–95, 521.

47. Roy Acheson and Elizabeth Fee, "Introduction," in Elizabeth Fee and Roy Acheson, eds., *A History of Education in Public Health: Health That Mocks the Doctors' Rules* (Oxford: Oxford University Press, 1991), 1.

48. Cassedy, *American Medicine and Statistical Thinking.*

49. A fifth, scheduled to be held in Cincinnati, was canceled because of the outbreak of the Civil War. Rosen, *A History of Public Health,* 241–43.

50. Cassedy, *American Medicine and Statistical Thinking,* 220–21.

51. Cordell, *Annals,* 666.

52. Brugger, *Maryland,* 142 (see chap. 2, n. 2).

53. Howard, *Public Health Administration,* 126.

54. Ibid., 126–28.

55. Ibid., 128.

56. Williams and McKinsey, *History of Frederick County,* 210–11.

57. Robert I. Cottom Jr. and Mary Ellen Hayward, *Maryland in the Civil War: A House Divided* (Baltimore: Maryland Historical Society, 1994), 10.

58. Williams and McKinsey, *History of Frederick County,* 269.

59. Brugger, *Maryland,* 274–76; Cottom and Hayward, *Maryland in the Civil War,* 29–32.

60. Daniel Carroll Toomey, *The Civil War in Maryland,* 7th ed. (Baltimore: Toomey Press, 1994), 39.

61. Ibid., 61–63. Brugger, *Maryland,* provides the best source on the state's involvement in the war. See chapter 6.

62. Toomey, *The Civil War in Maryland,* 98–99, 148–49.

63. "Antietam Recalls Founder of the American Red Cross," *Frederick [Maryland] News,* Dec. 8, 1960.

64. Ibid.; "Location of Clara Barton's Headquarters during Antietam Now Established," *Frederick [Maryland] Post,* Sept. 19, 1962.

65. George Worthington Adams, *Doctors in Blue: The Medical History of the Union Army in the Civil War* (New York: Henry Schuman, 1952), 4–9.

66. Ibid., 3, 14; Duffy, *The Sanitarians,* 110.

67. "U.S. Hospital—1862," Frederick Historical Society, File: Civil War: Hospitals; E. R. Goldsborough, "Military Hospitals, 1862," Aug. 4, 1936, Frederick Historical Society, File: Civil War: Hospitals.

68. Cottom and Hayward, *Maryland in the Civil War,* 104–5.

69. Williams and McKinsey, *History of Frederick County,* 566–68.

70. For background on the incidence of diphtheria in America, see Duffy, *The Sanitarians,* 11; "Occasional Notes: To End an Epidemic. Lessons from the History of Diphtheria," *New England Journal of Medicine* 326, no. 11 (1992): 773.

71. F. B. Smith, "Report on Sanitary Condition of Frederick County," quoted in Williams and McKinsey, *History of Frederick County,* 569.

72. Ibid., 569, 570.

73. "Memorial of the Mercantile Association," quoted in full in Williams and McKinsey, *History of Frederick County,* 573.

74. "Resolution of Board of Aldermen," in Williams and McKinsey, *History of Frederick County,* 573–77; Williams and McKinsey, *History of Frederick County,* 578–79; "Resolution of the Mercantile Association," in Williams and McKinsey, *History of Frederick County,* 579.

75. On the various ideas about the cause of the disease, see Peter C. English, "Diphtheria and Theories of Infectious Disease: Centennial Appreciation of the Critical Role of Diphtheria in the History of Medicine," *Pediatrics* 76, no. 1 (1985): 3–4.

76. William H. Welch, "The Cause of Diphtheria," *Medical News* 58 (1891): 551–60.

77. Harry F. Dowling, *Fighting Infection: Conquests of the Twentieth Century* (Cambridge: Harvard University Press, 1977), 20; Louis Galambos, with Jane Eliot Sewell, *Networks of Innovation: Vaccine Development at Merck, Sharp & Dohme and Mulford, 1895–1995* (New York: Cambridge University Press, 1995), 7–8, 15–16.

78. George Rosen, *Preventive Medicine in the United States, 1900–1975: Trends and Interpretations* (New York: Science History Publications, 1975), 3–13; Samuel H. Peterson and Michael R. Haines, *Fatal Years: Child Mortality in Late Nineteenth-Century America* (Princeton: Princeton University Press, 1991).

79. English, "Diphtheria and Theories," 1.

80. Rosen, *A History of Public Health,* 304–11.

81. René J. Dubos, *Louis Pasteur* (Boston: Little, Brown, 1950), 233–330; W. D. Foster, *A History of Medical Bacteriology and Immunology* (London: Heinemann Medical Books, 1970); Allan Chase, *Magic Shots: A Human and Scientific Account of the Long and Continuing Struggle to Eradicate Infectious Diseases by Vaccination* (New York: Morrow, 1982), 133–38.

82. F. M. Levy, "A Corner of History: The Fiftieth Anniversary of Diphtheria and Tetanus Immunization," *Preventive Medicine* 4 (1975): 226.

83. Emil von Behring and Shibasaburo Kitasato, "Über das Zustandekommen der Diphtherie-Immunität bei Thieren," *Deutsche Medicinische Wochenschrift* 16, no. 49 (1890): 1113–15; Emil von Bering, "Untersuchungen über das Zustandekommen der Diphtherie-Immunität bei Thieren," *Deutsche Medicinische Wochenschrift* 16, no. 50 (1890): 1145–48; Henry James Parish, *Victory with Vaccines: The Story of Immunization* (Edinburgh: E. and S. Livingstone, 1968), 44–51; Rob Roy Macgregor, "*Corynebacterium diphtheriae,*" in Gerald L. Mandell, R. Gordon Douglas Jr., and John E. Bennett, eds., *Principles and Practice of Infectious Diseases,* 3d ed. (New York: Churchill Livingstone, 1990), 1574–81.

84. M. J. White, Acting Surgeon General, Washington, D.C., to Assistant Surgeon General Rupert Blue, Paris, Oct. 6, 1923, Records of the Public Health Service, RG90, General Subject File 1924–35, box 056, NC-34, entry 10, file 0475. Blue was in Paris for the October session of the Office International d'Hygiene Publique.

85. Alan D. Anderson, *Origin and Resolution of an Urban Crisis: Baltimore, 1890–1930* (Baltimore: Johns Hopkins University Press, 1977), 18–19.

SEVEN: Public Health: Professional Responses to the Rise of
Scientific Medicine, 1900–1940

1. Anderson, *Origin and Resolution of an Urban Crisis,* 20–31 (see chap. 6, n. 85).

2. Edward F. Keuchel, "Chemicals and Meat: The Embalmed Beef Scandal of the Spanish-American War," *Bulletin of the History of Medicine* 48 (1974): 249–64.

3. On the debates and, in particular, the opposition of business interests to regulation, see *Congressional Record,* 59th Cong., 1st sess., 8897–8984. Thomas A. Smith, a prominent Maryland canner, added his angry voice to the House debate, opposing regulation. Various reform-oriented, muck-raking articles and books on business practices generated ever stronger public support for regulation.

4. James Harvey Young, *Pure Food: Securing the Federal Food and Drugs Act of 1906* (Princeton: Princeton University Press, 1989), 253–72, 3–6.

5. "Maryland Needs a Pure Food and Drug Law," *Bulletin of the Medical and Chirurgical Faculty of Maryland* 2, no. 3 (1909): 49, 50.

6. "State Board of Health Must Administer the Pure Food Law," *Bulletin of the Medical and Chirurgical Faculty of Maryland* 2, no. 7 (1910): 126–27.

7. Ibid., 50–51; "The Pure Food Question in Maryland," *Bulletin of the Medical and Chirurgical Faculty of Maryland* 2, no. 7 (1910): 124–25.

8. Harvey W. Wiley, "Pure Food Legislation," *Bulletin of the Medical and Chirurgical Faculty of Maryland* 2, no. 7 (1910): 135, 136.

9. Lyman F. Kebler, "Pure Drug Legislation," *Bulletin of the Medical and Chirurgical Faculty of Maryland* 2, no. 7 (1910): 138–41.

10. "Faculty Will Support the Pure Food Bill of the Governor's Commission," *Bulletin of the Medical and Chirurgical Faculty of Maryland* 2, no. 8 (1910): 163–64. The American Medical Association had played a similar role in the passage of the federal law in 1906.

11. "Report of the Pure Food Committee of the Faculty," *Bulletin of the Medical and Chirurgical Faculty of Maryland* 3, no. 7 (1911): 90–91.

12. C. Hampson Jones, "Our Milk Supply," *Bulletin of the Medical and Chirurgical Faculty of Maryland* 4, no. 4 (1911): 54–57.

13. "The Farm End of the Milk Problem," *Bulletin of the Medical and Chirurgical Faculty of Maryland* 5, no. 1 (1912): 3.

14. Ibid.

15. Fred C. Blanck, "Baltimore's Milk Supply," *Bulletin of the Medical and Chirurgical Faculty of Maryland* 5 (1912): 5.

16. "Milk and Infant Mortality," *Bulletin of the Medical and Chirurgical Faculty of Maryland* 5, no. 1 (1912): 1–2.

17. "The Milk Supply of Baltimore," *Baltimore Health News* 1, no. 3 (1924): 20–21.

18. "No Milk-Borne Disease in Baltimore since 1917," *Baltimore Health News* 13, no. 9 (1936): 55.

19. Mary P. Ryan, *Womanhood in America: From Colonial Times to the Present* (New York: Franklin Watts, 1983); Elizabeth Fee and Dorothy Porter, "Public Health, Preventive Medicine and Professionalization: Britain and the United States in the Nineteenth Century," in Fee and Acheson, *History of Education in Public Health,* 22–23 (see chap. 6, n. 47); Anderson, *Origin and Resolution of an Urban Crisis,* 9–15.

20. Elizabeth Fee, *Disease and Discovery: A History of the Johns Hopkins School of Hygiene and Public Health, 1916–1939* (Baltimore: Johns Hopkins University Press, 1987), 5–7, 41.

21. For background on early nineteenth-century conditions, see Cassedy, *American Medicine and Statistical Thinking,* 220 (see chap. 6, n. 3).

22. C. Hampson Jones, "The Good to be Derived from Our Sanitary Sewerage System," *Bulletin of the Medical and Chirurgical Faculty of Maryland* 4, no. 6 (1912): 91–92; Anderson, *Origin and Resolution of an Urban Crisis.*

23. William Royal Stokes, "The Disposal of Sewage in Small Towns and Country Dwellings," *Bulletin of the Medical and Chirurgical Faculty of Maryland* 4 (1912): 88–90.

24. Anderson, *Origin and Resolution of an Urban Crisis,* 18–19.

25. For an outstanding exposition of the cultural aspects of tuberculosis, see JoAnne Brown, "Matters of Life and Death: Hygiene and Political Culture in the United States, 1865–1945" (unpublished manuscript, courtesy of the author).

26. Christine R. Whittaker, "Chasing the Cure: Irving Fisher's Experience as a Tuberculosis Patient," *Bulletin of the History of Medicine* 48 (1974): 398–99.

27. "Report of Committee on Tuberculosis, 1909," *Bulletin of the Medical and Chirurgical Faculty of Maryland* 2, no. 9 (1910): 189; John Girdwood, "Report of the

Committee on Tuberculosis, 1910," *Bulletin of the Medical and Chirurgical Faculty of Maryland* 3, no. 7 (1911): 88.

28. Girdwood, "Committee on Tuberculosis, 1910," 88–89.

29. "Report of Committee on Tuberculosis, 1909," 186–87.

30. Ibid., 187.

31. Whittaker, "Chasing the Cure," 400–401.

32. Ibid., 402–7.

33. "The Maryland State Tuberculosis Sanitorium—Sabillasville: A Struggle in the Wilderness," *Bicentennial Supplement to the Frederick, MD, News-Post,* Nov. 25, 1975, 6.

34. "Maryland Tuberculosis Sanatorium, Colored Branch, Henryton, MD," *Baltimore Health News* 1, no. 7 (1924): 61.

35. Ibid.

36. Chase, *Magic Shots,* 196–97 (see chap. 6, n. 81); Robert F. Betts and R. Gordon Douglas Jr., "Influenza Virus," in Gerald L. Mandell, R. Gordan Douglas, and John E. Barnett, eds., *Principles and Practice of Infectious Diseases,* 3d ed. (New York: Churchill Livingstone, 1990), 1306.

37. Macfarlane Burnet and David O. White, *Natural History of Infectious Disease* (Cambridge: Cambridge University Press, 1972), 202–4. Because the responsible virus was not isolated until 1933, however, retrospective diagnosis is, in this case, fundamentally ahistorical.

38. Dowling, *Fighting Infection,* 195 (see chap. 6, n. 77); Alfred W. Crosby Jr., *Epidemic and Peace, 1918* (Westport, Conn.: Greenwood Press, 1976).

39. Dowling, *Fighting Infection,* 195–96.

40. Peter Radetsky, *The Invisible Invaders: The Story of the Emerging Age of Viruses* (Boston: Little, Brown, 1991), 229–31.

41. Victor Vaughn, "The Responsibilities of the Medical Profession in This War," *Bulletin of the Medical and Chirurgical Faculty of Maryland* 10, no. 4 (1918): 61.

42. "Volunteer Medical Service Corps," *Bulletin of the Medical and Chirurgical Faculty of Maryland* 10, no. 5 (1918): 81. The influenza pandemic became known as the "Spanish flu" because, when it had erupted in Europe, the Spanish had been particularly afflicted.

43. "The Influenza Epidemic," *Bulletin of the Medical and Chirurgical Faculty of Maryland* 10, no. 6 (1919): 89.

44. Chase, *Magic Shots,* 197–98.

45. "The Influenza Epidemic," 82.

46. George W. Comstock, "Commentary," in Richard V. Kasius, ed., *The Challenge of Facts: Selected Public Health Papers of Edgar Sydenstricker* (New York: Prodist, 1974), 165. As Sydenstricker explained, he and his collaborators selected the western Maryland town for several reasons. It seemed representative of much of America at the time, it had already participated in a health demonstration project, and it was conveniently close to his Washington-based team.

47. Edgar Sydenstricker, "A Study of Illness in a General Population Group.

Hagerstown Morbidity Studies No. I: The Method of Study and General Results," in Kasius, *Challenge of Facts,* 204–27; Edgar Sydenstricker, "The Incidence of Influenza among Persons of Different Economic Status during the Epidemic of 1918," in Kasius, *Challenge of Facts,* 314–32.

48. Fee and Porter, "Public Health, Preventive Medicine and Professionalization," 37.

49. Fee, *Disease and Discovery,* 24.

50. William Henry Welch, "Sanitation in Relation to the Poor: An Address to the Sanitation Organization Society of Baltimore, November 1892," in William Henry Welch, *Papers and Addresses* (Baltimore: Johns Hopkins University Press, 1920), 3:598.

51. Fee, *Disease and Discovery,* 19.

52. Ibid., 26–36.

53. Ibid., 37–51.

54. Elizabeth Fee, "Designing Schools of Public Health for the United States," in Fee and Acheson, *History of Education in Public Health,* 181.

55. Ibid., 182–83.

56. Elmer Verner McCollum, *A History of Nutrition: The Sequence of Ideas in Nutrition Investigations* (Cambridge, Mass.: Riverside Press, 1957), 211–301; Elmer Verner McCollum, *From Kansas Farm Boy to Scientist: The Autobiography of Elmer Verner McCollum* (Lawrenceville: University of Kansas Press, 1964).

57. Fee, *Disease and Discovery,* 96–115.

58. Records of the Public Health Service, RG90, General Records, General Subject File, 1924–35, Washington, D.C., Epidemiology Studies to the National Institutes of Health, box 055, NC-34, entry 10.

59. See, e.g., "Report of Committee on Public Instruction," *Bulletin of the Medical and Chirurgical Faculty of Maryland* 3, no. 6 (1910): 72, 73–74.

60. William H. F. Warthen, "The Baby Welfare and Pre-School Clinics," *Baltimore Health News* 2, no. 1 (1925): 36–37.

61. "General Death Rate of Baltimore City," *Baltimore Health News* 1 (1924): 11.

62. These figures were for the 1920s. Although they were partially an artifact of relatively thorough reporting, that could not entirely explain away the dismal mortality statistics. See "Negro Death Rate in Maryland Higher than in Any Other State," *Baltimore Health News* 1 (1924): 6. See also V. L. Ellicott, "Excessive Death Rate among Negroes: A Study to Determine Factors Responsible for High Rate," *Baltimore Health News* 1 (1924): 5.

EIGHT: Modern Medicine: Strains and Successes in Maryland
Health Care, 1940–1999

1. This program on WFBR was entitled *The Endless Chain;* the *Keeping Well* series was aired on Saturday evenings. The "chain" was "endless" as a result of the

quackery and poor reporting that left infected persons unidentified and likely to transmit to others such sexual diseases as syphilis.

2. The drama continued:

The young man asks, "Say, what does that red light mean?"

QUACK: "It means that the organism *Treponema pallidum* has entered your blood stream."

MAN: "What's that mean?"

QUACK: "It means that you have syphilis. The amber light burning steadily tells me that the center of infection is near your heart. The flickering of the purple light means that your central nervous system is being threatened by the disease. In other words, that you may go crazy if not promptly treated."

MAN: "That sounds awful—are you sure everything will be all right?"

QUACK: "Yes—I will give you Specific 18 to clear up the primary infection and Horton's Liquid X-5 discovery to check the nervous disorder threatened. Of course—this treatment is expensive."

MAN: "I'm not rich, Doc—maybe I can't afford this. You see, I've been saving now two years to get married and have a few hundred dollars in the bank."

QUACK: "I understand—if it were possible, my dear boy these treatments would not cost you a cent. In view of the special considerations in your case, I'm going to give you this entire treatment slightly less than cost— Give me $100 today to cover the cost of the diagnosis and your first series of medicines—the rest you can pay for by the week or month out of your income."

MAN: "That's mighty white of you, Doctor—then I'll still have enough left for us to get married on in June."

So as not to leave any doubt about the moral, WFBR's station announcer explained: "The Quack Doctor is public enemy no. 1 in the battle being waged to educate the public in the importance of a concerted fight to stamp out syphilis." Public enemy no. 2 in the "war" against syphilis was the licensed physician who, for personal or family reasons, did not accurately report cases of the disease.

3. James Harvey Young, *The Medical Messiahs: A Social History of Health Quackery in Twentieth-Century America* (Princeton: Princeton University Press, 1967).

4. See, e.g., the videotaped interview with Dr. Charles Williams, "Voices from the Past; Looking to the Future," produced by and available in the library of the Baltimore County Medical Association (BCMA). Williams was president

of the BCMA in 1952 and worked as a family doctor during the 1940s through 1960s, with his office in Pikesville.

5. Videotape "Voices from the Past; Looking to the Future," Baltimore County Medical Association. O'Donnell, who was president of the BCMA in 1953, later served as president of the Medical and Chirurgical Faculty.

6. "Doctors Available for Defense Listed," *Baltimore Evening Sun,* July 26, 1940; "Groups to Pick State Doctors for Armed Duty," *Baltimore Sun,* June 10, 1941; "The State's Doctors," *Baltimore Evening Sun,* June 18, 1941; "Finding Doctors for the Armed Forces," *Baltimore Evening Sun,* July 11, 1941; *Celebration of the Sesquicentennial of the Medical and Chirurgical Faculty of the State of Maryland, 1799–1949* (Baltimore: Medical and Chirurgical Faculty of Maryland, 1949), 55.

7. "Says State Is Meeting Call for Doctors in Armed Forces," *Baltimore Sun,* June 11, 1942. The shortage of doctors was so serious that the Maryland's attorney general's office passed a ruling that permitted German and Italian immigrant doctors to practice in the state without restrictions. See "Alien Doctors May Practice," *Baltimore Evening Sun,* March 10, 1942.

8. "Hopkins Hospital Report," *Baltimore Evening Sun,* Jan. 18, 1944. Dr. Winford H. Smith, executive vice-president of Johns Hopkins Hospital, reported that during 1943 there had been a constant and severe shortage of doctors, nurses, and other employees.

9. Suzanne Ellery Greene Chapelle, Jean H. Baker, Dean R. Esslinger, Whitman H. Ridgway, Jean B. Russo, Constance B. Schulz, and Gregory A. Stiverson, *Maryland: A History of Its People* (Baltimore: Johns Hopkins University Press, 1986), 248–49.

10. Brugger, *Maryland,* 528–51 (see chap. 2, n. 2), provides an excellent source on the experiences of the state and its citizens during the war. Brugger, a combat veteran of a later war, is particularly effective when he is discussing the military life.

11. Chapelle et al., *Maryland,* 249. The Johns Hopkins School of Hygiene and Public Health offered a new course in 1942 on "Industrial Health." *Bulletin of the Medical and Chirurgical Faculty of the State of Maryland,* Oct. 1942, 2.

12. Chapelle et al., *Maryland,* 251.

13. Harvey et al., *A Model of Its Kind,* 1:231 (see chap. 5, n. 5).

14. Douglas Carroll, "History of the Baltimore City Hospitals," *Maryland State Medical Journal* 15 (1966): 28–29; Chapelle et al., *Maryland,* 252; *Baltimore Sun,* July 26, 1940, June 11, 1942; *Baltimore Evening Sun,* June 18, 1941. Maryland sent 718 physicians into service, 577 from Baltimore and 141 from the counties. *Baltimore Evening Sun,* July 11, 1941; *Celebration of the Sesquicentennial of the Medical and Chirurgical Faculty of the State of Maryland,* Baltimore, 1949, 55.

15. *Celebration of the Sesquicentennial,* 530, 545–46; see esp. the author's story of the ill-fated fifty-sixth hospital unit. French, *A History of the University,* 455–56 (see chap. 2, n. 45); University of Maryland Medical System, *Yesterday and Today:*

An Historic Timeline, 1994, University of Maryland Health Sciences Library Historical Collection; Callcott, *History of the University of Maryland,* 336 (see chap. 2, n. 18); Augusta Tucker, *It Happened at Hopkins: A Teaching Hospital* (Baltimore: Johns Hopkins Hospital, 1973), 229.

16. U.S. Office of Scientific Research and Development, *Advances in Military Medicine Made by American Investigators Working under the Sponsorship of the Committee on Medical Research* (Boston: Little, Brown, 1948); U.S. Army Medical Service, *Preventive Medicine in World War II: Personal Health Measures and Immunization,* vol. 3 (Washington, D.C.: Office of the Surgeon General, Department of the Army, 1955); University of Maryland Medical System, *Yesterday and Today.*

17. Harvey et al., *A Model of Its Kind,* 1:75.

18. Chapelle et al., *Maryland,* 259.

19. "Rural Doctors Fewer," *Baltimore Evening Sun,* June 17, 1941.

20. Brugger, *Maryland,* 794–97; Chapelle et al., *Maryland,* 260–64.

21. For an example of how new surgical knowledge from wartime conditions was circulated back on the homefront, see the report of the semiannual meeting of the Baltimore City Medical Society in April 1942, at which there had been discussion of the newly published book by Dr. John J. Moorhead entitled *Traumatotherapy.* Moorhead described surgical procedures that had been undertaken at Pearl Harbor.

22. Victoria Harden, *Inventing the NIH: Federal Biomedical Research Policy, 1887–1937* (Baltimore: Johns Hopkins University Press, 1986).

23. Between 1947 and 1971, NIH's annual budget for research grants to universities and other research institutions increased from $4 million to $1.26 billion.

24. In the age of the computer and internet communications, the library can provide information to researchers throughout the United States and in other nations. In 1971, the NLM launched MEDLINE, a bibliographic service that connected 150 institutions and handled 140,000 searches in its first year of operations. Wyndham D. Miles, *A History of the National Library of Medicine: The Nation's Treasury of Medical Knowledge* (Bethesda, Md.: National Library of Medicine, 1982), 384–85.

25. Ibid., 1–40, 296–98. During World War II, concerns about the safety of the books and artifacts led the staff to decentralize the materials; they sent much of the rare material to the History of Medicine Division of the Cleveland Medical library in Ohio. This material was returned when the library opened in Bethesda in 1962.

26. Harvey et al., *A Model of Its Kind,* 76–80.

27. Ibid., 80–107, provides an overview.

28. Samuel P. Asper, "Evaluation of Dr. John Eager Howard's Contributions to Medicine," *Journal of the American Medical Association* 207, no. 4 (1969): 730–35; Harvey, *Adventures in Medical Research,* 355–60 (see chap. 2, n. 51).

29. The work of Lehninger (vol. 2, p. 767) and others on the Hopkins faculty

is described in A. McGehee Harvey, John L. Cameron, M. Daniel Lane, Guy M. McKhann, Victor A. McKusick, and Paul Talalay, *A Century of Biomedical Science at Johns Hopkins,* 2 vols. (Baltimore: Johns Hopkins University Press, 1993).

30. Thomas Bourne Turner, *Part of Medicine, Part of Me: Musings of a Johns Hopkins Dean* (Baltimore: Johns Hopkins University School of Medicine, 1981), 91–117. Dean Turner, who spent twenty-seven years with the medical faculty and twenty-one with the hygiene faculty, made this comparison: "The quality of research on the School of Hygiene side of the street as a whole never quite achieved the elegance or forward thrust of that of the School of Medicine" (99). See, e.g., Lewis Kuller, Abraham Lilienfeld, and Russell Fisher, "Sudden and Unexpected Deaths in Young Adults," *Journal of the American Medical Association* 198, no. 3 (1966): 158–62, which reported on a study jointly conducted by personnel from the School of Hygiene and Public Health, the Office of the Chief Medical Examiner of Maryland, and the Maryland Medical Legal Foundation. For a contrasting project see "Medical News," *Journal of the American Medical Association* 139, no. 9 (1951): 596.

31. University of Maryland Medical System, *Yesterday and Today.* During these years, Dr. Mark Ravitch was a surgeon at Baltimore City Hospitals, where Dr. Ronald H. Fishbein was chief resident. Ravitch introduced surgical stapling to the United States. He had been in the Soviet Union and had seen the application of staples rather than sutures. In Leningrad, he managed to purchase a staple machine, which he brought back to the United States and demonstrated for his colleagues. The practice quickly engendered enthusiasm, and stapling soon became a standard method of closure. Interview, Dr. Ronald Harrison Fishbein, Sept. 23, 1997.

32. The *R* in Cowley's name has no period. That is as it appears on his birth certificate and as it was intended by his mother. Jon Franklin and Alan Doelp, *Shock-Trauma* (New York: St. Martin's Press, 1980), viii.

33. Ibid., 8–9.

34. Cowley was able to conduct open-heart surgery even before the employment of heart-lung machines. Operating with alacrity on patients who had been cooled to reduce the metabolic rate, he was able to cut, repair, and close before the brain succumbed to oxygen deficiency.

35. Franklin and Doelp, *Shock-Trauma,* 7.

36. Ibid., 17–22, 71. Cowley's interest in trauma-related shock was wide ranging. In the mid-1960s, when he was chief of heart surgery at University Hospital, he went out on a limb with his budget to support what he thought would be a significant improvement in survival rates. Working with him at that time was Dr. T. Crawford McAslan, who had become convinced that the Swedish-made Engstrom respirator would prevent a great many deaths from shock lung.

Shock lung was first identified in World War I, but it was not until the wars in Korea and Vietnam that more patients succumbed to that complication—circulatory collapse due to deep shock—than to gangrene or blood loss. McAslan saw a similar process at work in patients who had been on heart-lung machines for extended periods (identified as postpump lung). Convinced that with better equipment he could save lives, McAslan worked with Cowley to purchase an expensive Engstrom machine to replace the cheaper respirators they were using. By 1972, McAslan had proved its worth by sharply reducing the death rates in their unit. Ibid., 29–35.

37. Cowley loudly decried the conditions that existed: "The God's truth is that most emergency rooms are awful. I get into trouble every time I say that and some miserable son of a bitch quotes me in the newspaper, but it's true. Even today [in the late 1970s] you live or die depending on where you have your accident, because in most places they take you to the nearest hospital." Ibid., 17. On the obstacles Cowley encountered and the factors that contributed to his eventual success, see ibid., 72–76, 135–51. Out of Shock Trauma came SYSCOM (Systems Communications Center), the statewide emergency medical services system. "SYSCOM: A New Resource," *EMS Newsletter* 2 (June 19, 1978): 1, 3.

By 1985, a $21 million grant was to be extended to the University of Maryland Medical System to start construction on a new six-story Shock Trauma Center. Governor Harry Hughes had also pledged substantial state support for the project. "New STC Building before Legislature," *Maryland EMS News* 11, no. 8 (1985): 1–2; "Legislature OKs New Shock Trauma Building," *Maryland EMS News* 11, no. 11 (1985): 1. By January 1989, the new R Adams Cowley, M.D., Shock Trauma Center began to receive patients. This state-of-the-art facility includes space on the roof for four Med-Evac helicopters, ten admitting areas equipped for resuscitation and stabilization, seventy-two beds (with an additional sixty-six beds on the adjacent fourth floor of the hospital), and an isolation room. "Shock Trauma Center Opens," *Bulletin* (of the University of Maryland at Baltimore) 73, no. 3 (1989): 1–2. Cowley lived to see his vision materialize; he died at the age of seventy-four in 1991. "Shock Trauma Founder Is Dead," *Baltimore Sun,* Oct. 28, 1991; "Man Who Saved So Many from Death Is Buried," Nov. 5, 1991.

38. Provident Hospital and Free Dispensary, *First Report of the 1954 Survey Committee,* Dec. 13, 1954, University of Maryland Health Sciences Library Historical Collection. Dr. Alan M. Chesney, an expert in infectious diseases from Johns Hopkins, chaired the committee that conducted this survey.

39. Ibid., 26–61. In 1950, "nonwhites" constituted 23.9 percent of Baltimore's total population of 950,000.

40. *Bulletin of the Medical and Chirurgical Faculty of the State of Maryland,* Nov. 1947, 2. The Blue Cross plans had been in active operation only since the end of the 1930s in most parts of the country. See "Blue Cross Plans Face a Challenge," *Bulletin of the Medical and Chirurgical Faculty of the State of Maryland,* Nov. 1942, 2. See also Maryland House of Delegates Minutes, Report to the Council of the Medical and Chirurgical Faculty on Proposed Revisions in Blue Shield

Plan, 1952. On a national level by 1940, in the thirty-nine states that had Blue Cross plans in place, over six million people had enrolled. See Starr, *Social Transformation of American Medicine,* 295–98 (see chap. 1, n. 23).

41. *Maryland State Medical Journal* 1, no. 1 (1952): 40.

42. Provident Hospital and Free Dispensary, *First Report of the 1954 Survey Committee,* 33–34. The committee that drafted the report was concerned because the percentage of African Americans in the city's population was increasing, as was the number enrolled under the state's Medical Care Program. Since 95 percent of the enrollees were being taken care of by African-American physicians, "the problem is a formidable one here and now. If that is so in 1954 how much more formidable will it be in 1970, which is less than a generation hence." Since city and state payments did not cover the full cost of care, the outlook was bleak (62–64).

43. *Laws of Maryland,* chapter 210, 1945; *Maryland State Medical Journal* 1, no. 1 (1952): 113–15.

44. *Maryland State Medical Journal* 1, no. 1 (1952): 40–42. The amount of federal support for construction varied from 33.33 to 44 percent during these years.

45. See, e.g., Lillian M. Snyder, "The Merits of Discharge Planning in Shortening the Hospitalization of Free Patients," *Maryland State Medical Journal* 2, no. 2 (1962): 10–17.

46. During the war, the armed services employed psychiatrists to deal with the various mental illnesses that occurred among military personnel. Two important aspects of their professional role were to weed out the malingers from the mentally ill and to develop means of bolstering morale. See Karl M. Bowman, "Trimble Lecture: Psychiatry and Morale," *Bulletin of the Medical and Chirurgical Faculty of the State of Maryland,* April 1941, 20 (abstract). See also Maryland House of Delegates Minutes, 1945, remarks by Dr. Kenneth B. Jones.

47. Gerald N. Grob, "The Origins of American Psychiatric Epidemiology," *American Journal of Public Health* 75, no. 3 (1985): 235. The best guide to these developments is Gerald N. Grob, *From Asylum to Community: Mental Health Policy in Modern America* (Princeton: Princeton University Press, 1991).

48. Interim Report of the Committee on Medical Care, Maryland State Planning Commission, Jan. 1947; *Maryland State Medical Journal* 1, no. 1 (1952): 113.

49. *Maryland State Medical Journal* 6, no. 2 (1957): 163.

50. Maryland State Department of Health, "Study of Organization and Operations," Feb. 25, 1966. A management consulting firm prepared the report for the state.

51. By 1967, about 30 percent of the state's preschoolers had not received adequate immunization against polio. *Maryland's Health* 39, no. 4 (1967): 4. On the development of the vaccines and the immunization campaigns, see Jane S. Smith, *Patenting the Sun: Polio and the Salk Vaccine* (New York: William Morrow, 1991); Tom Rivers, *Reflections on a Life in Medicine and Science* (Cambridge: MIT Press, 1967); Thomas M. Daniel and Frederick C. Robbins, eds., *Polio* (Rochester:

University of Rochester Press, 1997); Kathryn Black, *In the Shadow of Polio: A Personal and Social History* (Reading, Mass.: Addison-Wesley Publishing, 1996); Tony Gould, *A Summer Plague: Polio and Its Survivors* (New Haven: Yale University Press, 1995).

52. Gould, *A Summer Plague,* 4–8. "Careful planning and budgeting, free vaccine for the pre-school children, absorption of certain costs by the State and local health departments, and the Medical and Chirurgical Faculty's contribution $15,000 for education and promotion made it possible for the End Measles Menace campaign to 'break even.'"

53. See, e.g., the discussion by Zorayda Lee-Llacer (medical director of critical care medicine at Doctors Community Hospital, Lanham, Md.) of "Physician Strategies in a Managed Care Environment," *Maryland Medical Journal* 45, no. 3 (1996): 197–200. See also Gerald D. Klee, "Hippocrates on HMOs," *Maryland Medical Journal* 45, no. 4 (1996): 289–91.

54. See, e.g., Department of Health and Mental Hygiene, "1992 Executive Plan," Maryland State Archives, Annapolis. Also see the following articles in the *Baltimore Sun:* "Health Plan Likely to Shut Baltimore-Area Hospitals," Sept. 26, 1993; "Retooling Hopkins," May 15, 1994; "Operating Independently," July 25, 1995; "Bills Worry Doctors, Too," Sept. 7, 1997.

55. Health Manpower and Planning Committee, "Characteristics of Physician Practice Patterns in Maryland, 1981–1982," *Maryland State Medical Journal* 33, no. 9 (1984): 697–700; James Studnicki and Charles E. Stevens, "An Approach to the Assessment of Emergency Medical Care Utilization," *Maryland State Medical Journal* 31, no. 9 (1982): 45.

56. This was the central theme of "Operating Independently," *Baltimore Sun,* July 25, 1995.

57. Grob, *From Asylum to Community; Baltimore Sun,* Sept. 26, 1993.

58. Joseph M. Miller, "The Growth and Metamorphosis of Provident Hospital and Free Dispensary into the Liberty Health System, Inc.," *Maryland Medical Journal* 46, no. 4 (1997): 193–97. In the same issue see David C. Daneker and Lawrence Rychlak, "Dealing with Uncompensated Care: A Hospital Board Perspective," 191–92. The problem was national in scope. Jennifer Preston, "Hospitals Look on Charity Care as Unaffordable Option of Past," *New York Times,* April 14, 1996.

59. See the early commentary in Howard L. Tolson, "Are We Practicing Medicine or Specialties?" *Maryland State Medical Journal* 6, no. 2 (1957), 51.

60. Interview, Dr. Ronald Harrison Fishbein, Sept. 23, 1997. In his current position as chairman of the Health Professions Recommendation Committee in the Office of Academic Advising at Johns Hopkins, Fishbein takes these changes into consideration when he counsels undergraduates who are looking toward careers in medicine. In particular, he advises them not to specialize too early in their careers.

61. D. J. Kevles, "From Eugenics to Genetic Manipulation," 301–18; P. G.

Abir-Am, "The Molecular Transformation of Twentieth-Century Biology," 495–524; H. Kamminga, "Biochemistry, Molecules and Macromolecules," 525–46; all in John Krige and Dominique Pestre, eds., *Science in the Twentieth Century* (Amsterdam: Harwood Academic Publishers, 1997). For a broad overview of clinical research in the twentieth century, see Christopher Lawrence, "Clinical Research," in Krige and Pestre, *Science in the Twentieth Century,* 439–59.

62. The best source is Harvey et al., *A Century of Biomedical Science.* See also *Hopkins Medical News,* Nov. 1980, 1–3; winter 1996, 14–15; spring/summer 1997, 37–43; *Journal of the American Medical Association* 252, no. 8 (1984): 1041–48.

63. Susan Wright, *Molecular Politics: Developing American and British Regulatory Policy for Genetic Engineering, 1972–1982* (Chicago: University of Chicago Press, 1994); Luigi Orsenigo, *The Emergence of Biotechnology: Institutions and Markets in Industrial Innovation* (New York: St. Martin's Press, 1989); Maureen McKelvey, *Evolutionary Innovations: The Business of Biotechnology* (Oxford: Oxford University Press, 1996).

64. See, e.g., *Hopkins Medical News,* fall 1985, 16–18; summer 1988, 30–31; winter 1994, 5–6; winter 1995, 8, 11.

65. *Dome,* Jan. 1981, 1–2; Feb. 1985, 1–2; Nov. 1988, 1, 3; summer 1996, 1, 10; *Hopkins Medical News,* March 1979, 2–4; Sept. 1979, 1–2; Sept. 1980, 2–5; fall 1992, 19–31, 33–39.

66. L. Cavagnaro provided these statistics on the situation at Hopkins.

67. *Baltimore Evening Sun,* April 19, 1975. At Hopkins, however, there was a positive shift in the number of graduates as early as 1973 and 1974. I am grateful to Archivist William R. Day Jr. for providing this information.

68. *Maryland State Medical Journal* 32, no. 8 (1983): 572–74. The career of Vivien Thomas indicates how much had changed between the 1940s and the 1980s. Thomas, who had been forced to drop out of Tennessee State College because of financial difficulties, went to Hopkins in 1940 to work as a technician under Dr. Alfred Blalock. Operating closely with Blalock and Dr. Helen Taussig, Thomas helped develop the Blalock-Taussig shunt that, in 1944, was used in the first blue-baby surgery. Thomas had such a clear grasp of how the procedure should be performed that he stood behind Blalock during the initial operations, offering suggestions. The technician went on to work at Johns Hopkins for forty-five years. Although he never became an M.D., in 1976 the university appointed him as a surgical instructor and awarded him an honorary degree as Doctor of Law. *Hopkins Medical News,* July 1976, 3; Harvey, *Adventures in Medical Research,* 284–85.

69. W. Houston Toulson, M.D., to Dr. George H. Lull, Secretary, American Medical Association, Chicago, Med Chi Library.

70. Randi Henderson, "Up from Bigotry," *Hopkins Medical News,* winter 1995, 26–28.

71. "Hopkins Has Something of Substance for Young Blacks," *Hopkins Medical News,* May 1979, 1, 3.

72. Ben Carson with Cecil Murphey, *Gifted Hands: The Ben Carson Story* (Grand Rapids, Mich.: Zondervan Publishing House, 1990); "For Many, Pediatric Neurosurgeon Is a Folk Hero," *New York Times,* June 8, 1993. Carson's research and clinical work have focused on brain tumors in children, achondroplasia, and congenital deformities of the spine.

73. See Membership Meeting, "Maryland Physician Demographics, May 15, 1997," Med Chi Library.

74. Harvey et al., *A Model of Its Kind,* 151, 268–70. Chapter 11 of this book is devoted to "Women at the Medical School."

75. University of Maryland, Complementary Medicine Program, Report, September 1991 through August 1997, University of Maryland Health Sciences Library Historical Collection.

76. Ibid. Also see telephone interview with the author, Susan Berman, Nov. 1997. For press coverage of alternative medicine, see *Baltimore Sun,* April 4, 1995; January 20, 1998; *Annapolis Capital,* Feb. 24, 1998.

77. Grob, *From Asylum to Community,* esp. chaps. 9 and 10; Neil Solomon, "A Message from the Secretary of Health and Mental Hygiene," *Maryland's Health* 42, no. 1 (1970): 2.

78. John McAvinue, "October: Immunization Month," *Maryland State Medical Journal* 26, no. 9 (1977): 22; *Journal of the American Medical Association* 250, no. 2 (1983): 159–60.

79. Galambos with Sewell, *Networks of Innovation* (see chap. 6, n. 77). See also Allen Chase, *Magic Shots* (see chap. 6, n. 81).

80. C. Everett Koop, "The Early Days of AIDS . . . ," in Caroline Hannaway, Victoria A. Harden, and John Parascandola, eds., *AIDS and the Public Debate: Historical and Contemporary Perspectives* (Amsterdam: IOS Press, 1995), 9.

81. B. Frank Polk, "Epidemiologic and Clinical Aspects," *Maryland Medical Journal* 36, no. 1 (1987): 31.

82. Department of Health and Mental Hygiene: FY 1989–1991 Executive Plan, Adele Wilzack (Secretary), William Donald Schaefer (Governor), Jan. 1988, iii.

83. *Mortality and Morbidity Weekly Report* 40 (1991): 358–69.

84. C. Everett Koop, "The Early Days of AIDS as I Remember Them," 9, and Mark Smith, "AIDS and Minority Health," 102, in Hannaway et al., *AIDS and the Public Debate.*

85. See, e.g., material about Ryan White, a hemophiliac schoolboy, in *Newsweek,* March 3, 1986, 6; *Time,* Sept. 8, 1986, 68; *U.S. News and World Report,* Sept. 8, 1986, 10; and *People Weekly,* Aug. 3, 1987, 61–64. Also see Allan M. Brandt, "AIDS: From Social History to Social Policy," in Elizabeth Fee and Daniel M. Fox, eds., *AIDS: The Burdens of History* (Berkeley and Los Angeles: University of California Press, 1988), 154–55.

86. James W. Curran, "The CDC and the Investigation of the Epidemiology of AIDS," in Hannaway et al., *AIDS and the Public Debate,* 19–29.

87. Edward N. Brandt, "The Governor's Task Force on AIDS," *Maryland Medical Journal* 36, no. 1 (1987): 47. By 1987, there were regulations in all states that required the reporting of AIDS, syphilis, gonorrhea, chanchroid, lymphogranuloma venereum, and granuloma inguinale. There were, however, still difficulties in relation to enforcement of the regulations, and not all STDs were included. Hepatitis B, chlamydia, and genital herpes were reported only sporadically. Baltimore, e.g., required that herpes be reported, but the state did not. John C. Hume, "Prevention and Sexually Transmitted Diseases," *Maryland Medical Journal* 36, no. 1 (1987): 28.

88. The programs against syphilis in the 1940s have many things in common with those directed against HIV/AIDS in the recent past. In the 1940 Baltimore radio broadcast quoted at the beginning of this chapter, one section of the drama dealt with reporting.

> DOCTOR SAXON: "What is syphilis but an endless chain that has been handed down through the ages."

> DOCTOR ASHLEY: "I agree with you—but the average doctor does not have time for the elaborate contact investigation that seems so necessary."

Doctor Saxon sympathetically described how he had handled a case in Baltimore along investigational lines. A young woman he identified as "Little Buttercup" had a positive blood test for syphilis. Saxon pointed out that she could have been treated successfully as an individual patient but that such a narrow perspective would have been a public health fiasco. As Saxon explained, "Little Buttercup" had disclosed that within three months she had engaged in sex with fifteen youths and men. All contacts were located, and eleven of them showed positive blood tests. Following this trail, all the sexual contacts of those eleven were also tracked, and so on. By the end of this quest, Saxon noted, the clinic had ended up with a total of forty new patients. Those who have read Randy Shilts's book (or seen the movie) *And the Band Played On: Politics, People, and the AIDS Epidemic* (New York: St. Martin's Press, 1987) will find this story familiar.

89. Diane L. Matuszak, Ebenezah Israel, Joseph T. Horman, and J. Mehsen Joseph, "HIV Antibody Testing," *Maryland Medical Journal* 36, no. 1 (1987): 40–43.

90. F. Barre-Sinoussi, J. C. Chermann, F. Rey, M. T. Nugeyre, S. Chamaret, J. Gruest, C. Dauguet, C. Axler-Blin, F. Vezinet-Brun, C. Rouzioux, W. Rozenbaum, and L. Montagnier, "Isolation of a T-lymphotropic Retrovirus from a Patient at Risk for Acquired Immûne Deficiency Syndrome (AIDS)," *Science* 220 (1983): 868–71; Robert C. Gallo, Syed Z. Salahuddin, Mikulas Popovic, Gene M. Shearer, Mark Kaplan, Barton F. Hayes, Thomas J. Palker, Robert Redfield, James Oleske, Bijan Safai, Bilbert White, Paul Foster, and Phillip D. Markham, "Frequent Detection and Isolation of Cytopathic Retroviruses (HTLV-III) from Patients with AIDS and at Risk for AIDS," *Science* 224 (1984): 500–502. Gallo is now working on AIDS at the University of Maryland.

91. See, e.g., the information from the Baltimore City Sexually Transmitted Training Center. The center's Instruction Folder, which includes numerous articles about STDs, is provided to all participating members of the training sessions.

92. Kenneth B. Morgen, "Counseling and HIV: Test Results and Risk Reduction," *Maryland Medical Journal* 36, no. 1 (1987): 44–46.

Index

Bloodletting, 3, 14, 17, 19, 68

Blue Cross, 161

Bond, Thomas E., 80

Booker, William D., 109

Bosworth, Sgt., 16

Botanic medicine, 1, 5, 169

Bourne, Thomas, 180n. 20

Bowditch, Henry Pickering, 88–9

Brace, C. H., 62

Bressler Research Laboratory, 105

Briggs, Isaac, Jr., 15

Broca, Pierre-Paul, 15

Brown, George, 181n. 20

Brown, Gustavus, 180n. 20

Brown, Gustavus Richard, 180n. 20

Brown, John F., 114

Brown, Thomas H., 114

Browne, Bennet Bernard, 48, 50, 109

Browne, Morgan, Jr., 180n. 20

Brush, Edward N., 56

Buchanan, George, 71, 181n. 20

Bull Run, Clara Barton at, 131

Bulletin of the Medical and Chirurgical Faculty of Maryland, 146–7

Bureau of Child Welfare, 151

Burking (murder for dissection), 70

Califano, Joseph, 171

Calomel, 14

Cancer, 59, 178

Carey, Francis King, 37, 54

Carnegie Foundation, 104, 149

Carnegie Outpatient Building, 41

Carr, William, 53

Carroll Creek, 133

Carson, Benjamin S., 168

Carter, Jimmy, 171

Carven, John K., Mrs., 108

Catholicism among immigrants, 121

Cedar Mountain, 131

Cell tissue culture, 157

Centers for Alternative Medicine, 170

Centers for Disease Control, 171–2

Centralization, 62, 111, 114, 166, 171–3, 177

Chadwick, Edwin, 127

Chapman, John Lee, 47

Chapman, Ross Mc., 57

Chemistry courses, 102, 109

Chesapeake Bay, 37, 74

Chesney, Alan Mason, 100, 200n. 47

Chestertown, 19

Chew, S. C., 29

Chinese medicine, 170

Chiropractic, 19, 185n. 58

Chisolm, J. J., 78

Cholera, 18, 23, 27, 116–24, 133, 145

Christian Commission, 131

Churchville, 65

Cinchona, 4

City Hospitals, 93, 161

Civil War, 32, 38, 77, 129–32

Clagett, Zachariah, 181n. 20

Clark, William M., 100

Clark University, 92

Claybrook, Erwin B., 62

Clerkships, 94

Clinical Shock Trauma Unit, 160

Coale, R. Dorsey, 45

Coale, Samuel Stringer, 2

Cocke, James, 71–2

Cohen, Joshua J., 29, 46

Cohnheim, Julius, 90

Cole, William M. A., 114

College of Medicine, Philadelphia, 5, 65

College of Medicine of Maryland (*see also* University of Maryland School of Medicine), 30, 68

University of Michigan, 92
University of Pennsylvania, 67, 90
Urbanization, 62, 108

Vaccination, 122, 125–7, 151, 156, 163, 166, 171, 173
Vanderbilt Medical School, 168
Venesection (*see also* Bloodletting), 3, 68
Veronal, 48
Version in childbirth, 21
Veterinary science, 112
Victor Cullen Center, 144
Vitamins, 150, 169
Vitriol (sulfuric acid), 5
Volatole tincture, 1
Voluntary hospitals, 51
Volunteer Medical Service Corps, 146

Walsh, William E., 62
Waltz, Peter, 181n. 20
Warfield, Charles Alexander, 180n. 20
Warrell, Edward, 180n. 20
Washington, George, false teeth of, 79
Washington Medical College, 76, 126–7
Water: in Frederick, 133; municipalization of, 127–9
Waters, Charles E., Mrs., 108
Waters, Wilson, 180n. 20
Watkins, Levi, 167–8
Weed, Lewis H., 100
Weir, R. F., 132
Welch, William H., 39–40, 88, 90–2, 94–5, 100, 135, 145–6, 148–9
Wells, John, 181n. 20
West, William M., 114
Western Female High School, 110

Western Maryland, 162
Westminster, 11
WFBR radio, 154
White, Edward, 181n. 20
Wiesenthal, Andrew, 71
Wiesenthal, Charles Frederick, 6–8, 70–2
Wiley, Harvey W., 139–40
Williams, Anita R., 54
Williams, Hannah, 23
Wilmer Eye Institute, 41
Wilmer Ophthalmological Institute, 100
Wilmington, Del., 19
Wilson, William T., 29
Winslow, Randolph, 108–9
Woltereck, Gustav, 151
Woman's Medical College of Baltimore, 108–11
Woman's Medical College of Chicago, 109
Woman's Medical College of Pennsylvania, 109
Women: as activists, 131–2, 141; as medical students, 87–8, 92, 96–7, 108–10; treatment of, 48–52
Women's Civic League, 141
Women's Fund Committee, Johns Hopkins, 88
Women's Medical College, 50
Wood, Gerard, 180n. 20
Woodward, Lewis, 11
Woodward, Theodore E., 159
Woolford, John, 181n. 20
World War I, 41, 100, 145
World War II, 155–6
Worthington, Charles, 181n. 20
Wyvill, Dorsey, 181n. 20

Yellow fever, 116–8, 205n. 10

Library of Congress Cataloging-in-Publication Data

Sewell, Jane Eliot.

Medicine in Maryland : the practice and the profession, 1799–1999 /
Jane Eliot Sewell.

    p.   cm.

Includes bibliographical references and index.

ISBN 0-8018-6127-6 (alk. paper)

1. Medicine—Maryland—History—19th century. 2. Medicine—Maryland—
History—20th century. 3. Medical care—Maryland—History—19th century.
4. Medical care—Maryland—History—20th century. 5. Medical education—
Maryland—History—19th century. 6. Medical education—Maryland—History—
20th century. I. Title.

[DNLM: 1. Delivery of Health Care—history—Maryland. 2. Education,
Medical—history—Maryland. 3. Public Health—history—Maryland.
WZ 70 AM3 S516m 1999]

R241.S49 1999

362.1′09752—dc21

DNLM/DLC

for Library of Congress   98-43609